# B-24
# BRIDGE
# BUSTERS

# B-24
# BRIDGE
# BUSTERS
## RAF LIBERATORS OVER BURMA

COLIN PATEMAN

FONTHILL

*This book is dedicated to my father and his older brother. Unaware of their sibling connection, both served in the Royal Air Force in Burma and were eventually united by family research in 1999.*

Fonthill Media Language Policy

Fonthill Media publishes in the international English language market. One language edition is published worldwide. As there are minor differences in spelling and presentation, especially with regard to American English and British English, a policy is necessary to define which form of English to use. The Fonthill Policy is to use the form of English native to the author. Colin Pateman was born and educated in Sussex; therefore British English has been adopted in this publication.

Fonthill Media Limited
Fonthill Media LLC
www.fonthillmedia.com
office@fonthillmedia.com

First published in the United Kingdom and the United States of America 2016

British Library Cataloguing in Publication Data:
A catalogue record for this book is available from the British Library

Typeset in 10.5pt on 13pt Minion Pro
Printed and bound by CPI Group (UK) Ltd, Croydon, CR0 4YY

# Acknowledgements

The author would seek to acknowledge David Arthur Jones, Lucian Brett Ercolani, and Thomas Francis Reynolds, who are the original compilers of the flying logbooks and other associated material that has been used to assemble the foundation of this work.

Matthew J. Poole, Robert Quirk, and Martin Bond deserve recognition for their contributions of work associated to the B-24 and their willingness to share information. Terry Manttan at the Thailand-Burma Railway Centre, Kanchanaburi; Steve Fogden for the Rangoon jail muster roll; and Nicky Swann for the material on Frank Holden. Additional photographs have been included from the author's collection, alongside other contributors who have been duly accredited. The terms of the Open Government License facilitates the use of historic material from the National Archives, while other material, particularly photographic work, sits within the public domain created by the government prior to 1957. Finally, I would like to acknowledge the assistance of my wife Sarah-Jane, who endeavours to support my passion for collecting, researching, and writing.

# CONTENTS

# Introduction

Despite the 1937 Constitution that administratively separated Burma from British India, the provisional and developing home rule measures in place were insufficient to separate that country from being a British Crown Colony. Burma was therefore automatically at war with the Axis powers upon the British government's declaration of war on 3 September 1939. The Burma nationalist movements ensured that their discontented voices were heard, ensuring Burma was far from being a stable platform to wage war against the belligerent Japanese. Burma was important territory that featured within the Japanese vision of a 'Greater East Asia Co-Prosperity Sphere'.

The Japanese onslaught of forcibly occupying Asian territory, including Burma, resulted in the necessity for the Japanese to construct the Thailand to Burma railway; this was in order to supply the machine of war and facilitate their intention to invade British India. The railway was forcibly built by prisoners of war and impressed labour under the command of the Imperial Japanese Army. The challenging construction was forged through the jungle, with hard labour supplied by 300,000 men. Each mile of the railway required 2,200 hardwood railway sleepers to be laid, with each sleeper embedded into the ground at an immeasurable cost in human life. In 1946, a Canadian Military Intelligence Officer, Lieutenant C. C. Brett, reflected upon the railway and estimated that those men suffered a mortality rate of immense stature, quite possibly a figure of around 100,000. The railway, 260 miles in length, required 688 bridges to be built. Those bridges would become fertile targets to be destroyed by Allied airmen who flew inordinately lengthy bombing operations from airfields far away in India.

An understanding of the history associated to the famous 'Bridge on the River Kwai' and specifically the lives of three Allied aviators are explored in this book. The Japanese military infrastructure of railways, bridges, shipping, and the planting of aerial sea mines in Japanese held waters were of paramount importance to the Allied war mounted in the Far East.

Factual evidence written during the war explains the journeys taken by those three men and many others, predominantly from 99 and 159 Squadron. They served alongside each other in the air during the campaign to retake Burma and intrude deep into Thailand. American-built B-24 aircraft were supplied to the British government under authority of the lend-lease bill. These machines, known as Liberators, became the ideal aircraft to conduct those courageous long-range operations. Ultimately, the Liberator aircraft became responsible for the destruction of many Japanese targets, including the disablement of the significantly important Thailand to Burma railway. British and Commonwealth crews eventually destroyed the steel spans of the strategically important railway bridge at Kanchanaburi in June 1945. That final 'bridge busting' operation by the Royal Air Force represented the eventual demise of the Japanese vision of Far East supremacy in Burma. Now recognised all over the world as the 'Bridge on the River Kwai', the original and remaining six bridge spans still stand—some steel girders bearing the words 'Made in Japan'.

British and Commonwealth personnel who flew on those dangerous operations were issued with individual flying logbooks and were required to keep detailed records within them. During the immediate post-war months, the vast majority of flying logbooks were in accordance with instructions, recovered by the Air Ministry and subsequently placed into storage as official documents. The accumulation of recovered record books was substantial and, due to the fact storage became a problem, the Air Ministry later let it become known that they could be returned to the individuals who had compiled them. By 1959, in spite of announcements in national newspapers, the vast majority of logbooks remained unclaimed.

The governments' paper committee later recommended the destruction of the stored logbooks. Irreplaceable historical documents were destroyed and have subsequently been denied to the generations that have followed those brave young men who had created them. The books that remain represent valuable time capsules of operational duty, each without distortion of fact or historical misinterpretation. For this reason alone, surviving flying logbooks are treasured as rare possessions. This book has been primarily composed from entries made within surviving record books and supported by other official historical documents.

# 1

# The River Kwai

Burma would best be described as being wedged between India and China with an extensive border with Thailand. Geographically, the country covers an area approximately the size of France and Belgium combined. With a population of around 17 million people in 1941, the popular perception of Burma was of a land densely covered by jungle. However, the terrain fought over in the Second World War (between 1942 and 1945) was in fact fairly varied, but inevitably it was inhospitable. Communication routes within Burma were generally poor, with few roads or railways. The country tended to be dominated by the main waterways, almost all of which ran north–south, following the natural geographical topography of the country.

Despite the fact that one river—now famously known as the River Kwai—is one of the most well-known rivers in the world, it is unremarkable. In the context of the Far East theatre of war, the relatively insignificant River Kwai is dwarfed by far greater water courses. The extensive coastline of Burma consists of vast tracts of mangrove swamp and significant river deltas that form at the mouth of each of its primary rivers.

Central Burma consists of large valleys, which in the wet season feed water into the Irrawaddy, Chindwin, and Sittang rivers. The mighty River Irrawaddy rises in the Himalayas and flows down the central sector of the country, being joined by its tributary, the Chindwin, near Pakokku, south of Mandalay, and onto the delta at Rangoon. Its central course is across a wide plain that receives little rainfall until the monsoon period and is therefore baked dry in the hot season. Likewise, the Chindwin rises in the far north, near the Assam border, and flows south west on the eastern side of the Naga and Chin Hills. For much of its length, the river flows through dense jungle. The Sittang also flows north–south to the Gulf of Martaban, and it has similar characteristics to the Irrawaddy. The fourth river, the Salween, flows through the eastern area, having risen in China, and eventually flows through extensive and impassable deep gorges into the Gulf of Martaban at Moulmein.

The River Kwai at Kanchanaburi has become an iconic place firmly set in the history of the Second World War. For the many hundreds of pilots and air crews who attended endless briefings, tasked with attacking selected targets on the Japanese railways, it was simply another target in the state of Thailand, which until 1939 had been known as Siam. Like all waterways in that part of Southeast Asia, it has two contrasting conditions. Five months of the rainy monsoon season transforms its demeanour, having to consume inordinate volumes of water that swell its banks, the fierce flows attacking the rapids and falling sections of terrain creating torrid waterways of immense strength. As the weather changes, the river eventually reduces to a slower flow and gradually, as the waters recede, it exposes gentle banks and flat sandy expanses for a genteel existence until the great rains inevitably arrive once again several months later.

The River Kwai begins its own existence at the convergence of the Ranti, Songkalia, and Bikhli Rivers. At Kanchanaburi, a location now historically linked to the Bridge on the River Kwai, the river merges with the Khwae Yai River to form the larger Mae Klong River. At its confluence, the river becomes significantly wide, capable of disgorging monumental quantities of water during the wet season. Huge quantities of silt-mud collect here, making the river wide, but not deep. Subsequently, the waterway empties itself into the Gulf of Thailand at Samut Songkhram. The stretch of river, which frequently focuses on the events within this book, was known locally as the Mae Khloung or Mae Klong. The rivers tributary, the Khwae Noi, is where—at a location known as Tamakan, near Kanchanaburi—the famous bridge was actually constructed.

For many thousands of years, the Khwae valley had been a route for traders and missionaries who commuted between the Gulf of Martaban, Burma, and the central expanses of what is now Thailand. The word Khwae, meaning branch or tributary, and Noi, meaning small, was frequently mispronounced by English speakers as Kwai—this became the fundamental reason as to the name in which we identify the river today.

Post-war and thence permanently, the river has continued to live its life as the River Kwai and is now probably one of the most recognised rivers in the world, a significant part of that notoriety due to the worldwide recognition provided by the award winning film, *The Bridge on the River Kwai* by David Lean and Sam Spiegel, released in 1960.

A lesser-known fact concerning this area were the historical surveys commissioned to explore the development of a railway through Thailand and Burma towards India, a proposed route that sought to link some of the most important empires in the world. The British colonial administrator Holt S. Hallett explored the region in the early nineteenth century, promoting a railway connection in order to take British goods from the Gulf of Martaban, Burma, through Thailand to Southern China. This ambitious proposal was never constructed. It was thought to have been virtually impossible because of the geographical conditions that required momentous levels of engineering to cut through rock and cross large expanses of waterways.

Between 1887 and 1888, the British Railway Contractor Punchard and Company was commissioned by the then Siamese government to survey a proposed railway line from Bangkok to Ayutthaya, a location ideally situated with an equal distance between India and China. The railway, initially short in distance, was extended further to Korat, situated on Thailand's north-eastern plateau lying northeast of Bangkok. Korat served as the gateway to the lower north-eastern regions. This development proceeded and was constructed to form the foundation for the initial development of the rudimentary railway network that still exists today. It was in 1886 that the British rule in Burma was consolidated as part of British India and remained so until 1935, when the governance changed towards a route of independence that would not be achieved until after the Second World War.

Overland routes with bordering countries were almost non-existent, and virtually all communication routes ran north–south following the natural geography, including the Rangoon to Mandalay railway. Other railway lines ran from Mandalay to Lashio, from Rangoon to Prome (also known as Pyay), and from Pegu (present-day Bago) across the Sittang to Martaban, connecting to Moulmein and the line through Tenasserim to Ye by rail-ferry. The most important internal communication route was the river traffic on the Irrawaddy and the Chindwin. Services were provided by the fleet of assorted river craft operated by the Irrawaddy Flotilla Company. Due to the accessible sea communications with India across the Bay of Bengal, there had been little need to develop overland routes between India and Burma. There were no roads as such through the mountainous border areas, therefore, access to India was restricted to a few precarious tracks.

To facilitate their plans to invade India, the Japanese needed to construct a strategic railway supplies route from Thailand into neighbouring Burma and beyond. The River Kwai itself would need to be bridged as the proposed railway travelled through that region containing many rivers, streams, and gullies. Some 688 bridges were to be constructed along the railways length. Only eight bridges were constructed from steel, one being the famous Bridge on the River Kwai.

## Japanese Politics and Alliances

The Sino-Japanese War, which started in 1937, proved to be costly in every respect; not only did Japan fail in its objective of economically exploiting China, but the war became a major drain on Japan's economy. By 1938, the Japanese were manufacturing only a fraction of the material needed to continue its offensive with China. In early 1939, Japan had occupied the Hainan and Spratly Islands, which became launching bases for aggressive military offensives against South China and French Indochina. By 1940, Japan became more needful than ever on the west for the vital resources it sought to continue its offensive, but it was a western world that was more inclined to side with China than with Japan.

In Europe, the fall of France in 1940 gave the Japanese the opportunity to look towards other territories. An agreement with Vichy-France in July 1940 saw the recognition of what were described as the special requirements of Japanese troops in China. It additionally saw an acceptance of the military occupation of the northern area of the French Indochinese states, Laos and Vietnam. These actions were significant in the objective for Japan to significantly restrict the supply routes for Chinese Nationalist forces, which were further progressed by Japan's non-aggression treaty with Thailand.

The German occupancy of Holland saw Japan commence negotiations with the Dutch Colonial regime in Indonesia for its oil and rubber. It also sought to explore diplomatically acceptable routes for military expansion, in particular for its navy and air force.

On 27 September 1940, Japan joined Germany and Italy in what became known as the Tripartite Pact, or Pact of Berlin. The main objectives of the Pact were to enforce America to remain neutral, while Germany was provided with an opportunity for a swift victory against the British. For Japan, it meant they would be able to expand into Southeast Asia without American interference and Japan additionally hoped to gain from the Pact by improved relations with Russia through established German mediation.

The Tripartite Pact was the foundation on which the relationship between Germany and Japan was built upon and which remained with them until 1945. It also facilitated in the successful non-aggression pact that Japan sought with Russia, which was eventually signed in 1941. Interestingly, the term Axis frequently adopted to describe the alliance was never an official term; it was a phrase used by Benito Mussolini, the Italian prime minister from 1922 until 1943, which is now used extensively to describe these allies of Adolf Hitler.

The relationship between Burma and the Japanese Imperial Army was soon to be understood as their conquest of Southeast Asia and the obliteration of Western control in India was rapidly becoming a military objective. Following the German offensive against Russia in June 1941, French-controlled Indochina became a realistic objective for Japan. However, Japan's actions in this respect brought responses from America, Britain, and Holland, which resulted in Japan suffering embargo restrictions. Those embargos were attempting to freeze valuable resources, in particular, the most valued of all, oil. However, the vison of Japan was set, she was at that time one of the worlds' largest merchant fleet operatives and saw trade opportunities as being unrestrictive. What followed would be a most fundamental development in the rapidly changing events of those times. Japan was set with just two courses to follow: a withdrawal from China to appease the British, Dutch, and Americans to facilitate the removal of the embargo, or engage in the military offensive to seize the resources they required from the Dutch East Indies. The war minister in Japan clashed with the prime minister of Japan over the matter, forcing his resignation. Japan saw no reason to suffer a humiliating stand down from its ambitions against China and decided to take by military force the resources it desired. The war against the Western Allies was about to be cast, the wider objectives for Japan were to replace Western imperialism in China and Southeast Asia with independence granted under Japanese control. Clever terminology phrased by Japan's Foreign Minister Arita enhanced Japan's vision of creating the 'Greater East Asia Co-Prosperity Sphere'. To be simply achieved by her economic domination across French Indochina, Burma, Thailand, and India.

Towards the end of 1941, the German Army, having gained massive swathes of territory, was knocking on the door of Moscow. The powerbases of Europe were occupied by German forces leaving Southeast Asia as ripe for picking. Britain was surrounded by seas occupied by marauding packs of German submarines, which were strangling the supply of food and materials. Supply convoys were being progressively sent to the bottom of the sea. Japan at that time wrongly assumed the threat from Britain and Russia had all but been extinguished.

These events were on the backdrop of other political actions taken in 1940. The military occupation of the northern areas of the French Indochinese states of Laos and Vietnam effectively separated Thailand and China. Laos bordered Burma, which was seen to be extremely valuable, and Japan had completed the military occupation of French Indochina by July 1941. This series of events, combined with a non-aggression treaty with Thailand, created a significant border along the boundaries of Burma. Thailand subsequently declared war against the Western Allies in December 1941. The importance of Burma was now fundamentally enhanced. The great Burma Road, built and completed in December 1938 by the British using Chinese labourers and American aid, had been a feat of great engineering and physical endurance. This unique road had become the sole remaining land supply route to assist Nationalist China forces fighting against the Japanese.

The possibility of an attack on Burma across her eastern frontier had for long been regarded as a remote possibility. In August 1940, the military Chiefs of Staff reviewed the situation in the Far East and concluded that, though a Japanese occupation of Thailand would bring the threat of air attack on Burma closer, the invasion of Burmese territory would still be a comparatively remote threat. The Japanese, however, had laid plans to support an organisation named the 'Minami Organ'. Primarily, this organisation was integral to the numerous Burmese resistance and nationalist groups. The Japanese sought to activate the closure of the Burma Road to China by assisting the Minami Organ. The United States were directly shipping lend-lease materiel by sea into the Burmese port of Rangoon, it was then transferred on the railway to northern Burma and finally carried by truck over the narrow and winding 700-mile-long Burma Road into China. The Japanese objective was to cut off that valuable and essential munitions and materiel supply route for the Chinese Army.

After two years and three months of bloody conflict that had taken place in the European War, the Japanese attacked the United States of America at Pearl Harbor. The international dateline, however, influenced the timing of the Japanese acts of war against Western powers. The insurgents into Thailand and Malay in the early hours of

8 December 1941 actually took place before the aerial attack at Pearl Harbor because they were on the other side of the international dateline.

Colonel Suzuki Keiji, at the Imperial General Headquarters in Japan, drew up a plan for the Japanese conquest of Burma in December 1941. The Japanese-Thailand non-aggression agreement had been signed on 8 December and Japanese bombing raids commenced on Rangoon on 23 December. The objective and summary of Japan's enforcement towards Burma were very explicit; Colonel Suzuki Keiji is described within the translated Japanese Military Administration Document as the Chief of the Minami Organ. That document translated by the academic Won Zoon Yoon, assisted by Thomas Winant, read:

> In concert with the military advance into Burma, the objective is to stir up disturbances throughout Burma in order to hamper the enemy operations and to induce the Burmese to co-operate wholeheartedly with Japan.
>
> The Minami Organ shall direct the members of the Burma Independence Party in organizing a rebel army. Their task shall be to destroy political organizations and create turbulence in the country. The Minami Organ shall also organise a volunteer army, form a capable core of members for the Independent regime, and establish a provisional government after suppression of the Tenasserim region. [The narrow coastal region of south eastern Burma, bordered by Thailand and to the west by the Andaman Sea.] The Minami Organ, moreover, shall promptly conquer the Rangoon region, destroy the centre of British rule in Burma, establish the foundation of an independent regime and complete the independence of Burma following the suppression of Upper Burma. This plan shall be executed in close connection with military operations in Burma.

This initial military organisation of Burma would later be dissolved upon the formation of what became the Burma Independence Army, the Japanese utilising a fitting title to their vision of rule over occupied Burma. The offensive military actions signalled the progressive falling of other territories, which were conquered one by one.

Hong Kong fell on Christmas day 1941; by the end of January 1942, the long, narrow southern part of Burma, the Kra Isthmus, Tenasserim, with its useful ports and airfields of Mergui (present-day Myeik), Tavoy (present-day Dawei), and Moulmein had also fallen. Singapore fell on the 15 February 1942 and by mid-March Sumatra and Java had also fallen. Thousands upon thousands of Allied soldiers became prisoners of war, as did enormous numbers of civilians, categorised as alien to the native territories whom became a valuable workforce for the Japanese.

The Geneva Convention of 1929 held the important basic rights for all prisoners of war. The lives of Allied prisoners of war should have been influenced and controlled by the Geneva Convention, with agreement that held no boundaries regardless as to whatever army, navy, or air force they were engaged within.

Japan had signed, but never ratified the Geneva Convention and additionally during the Second World War they saw no reason to treat any prisoners of war in accordance with the international agreements of the Hague Conventions, 1899 and 1907. Primarily, this was because the Japanese viewed surrender as dishonourable in all respects, suicide was superior and desirable to them in all acts of battle. Moreover, according to a directive ratified by Emperor Hirohito, 5 August 1937, the constraints of the Hague Conventions were explicitly removed in relation to their treatment of Chinese prisoners.

Allied Prisoners of war held by the Japanese armed forces were subject to brutal treatment, forced labour, starvation rations, and negligible medical treatment. The most notorious use of forced labour was during the enforced construction of the Burma to Thailand Railway.

On 13 August 1942, Japan passed the Enemy Airmen's Act, which stated that Allied pilots who bombed non-military targets in the Pacific Theatres and were captured on land or at sea by Japanese forces were to be subject to trial and punishment. This was despite the fact there was no international law that contained provisions regarding to aerial warfare. All of these matters induced great fear and trepidation towards the Japanese, who had potential for extreme penalties. The Japanese Command functioned upon every order emanating from their emperor, regardless of circumstance or the utterer. Within the Imperial Japanese Army they had an equivalent of the infamous German Gestapo, the *Kempeitai*. These men had great influence in matters associated to captured prisoners of war—their brutality was exceptional. The *Kempeitai* were ultimately responsible for all prisoners and forced-labour camps. They implemented the 1941 Imperial Japanese Army's Penal Regulations for Far Eastern Prisoners, Article IV of which stated:

> Those who injure or give a blow or menace to those who are on duty of superintending or warding or escorting will be sentenced to death or penal servitude or imprisoned for life or for the period of two years or longer.
>
> When a group of men commit the same, the ringleader will be sentenced to death, or penal servitude or imprisonment for life, and the rest will be sentenced to penal servitude or imprisoned for the period of three years or longer.
>
> Those who commit the foregoing two crimes and cause death will be sentenced to death.

A chilling account of the Japanese interpretation of Article IV is provided within document 1349 at the IWM archives, London. That document holds the testimony of Sergeant Innes-Ker, a British prisoner of war from the 1st Battalion Straits Settlement, Volunteer Force. As a prisoner of war, he was forced to work on the Burma to Thailand Railway and later provided primary evidence of seeing a fellow prisoner simply drop a rope that was being used to raise a railway bridge timber. A Japanese engineer started beating the prisoner who had dropped the rope—the prisoner had simply raised his arm to protect himself. The prisoner was subsequently tied to a tree in crucifix fashion, where he remained for four days without food or water until he died.

# 2

# The Invasion of Burma

Towards the end of 1939, a number of aerodromes were under construction by the British within Burma. These valuable, yet basic facilities needed to be protected and so military detachments had to be found from within the home forces. The Burma Frontier Force had been formed following the separation of Burma from India, with units coming from the Burma Military Police. This force consisted of battalions of men, mainly Gurkhas and Indians, who were administered by the Defence Department of the Government of Burma. In 1940, a new battalion was formed, the Kokine Battalion, who were ordered to specifically carry out the specialised duties of defending the airfields at Akyab (present-day Sittwe), Moulmein (present-day Mawlamyine), Tavoy, Mergui, Victoria Point, and Lashio.

Shortly after the bombing of Pearl Harbor, Japanese planes took off from airfield bases in Thailand and commenced offensive operations against Burma. Japanese aircraft bombed the Tavoy airfield on the British island outpost in the Andaman Sea. The Andaman Sea is a body of water to the southeast of the Bay of Bengal, south of Burma, west of Thailand, and east of the Andaman Islands. The Japanese air crews were well-trained and equipped with effective aircraft, something that came as a surprise to many, especially following frequent derogatory reports and speculation uttered from many quarters upon the presumed deficiencies of the Japanese Air Force.

At 1.15 a.m. on the 8 December 1941, Japanese troops landed offensively at Kota Bharu in Malaya and at the same time commenced air raids upon Singapore and Hong Kong. Kota Bharu had been the site of an Allied airfield constructed in 1936 and built close to the coastline, one of three locations that the Japanese forces landed upon that day. Two days later, the Japanese Navy sank HMS *Prince of Wales* and *Repulse* off the Malayan coast, the might and ability of the enemy needing little more emphasis than those chilling events, which shocked the British nation. The Japanese Navy was no doubt capitalising from its countries denunciation from the Washington Naval Treaty in 1934, a treaty that had limited the tonnage of capital ships since 1922.

Mingaladon Airfield, near Rangoon, was the operational centre of the Royal Air Force, Air Defence of Burma. It was primly positioned, protecting the imperatively important port of Rangoon. The entire air support to that British-based army consisted of just thirty-seven front-line British and American aircraft. Of this small force, sixteen were American Brewster Buffalo fighters, short stubby aircraft that had been designed for the United States Navy. These were operational with the Royal Air Force in 67 Squadron. The remainder were American Tomahawks, part of the American Volunteer Group. Their pilots were employed by retired Major Chennault of the United States Army Air Corps who had been employed as the Air Advisor to the Chinese and charged with the protection of the Burma Road. His men numbered approximately 100 in strength, some of which had been detached to the defence of Rangoon, thus highlighting the importance of protecting that most significant port complex. The first air raids on Rangoon occurred on the 23 and 25 December, valiantly opposed by those meagre resources.

The Royal Air Force and her Commonwealth Air Forces were struggling to gain strength not only in aircraft, but particularly with trained pilots and air crews. Few were available for the Far East and those that were sent endured a tortuous transit journey, engaging with a convoy route from Liverpool to Takoradi on the West African coast, passenger flight across Africa to Cairo, Basra, Karachi, and Calcutta. From India, they were transferred to the island of Akyab in Burma, then onto Bangkok and Penang, before finally arriving at Singapore.

Singapore was firmly set in the sights of the invading Japanese forces, as was Rangoon and the progression north into Burma along the Bengal coast to central Assam. India was the ultimate jewel in the crown and it was that objective which forced such extraordinary measures to be deployed by the Japanese in their fight through Burma. On 14 January 1942, Japanese forces were surging south and were no more than 100 miles away from the British Fortress Island of Singapore. On 20 January, the Japanese Railway Regiments crossed into Burma from Thailand intent on making for Moulmein. This unit would be used in emergency repairs to the railways and later in constructing the Burma–Thailand Railway. The Royal Air Force mustered its beleaguered capability in order to defend Singapore, with great heroism taking place in the classical Vildebeest, Hudson, Bristol Blenheim, and Buffalo aircraft. By 31 January 1942, all British and Commonwealth forces had withdrawn from the Malay Peninsula onto Singapore Island. Seaborne evacuations from Singapore had begun in January and they continued as best they could until the last possible moments. On 8 February, the Japanese forces commanded by General Tomoyuki Yamashita landed in the north-west of the island. The Australian units were tasked with defending significant territory and fought with immense bravery. However, within six days, the Japanese were at the outskirts of Singapore city, which was by then under almost constant air attack.

On 15 February, Lieutenant-General Arthur Percival, the British commander in Singapore, called for a ceasefire and made the difficult decision to surrender. The official surrender document was signed that evening and, after days of desperate last stand fighting, all British Empire troops were to lay down their arms at 8.30 p.m. More than 90,000 troops immediately became prisoners of war, together with significant numbers of European civilians who were interned. Winston Churchill called the ignominious fall of Singapore to the Japanese the worst disaster and largest capitulation in British military history. It is appropriate to mention the significant loss of life that took place, with an estimated sixty ships damaged or sunk by the Japanese Air Force while attempting to escape from Singapore. Three ships were hastily refitted as best possible to serve as hospital ships and attached to each vessel was a contingent of nurses, many of whom were from the Australian Army Nursing Service. First to depart, on 10 February 1942, was the ship *Wah Sui*, which without any serious damage set sail to Batavia in Java.

The second ship, a Blue Star Line cargo liner, the *Empire Star*, slipped away in darkness the following night. The *Empire Star* was a vessel of over 11,000 tons and she had recently delivered a full load of supplies into Singapore. She carried over 2,000 people in her hold when she departed. Many of those men were Royal Air Force personnel who no longer had aircraft to fly or service on the ground. Captain Selwyn Capon commanded the *Empire Star*, which had sailed with the Blue Funnel Liner, *Gorgon*. They were escorted by HMS *Durban* and a smaller Armed Auxiliary Patrol vessel. This small convoy also made towards Batavia. During daylight, the Japanese Air Force sighted the convoy and a significant force of Japanese aircraft bombed the ships. In a consistent and prolonged attack, endured over two hours, serious damage and loss of life took place. The *Empire Star* sustained three direct bomb hits, which killed fourteen people and severely injured many others. Substantial damage had been caused and several fires had broken out. Despite this, the *Empire Star* survived, all of the vessels in the small convoy had deployed their machine gun defences and made a good account of themselves. The men and women in the holds of the ships endured sheer terror that continued with intermittent aerial attacks mounted by the Japanese over the coming hours. Two Australian nurses, Sister Margaret Anderson and Vera Torney, would eventually be rewarded with a George Medal and Order of the British Empire respectively for their bravery on the *Empire Star*. Quite remarkably, the convoy also made sanctuary in Batavia and eventually reached its destination—Australia.

On 12 February, the steam ship *Vyner Brooke* sailed from Singapore harbour vastly overcrowded with as many people as possible held in every conceivable space. The *Vyner Brooke* was at that time a British-registered cargo vessel originally named after the Third Rajah of Sarawak—Sir Charles Vyner Brooke. This vessel had been operating under the flag of the Sarawak Steamship Company until being requisitioned by the Royal Navy as an armed trader.

The *Vyner Brooke* had a crew of forty-seven and a high proportion of the passengers were women and children. Among the passengers were the last sixty-five Australian nurses to leave Singapore, led by matrons Paschke and Drummond. The nurses were deployed into several teams with responsibility for various areas of the vessel.

Initially, the ship was fortunate to have escaped without significant attacks against them, however that would change. The *Vyner Brook* subsequently received the full attention of the Japanese Air Force on 14 February while sailing in the Bangka Strait, heading for Palembang in Sumatra. It was a terrifying attack that caused the ship to sink within just thirty minutes. The loss of life was considerable and made worse by the enemy aircraft strafing the sea, shooting the struggling survivors in the water. Various individuals and small groups of survivors spent several hours in the water. One group of survivors, comprising of civilians, including children, soldiers, and some nurses, were washed ashore on the Island of Bangka. The island had already been occupied by the Japanese and most of them were immediately taken captive.

A terrifying fate awaited those that had been separated in the water and landed on Radji beach. They were befriended with another party of civilian survivors and a group of Commonwealth servicemen and merchant sailors, all of whom had made it ashore after their own vessels had become recent casualties to the Japanese Air Force. This group unsuccessfully sought assistance from local villagers. In desperation, a small group attempted to make contact with the Japanese. Many people were in need of treatment. All of the nurses remained with the injured and a party of Japanese troops arrived at Radji Beach a few hours later. The nurses and men surrendered to the Japanese troops, who immediately separated the men from the women. The Japanese troops took the men away along the beach, but returned shortly afterwards, obviously displaying that the male survivors had been shot and bayonetted to death by cleaning their bayonets.

The separated group of nurses were ordered to walk into the sea, where they were machine-gunned as they waded into the water. Only one nurse survived, despite being shot through her back. She was Sister Vivian Bullwinkel of the Australian Army Nursing Service. A bullet had passed through her body without striking any major organ. This remarkable nurse survived further traumatic circumstances at the hands of the Japanese and ultimately gave evidence of those who were brutally executed on the Island of Banka in 1942.

Vivian Bullwinkel's evidence was that when the women were up to their waists in water the Japanese started firing up and down the line with a machine gun. They just swept up and down the line and the girls fell one after the other. She had been towards the end of the line and a bullet struck her in the left loin and went straight through and came out towards the front. The force of it knocked her over into the water and there she lay—she did not lose consciousness. The waves brought her back onto the edge of the water. Having been there ten minutes and everything seeming quiet, she sat up and looked around and there was no sign of anybody. She got up and went up in the jungle and lay down and either slept or was unconscious for a couple of days (Australian War Memorial, AWM 1010/4/24).

Of the sixty-five Australian nurses who had embarked upon the *Vyner Brooke*, twelve had been killed in the aerial attack or drowned following the sinking. Twenty-one were murdered on the beach and the surviving thirty-two became internees.

Before the war was won, a further eight died during their imprisonment. After the war, Vivian Bullwinkel received the honour of an MBE and additionally received the coveted Florence Nightingale Medal. In 1992, she returned to Banka Island to unveil a memorial to the nurses who had not survived, Sister Vivian Bullwinkel MBE died on 3 July 2000.

It would be remiss not to mention events that took place at Singapore's Alexandra Hospital on 14 February 1942, just two days after the sailing of the steamer *Vyner Brooke*. What took place at the British Military Hospital was a war crime atrocity that paved the way forward in manifesting the fear of Japanese brutality. The callousness of those events would purvey deeply through the Allied forces in Southeast Asia and escalate well beyond that theatre of operation.

The Alexandra Hospital was equipped to cater for around 500 patients, but the casualties in defending Singapore had swollen the casualty figures to nearly double its capacity. Wounds of every nature were being treated by the men of the 32nd Company, Royal Army Medical Corps, and emergency lifesaving operations were being undertaken when the Japanese closed in upon the hospital. A British medical officer approached the advancing enemy, expecting to be awarded the protection of the internationally recognised Red Cross, but he was fired upon and the hospital was attacked on several quarters. Forcibly entering the hospital, the Japanese went from room to room indiscriminately shooting, bayoneting, and beating doctors, orderlies, and patients. An estimated fifty men were killed in these initial actions, while some 200 people were tied up and forcibly removed from the hospital and detained in small outbuildings overnight. The conditions were beyond comprehension, crammed into confined spaces, tied up, unable to move, and without water until the following morning. The Japanese extracted some small groups of the captive men and the motive became immediately clear as screams indicated that they were being systematically executed.

These events were reported upon after the war and investigated by the British Officer Colonel Cyril Wild. This man had been the officer who carried the white flag of surrender at Singapore and acted as the translator. Having met the Japanese commander General Tomoyuki Yamashita at the surrender of Singapore, he would meet him again in October 1945. Among several matters, Yamashita was interviewed about the killings at the Alexandra Hospital. Yamashita directed the investigation of that matter towards his subordinate, Lt-General Mutaguchi, the officer in charge of the 18th Division, which had advanced onto the hospital.

Colonel Wild investigated this war crime, securing evidence from Major Bull, a doctor who had witnessed the events. That evidence enabled Wild to interview Lt-General Mutaguchi and put to him the following facts:

> On 12 February troops of the 18th Division entered the hospital and started shooting and bayoneting everyone in sight. In the operating theatre they bayoneted a patient on the operating table and the surgeon who was operating on him. They killed both

of these, and wounded another medical officer and medical orderly. After killing a lot more medical personnel they collected over two hundred as prisoners from the hospital and took them half a mile away, where they locked them up in small rooms. The next day they took them out and machined gunned or bayoneted all but five who escaped and became prisoners of war.

The perpetrators of the Alexandra Hospital massacre escaped justice. Lt-General Mutaguchi was, through lack of evidence, released from custody on 5 June 1947. However, sufficient evidence was available against General Tomoyuki Yamashita, the commander who led the Japanese invasion force. He was hanged on 23 February 1946 after being convicted of many brutal war crime atrocities committed by the Japanese troops under his command.

Returning to 1942, with Singapore lost, the prolific Japanese forces completed their triumphs of overrunning the Dutch East Indies. They subsequently progressed into the western Pacific, and in doing so occupied the numerous island bases throughout that large geographical area, thus threatening the security of Australia. The Allies attention turned to the impending defence of Burma and the protection it provided to India. As previously mentioned, Rangoon was the lifeline for the country with its port and railway connections. Rangoon was the beating heart of Burma, a country that had elevated ranges separating Burma from India in the west, China in the north, and Thailand in the east.

The Royal Air Force in Burma at that time was within the Far East Command structure, with No. 221 Group formed in that group in April 1941. The Command was located in Rangoon to organise, among other matters, the emergency airfield construction required to defend Burma. There were seven airfields linking Lashio in the north and Rangoon in the south, with landing strips in Tenasserim and at Myitkyina. In December 1941, the Japanese invasion of Burma gathered force on what would eventually become the longest land campaign for Britain during the entire period of the Second World War.

In early January 1942, the previously requested Allied reinforcements of aircraft arrived for 221 Group. A squadron of Bristol Blenheim aircraft, supported by some old and well-worn Hawker Hurricanes, was sent from Egypt. The Blenheims bombed Japanese bases as far away as Bangkok. They destroyed many Japanese aircraft on the ground and the additional fighters proved essential in efforts to avoid total Japanese air supremacy. Their efforts enabled reinforcements for the Burma Army to be landed, while additionally protecting the essential work of demolition, acts preparatory in denying equipment and facilities to the Japanese invaders. During the last week of January, the Japanese Air Force made a determined effort to overwhelm the small fighter force defending Rangoon. They made repeated and sustained daylight attacks on the city and surprisingly, after losing some fifty bombers and fighters during the six-day offensive, they reverted to night raids.

On 16 January 1942, a Japanese battalion occupied Victoria Point at the southern tip of Burma. This gave them their first airfield inside the country. The Japanese, having captured Moulmein on 31 January 1942, headed north crossing the Bilin River, forcing an Allied withdrawal over the River Sittang. The important railway bridge over the river was blown up by British forces on 23 February 1942. Inopportunely, this action stranded a significant number of Allied Indian troops on the eastern bank of the river. The importance of river bridges and railway transportation was to become incredibly valuable to both sides as the war progressed in Burma. A vast track of the native population was making its way northwards, disorganised and in the main panic-stricken. Thousands were to die by the wayside from cholera, malaria, or simply from fatigue and hunger while making for the doubtful safety of India.

On 7 March 1942, the Allied Command issued orders to commence a withdrawal from Rangoon. The following day, as the last British train left, the Japanese marched into the city from the west. Organised demolition parties had attempted to destroy key facilities in Rangoon, in particular the railways. The District Locomotive Superintendent was Arthur Johnson. Having been responsible for the demolition of the extensive railway workshop just outside of Rangoon, he and his demolition party were on the last train to leave when it was ambushed by the Japanese. Although there was heavy firing at the train, Mr Johnson extricated a railway officer who was wounded and unable to move. He improvised stretchers for this officer and another wounded member of the party and organised a carrying party. Owing to the darkness they had to travel slowly, thus minimising the chances of escape. However, with the aid of Burmese guides, he was able to steer the stretcher party safely away from the scene of the ambush. Eventually, the survivors escaped and returned to Allied-held territory. Arthur Johnson's gallant action was to be acknowledged through being awarded the George Medal. *The London Gazette* publication on 29 January 1943 added:

> This was a very gallant exploit. Throughout the rest of the campaign he displayed outstanding energy, conspicuous leadership and self-sacrifice

After their impressive defence of Rangoon, the remaining British aircraft, along with the Flying Tigers, were relocated to Magwe in the Irrawaddy Valley, south of Mandalay. They were, however, to suffer significant losses at that airfield, which was then heavily attacked by the Japanese. It is appropriate to mention the monumental effort of the few Royal Air Force and American Volunteer Group Pilots who took part in the defence of Rangoon. Allied Command summed up their action with the following statement:

> It was thus possible for the last convoys of reinforcement to enter Rangoon and for the demolition and final evacuation to be completed without serious air interference. At the same time American P40 Tomahawks and Buffaloes, the range was too great for Hurricanes, attacked any enemy airfield within reach, and our few bombers ranged far into Siam. Rarely can so small an air force, have battled so gallantly and so effectively against the odds.

Four British Distinguished Flying Cross medals and one Distinguished Service Order were eventually awarded to five pilots who had flown within the American Volunteer Group.

The British withdrawal from Burma took place between 7 March and 26 May 1942. All Allied forces were led north through the jungles toward Mandalay. The Japanese supplied additional fighting troops in order to pressure the Allied withdrawal, moving north in three separate columns of strength, one through the Irrawaddy Valley, one along the Rangoon–Mandalay Road in the Sittang Valley, and the last column marched from Taunggyi in the east, pushing towards Lashio. The Allied forces finally retreated across the Indian border on 26 May 1942. As the beleaguered British crossed into India, it signalled the entire occupancy of Burma by the Japanese forces. The Japanese commanded the people of Burma and importantly accessed the capability to produce oil, rice, and valuable tungsten manganese. It was to prove fortunate that, with the advent of the monsoon season, coupled with difficulties of supplying such an extensive offensive force spread across such a wide front, the Japanese were prevented from pressing their advantage and pursuing their advance into India.

In Burma, the monsoon rains normally arrive from the south-west in early May. The winds are heavy with moisture that bursts from the sky with ferocity, instantly creating humidity, which can be overwhelming. Thereafter, the rains will fall for several hours each day, the humidity induces mould and materials often rot—leather shoes, in particular, will simply fall apart. Insects become even more active, consistent parasites that are almost impossible to thwart. The monsoon period had the capability to stop the progression of war both on the ground and in the air. The ground becomes exceptionally soft underfoot, making any form of progress tiring and debilitating.

The Japanese plans for the conquest and rule of Burma openly directed that the Burma Independence Party were to be tasked with destroying all opposing political organisations. Despite this, political instability would remain throughout Burma during the Second World War. Within those various political movements, some would seize opportunities to influence the desired freedom from British rule in Burma. General Tojo, the Japanese prime minister, announced on 28 January 1943 that Japan intended to recognise occupied Burma as an independent state.

3

# The Fight from India in Wellington Bombers, 1942–1944

Air Chief Marshal Richard Edmund Charles Peirse was appointed the Commanding Officer of the Royal Air Force in India in 1943. He immediately set about establishing, as best possible, a credible air defence of India, with the more long-term objectives of recapturing occupied territory. The Air Chief Marshal quickly appreciated the need to decentralise the command structure, so therefore created an Air Headquarters in Delhi where he was based alongside an additional Air Headquarters, which existed in Bengal to control the operations in the eastern part of India. The command structure comprised of three groups, all equipped with various aircraft types. No. 221 Group was responsible for the offensive bombing campaign, with operations conducted from within India, primarily to Burma and as far as Thailand. No. 222 Group was in Ceylon, re-establishing itself from the relentless onslaught it had received from the Japanese carrier-borne flying units. It was tasked with the patrolling of the entire Indian Ocean, while 224 Group controlled the fighter protection, both offensive and defensive deployments. In April 1943, the title of 'Royal' was officially bestowed upon the Indian Air Force. This home command and rather small Indian Air Force was able to provide vitally important Fighter Squadron capability.

India was not secure from strong and vociferous political voices—the country was far from stable. The respected opinion of Gandhi had voiced concern that the British were incapable of defending India, adding that their presence was in itself an incentive for the Japanese to invade their country. A significantly large campaign of civil disobedience existed in 1942, which effectively enhanced and supported the progression of independence for India. This would ultimately be achieved in the following years; however, Winston Churchill simply desired to achieve political stability and deal with the imminent danger posed by the Japanese who were threatening her borders.

With regard to the Allied bombing sorties conducted from India, the infrastructure and harsh conditions imposed upon the air and ground crews need to be understood.

India was an extensive country with a significantly large populace, which in itself provided an extensive labour force, but, in the main, an unskilled one. Almost all internal transportation over any distance within India took place on the railway, which was in many instances overburdened by the population, with both locomotives and rolling stock carriages in short supply. Additionally, track widths were not universal across the extensive territorial districts, which created complications that proved difficult to manage. Winston Churchill had requested immediate planning for the reconquest of Burma, and part of this was to construct a great many airfields. Geographically, the east of India provided the best options for heavy bombers to operate from, while across all of the country other airfields would provide protection on coastlines and internal communications. The logistics for such a mammoth task were almost insurmountable, bearing in mind the infrastructure of support required for each airfield and the requirement for repair and training facilities, which in themselves supported the entire operational structure. The pre-monsoon weather in India was inevitably always hot, but in 1942 conditions were excessively so, making it almost impossible to work in by the approach of mid-day. The weather eventually broke with the onset of the monsoon season, but this then inevitably created difficult ground conditions that induced prolonged misery for everyone who was working hard with the barest of equipment. Calcutta was the primary base for the Royal Air Force and, on 6 June 1942, 227 Group was formed at Lahore to centralise and deal with all aspects of training, a crucial component within the overall plan to build, plan, and supply all of the manpower and equipment that would hopefully be arriving across India. The majority of men who flew within the Royal Air Force from India came from Britain, many of whom had volunteered at the outset of war. There was, however, a significant number of men spread throughout the service that came from the Commonwealth countries of Australia, Canada, New Zealand, South Africa, and India. The vast majority of these men came from within the Commonwealth training schemes based in Canada and Rhodesia and to some extent within Britain. The United States Army Air Force in India would come under the command of the newly created 10th Air Force at Karachi; however, the United States aerial forces were very focused upon the conflict within China and many deployments were to engage with flying into China over the dangerous Pat-kai Mountains, known to all in India as 'flying over the hump'. The American-built B-24 bombers would eventually play a crucial role for the Royal Air Force, the aircraft being obtained by the British under the lend-lease scheme and later deployed across India.

The monsoon season severely restricted Allied air activity during 1942. Nevertheless, from April to December that year, the Royal Air Force flew 3,790 sorties, losing eighty-one aircraft in the process. The restructuring and development of India continued until the 16 November 1943, when the South East Asia Command was formed to take control of all Allied air operations in the Southeast Asia region.

Winston Churchill recognised the need for more heavy bombers in India and discussed matters with the United States, in the knowledge that Bomber Command in Europe was unlikely to be in a position to provide aircraft as their losses were in themselves problematical; the Middle East Command, likewise, had severe losses. The Royal Air Force was only able to muster a few tired Wellington bombers and one squadron of B-24 Liberators for India. The Liberators of 159 Squadron would eventually play a crucial role in the Far East conflict, arriving at Salbani, just west of Calcutta, in September that year. However, the story of 159 Squadron's arrival in India was not a simple one. It was formed in name only with personnel based at Molesworth, England, on 2 January 1942. They were posted to the Middle East the following month, though they had still not received any aircraft and then posted to India on 10 May 1942. The squadron's aircraft were flown to Palestine in July, where they carried out raids on North Africa, Italy, and Greece before finally leaving for India on 30 September 1942.

The first operation flown from India by the four-engined Liberator was on 17 November 1942. No. 215 Squadron's Wellingtons had arrived in April, followed by 99 Squadron, again with Wellingtons, who arrived later in October 1942. These faithful two-engined Wellington bombers were real workhorses despite many of them being old airframes, which had originated from the United Kingdom and the Middle East. These well-worn aircraft inflicted heavy maintenance requirements on the ground crews, who were in short supply of parts. The Royal Air Force would eventually be provided with an initial 366 American B-24 Liberator aircraft from the Americans. Many of the crews who flew in the Liberators had previously seen operational service in the steadfast Wellingtons. The B-24 Liberator aircraft were externally similar to the standard American B-24, which was known as the B-24D. Internally, however, they differed slightly, having been fitted with several items of British equipment, including the armament fittings where the Browning machine guns were preferred. The larger factory fitted twin .50-inch rear guns were frequently retained, primarily due to the range of fire provided by the significantly larger and more devastatingly powerful ammunition they fired.

Wellingtons and one squadron of Liberators were all that were available for night bombing operations from India. During November and December 1942, the operational squadrons were fully committed to flying sorties against airfields in Burma and equally as many against other military targets. Airfields remained a priority target for the Wellingtons and Liberators throughout operations into the New Year, disrupting and destroying Japanese Air Force aircraft. The Wellingtons concentrated on targets such as Akyab, Taungup, and Mandalay. The B-24 Liberators flew much further to selected targets in the Irrawaddy valley and even as far as Rangoon. With few radio aids to help them on their long flights, navigators had to rely partly on the stars, which were not always visible, especially during the treacherous climate conditions. Inevitably, some aircraft crashed and their crews were either killed or lost in the jungle. Tropical forests were dense, dark, and totally inhospitable, and any survivors from a crash stood little chance of being found. If an aircraft was to be forced down, the wreckage would frequently become overgrown in a matter of days, and it was little more than a week before the jungle swallowed it up completely. Individuals who took to a parachute may have fallen towards a lush green canopy, the appearance of which from the air could almost be described by some as beautiful; however, the jungle simply consumed them into an impenetrable environment. Once in the jungle, life would depend upon luck and surviving on the foods the instructors from the jungle survival training school had identified to them. Young fern leaves, roots of creeping vines, and infant bamboo were capable of providing some nutrition. Sidearms tended to be carried as a matter of routine by the majority of Australian and New Zealand crews on all flights that overflew enemy territory, however, the pistols were not universally popular and some men regarded them as a liability. It was known that Japanese soldiers regarded the carrying of a weapon as a reason to immediately open fire. Regardless of this perceived threat, a great many pilots and air crew who crashed into the jungle would have gained satisfaction at having some form of firearm defence against the enemy and wildlife predators. The dense jungles alone created lethal conditions, and many men who escaped death in the air by parachute were lost without trace in unknown tragic circumstances, denied the dignity of a proper grave.

Pilots from the European theatre would never experience such harsh circumstances or the atrocious life-threatening weather conditions that existed in the Far East. Frequently, air crews saw cloud formations so dense that aircraft were incapable of getting above or around them. These formidable conditions carried so much energy that they could simply flip over an aircraft with its violent air vortexes. The experienced pilots in Burma were anxious that all air crews arriving from the European theatre should be educated to understand the hazards of monsoon flying. In particular, they were told of the dangers of flying in squalls—daunting black clouds capable of extending just a few miles wide to over 100 miles wide. At night, crews only identified these as a result of the sudden violent bumping and jostling as they approached. Meteorological notes for air crews provided detailed advice on flying in the monsoon season and they advised of the three types of monsoon squall: the white, which in normal circumstances could not be flown through except at between 12,000 to 16,000 feet; the black squall, which could be flown through at very low heights of approximately 100 to 300 feet; and the brown squall, which was the most treacherous of all. It needed to be avoided at all cost, even if it entailed flying many miles to navigate around it. Should any pilot be forced to enter the squall, their flying instruments would become of little use. The aircraft would inevitably be thrust upwards at great velocity, creating sheer forces where water would penetrate through voids and joints in the fuselage and cockpit. The brown squall had the ability to throw the aircraft around at will, while engulfing the aircraft in a wall of water with lightning flashing along the wing lengths, particularly around the airscrews, which created unique and terrifying conditions. Ultimately, these situations had the ability to consume and destroy aircraft, resulting in a shocking loss of life. Another term used for these formidable circumstances was a 'thick squall', a reference frequently seen in period operational flying logbooks.

All members of the fighting services engaged in flying duties were required to keep a personal record of flights, and flying logbooks were issued to all members of any crew who flew within the Royal Air Force or the Commonwealth Air Forces during the Second World War. Each book was regarded as the property of the government and was required to be maintained with an accurate and detailed record of all flights undertaken on any service aircraft. Proficiency assessments were required to be completed annually, and the commanding officers or their deputies were tasked with inspecting and signing these books on a monthly basis. When these logbooks were being compiled, they were of utmost importance to the individual as they evidenced their qualifications and accumulative hours spent flying operationally—in the case of multi-crewed aircraft, the number of operational raids. The frequency of submission for inspection and endorsement meant that these books were regularly handled. The covering rubbed and the card beneath became exposed on the corners and the spines became worn. These signs immediately indicated that the owner had been in service for some time. Pilot flying logbooks were larger in dimension than the observers and air gunners flying logbooks as they required more detail to be recorded. As you would expect within military service, these books were identified by unique reference numbers—Form 1767 for observers and Form 414 for pilots. Other differentials existed within the basic format of these flying logbooks. Those issued in South Africa were supplied with a covering of red material for observers and green for pilots, which made them instantly recognisable. Those issued in India were supplied with a cream-coloured cloth covering. However, it was not uncommon to see any type of logbook covered in outer leather binding to preserve its integrity. This was frequently seen in the Far East, where the books suffered in the extreme humidity.

In early 1942, the Allied Air Forces had just four all-weather runways in India, each provided with good operational facilities. The surge of new constructions using native labour rapidly created new facilities, with 285 airfields completed by late 1943. Many of these were basic, but the important runways were capable in supporting the needs of various aircraft types.

India Air Command had made a plea for Handley Page Halifax bombers to be sent to the Far East. In October 1943, the Air Ministry made provision to send two Merlin-engined Halifaxes and two Lancasters to India for climatically controlled condition evaluations. The Royal Air Force Pilot Arthur Middleton, serving within the Special Duties Flight 1577, was tasked with the trials. He was a most experienced pilot, having been awarded the Distinguished Flying Cross for operations across Europe and the Middle East. Departing in Halifax DK263, he flew the aircraft on a ten-day transit to reach India where the extensive trials were to be undertaken. These trials included short-runway take-offs, landing exercises, and height tests. One of these trials was a sortie on 24 November 1943, where the Halifax DK263 carried a full bombload in a recorded heat of 92° Fahrenheit (34° Celsius). Tragedy would subsequently strike Halifax DK263 on 26 January 1944, when Flight Lieutenant Middleton flew the aircraft from Bombay with a full crew and six passengers and a light load of mail bags. This was a simple transit flight, but two engines failed on the aircraft and a forced-landing took place on Kamptee airstrip. This airstrip was only 600 yards in length and Flight Lieutenant Middleton was apparently unaware that the cleared ground fashioned for aircraft finished with a sudden drop of 80 feet into a riverbed. The Halifax landed successfully, but struck a pothole with its starboard wheel near the end of its landing run. Having been travelling relatively fast, it caused the Halifax to cartwheel into the river, landing on its back in a crumpled mess. Nine occupants of the aircraft had been killed in the crash, four crew and five passengers. The pilot Arthur Middleton survived and would eventually return to the United Kingdom. He later flew a third tour of duty in the Mitchell B-25 bomber, and this lucky survivor was eventually awarded the Distinguished Service Order by the end of war.

Aboard one of the Wellington bombers (HX591) that arrived in India in October 1942 was twenty-year-old David Arthur Jones from Cardiff, Wales. David was the eldest of three sons born to Rachel Edith Jones and John (his father), who worked on the Great Western Railways. David Jones was a gifted academic and was rewarded with a scholarship to the prestigious Colston's Collegiate School. The school's active cadet forces contingent for the Royal Air Force was where David first experienced the wearing of a military uniform. At that time, although he did not know it, his diligence in mathematics would eventually enable him to pass the selection procedures to become a navigator within the Royal Air Force.

The men who flew in the Second World War were all volunteers, and David commenced his service at the rank of leading aircraftsman under training, a status indicated by a white flash worn upon his side hat. Eventually, David took to the air on 28 August 1941, the date on which he commenced accumulating his flying hours within his own flying logbook. He would eventually carry that book with him to India a year later. Before then, he would undertake intensive training and gain experience in the Wellington bombers that equipped the Operational Training Unit at Moreton-in-Marsh, Gloucestershire. His skills in navigation would be tested in a most unexpected development; the training unit at Moreton was required to enhance the strength of Bomber Command in a raid to Bremen. The unit was required to supply competent crews to also participate in that operation on 25 June 1942. It proved to be David's first operational sortie and one which was successfully completed, enabling him to record a seven-hour-and-twenty-minute offensive operation into Germany. It was, however, to be his first and last engagement in Bomber Command. The following month, he was required to form part of another Wellington crew within the Overseas Air Delivery Unit and fly the aircraft to the Middle East.

The dangers associated with delivering bomber aircraft to the Middle East and Far East are vividly evidenced by an incident on 14 June 1942. Wellington DV547, crewed by 99 Squadron personnel who were detached from their Squadron and flying with the Overseas Air Delivery Unit, stopped over at Sharjah—a location where the airfield overlooked the Persian Gulf. This was an important Allied base and ideal for a staging post facilitating direct flights into India. The Wellington was captained by a New Zealander, Flying Officer Brown. His five crew members consisted of three British and two Australian airmen. The Wellington Bomber attempted to depart from Sharjah, but gained insufficient height and eventually struck an obstruction causing a crash, which resulted in the aircraft bursting into flames. All five men on board suffered serious burns and were admitted into Karachi hospital for treatment. One of the Australians, Sergeant Curr, eventually returned to operational flying ten months later; he was posted into 159 Squadron and flew against the Japanese in that unit's Liberators.

David Jones flew within Wellington HX591, which was the aircraft selected to be transported to the Far East. Jones was faced with the unenviable task of navigating the aircraft on a route from the United Kingdom to Gibraltar, Gambia, Gold Coast, Nigeria, Sudan, Iraq, and finally India. Departing on 28 July 1942, it proved to be an eventful transit. On 10 August they suffered a hydraulics failure, which caused damage to an airscrew propeller. On 2 September, in Sudan, an overshoot on landing damaged the tail plane and landing wheel, which eventually induced the crew to exchange aircraft in Iraq. The remaining transit would take place in Wellington HD977, the aircraft in which they eventually arrived safely in India. Both the crew and aircraft joined the strength of 99 Squadron, who were operating from Digri in Bengal, India.

The first full day on the squadron was spent in the briefing rooms talking to the available crews about what to look out for with cloud formations. There was no doubt amongst all the airmen that the worst enemy was the weather. The operational briefing procedure was explained, normally undertaken the previous day as the majority of sorties were undertaken within the early hours. The crews would gather in the large briefing room with all the participating personnel to be informed of the intended target, what bombs were to be carried, how high to be on the bombing run, what to expect from the opposition, and of course the weather. The respective crew members would then depart to be briefed in their special duties, such as navigation, bomb aimers, and air gunners. David Jones was a young man who had experienced just one operational sortie flying over Germany and two rather fraught landings in far off parts of the world. His flying logbook allows us to get a sense of the duties he undertook, both against the enemy and during various other flying duties. Using a red fountain pen, the dark, rich-coloured ink accounts for every night excursion undertaken to drop bombs and destroy as much as possible of the Japanese war infrastructure, with blue ink used to record, in the main, all other duties. The first notable entry for David to pen was on 11 November 1942; while on a flight to gain air experience and local landmark observation, the weather suddenly turned into a violent squall forcing them back to the safety of Digri.

The crews were adept at operating from other makeshift landing strips, which had been constructed a short distance from the main base; these temporary landing grounds, in essence, reduced flying time on actual operations against the enemy. No. 99 Squadron would eventually conduct its first operation from Indian soil on 18 November, when eight Wellingtons flew from the advance staging post at Fenni to attack a Japanese airfield at Meiktila. David Jones did not participate as the crews would normally fly on consecutive days, followed by non-flying rest days, so it frequently fell to luck as to which personnel would be involved. When full strength operations were required, the predicting factors were simply the number of aircraft serviced and fit to fly. It did, however, transpire that targets were frequently attacked on alternate nights by both 99 and 215 Squadrons. This would enable consistent attacks upon worthy targets.

These men had great loyalty towards the Wellington bomber, designed by Barnes Wallis and Rex Pierson of Vickers Aviation. The aircraft was known to all as the 'Wimpy', deriving that nickname from the Disney cartoon character, Wellington Wimpy. Those men who flew and maintained the aircraft frequently had cause to bless its strength provided by the geodetic construction—a criss-cross of airframe members that Wallis had invented. The aircraft's apparent fragility beguiled its capability of surviving serious damage while in the air. The Wellington aircraft, developed from the original specification, was designed to carry a 1,000-lb bombload for a distance of 720 miles. The capacity was increased to carry a 4,500-lb bombload for 2,500 miles, an impressive performance that contributed to the Wellington being the main aircraft used in Europe by Bomber Command for the first three years of the war. Even when superseded by four-engined types, it continued in production until 1945, with some 11,460 aircraft being been built. An assumption must be that those Wellington crews in India saw the B-24 Liberators as a more effective aircraft, with their multiple engines and large deep fuselages capable of taking the war right into Thailand. Nevertheless, until more Liberators were to arrive in India, the flights continued with the two-engined dope-canvas-sided Wellington bomber. Flying in formation was impractical and very dangerous in the monsoons because storms came up in a matter of minutes and in many instances without any warning at all. On these long Far East flights, which Wellingtons were not ideally designed for, it was vital that the crews flew according to the flight plan in order to conserve fuel.

David Jones witnessed the evident dangers to Wellington crews on the night of 22 November 1942, when seven fellow 99 Squadron crews attacked various important communication targets around the Meiktila area. The Japanese fighters singled out one Wellington (flown by Sergeant Stanley) and, during the aerial fight, his rear gunner Sergeant Austin defended his aircraft as admirably as possible. Badly damaged, the aircraft managed to return to Allied lines for an emergency landing at Chittagong. Unfortunately, the Wellington overshot the landing strip and became engulfed in fire, causing the death of Sergeant Austin and his fellow crewmember, Pilot Officer MacDonald. Compared to the great bombing campaign in Europe, the operations over Burma were almost negligible in respect of the numbers of participating aircraft, but the cost in lives was not. It must be remembered that many Allied air crews were also losing their lives flying smaller and outdated aircraft on offensive bombing operations from India.

An official report published to journalists by the Reference Division of the Ministry of Information detailed that, in November 1942, the number of raids made by the Royal Air Force over Burma had increased to thirty. Rangoon, and especially its principal airfield at Mingaladon, had been attacked by Allied bombers for the first time since the monsoon began, and other airfields, as well as railway objectives, were repeatedly raided. Low-level attacks on Japanese sea and river shipping had also become a feature of fighter aircraft operating from India. The most striking fact emerging from all this is the almost entire absence of any losses in aircraft. Among other objectives, Akyab was raided six times, Rangoon five times, Meiktila five times, Magwe four times, and Mandalay twice. Targets had been airfields, runways and buildings, oil installations, railway lines, stations yards trains, army huts, and other buildings in Japanese hands, as well as objectives in river areas and shipping. In some cases, fighter escort had been provided and bombing appears to have been accurate, with good results observed. On one night (21 November 1942), Mingaladon and Taungoo airfields were attacked by medium and heavy bombers operating on an increased scale; many thousands of pounds of high explosive were dropped, and fires started that were visible from 80 to 100 miles away. In both day and night raids, the only bombers specifically mentioned by name have been Blenheim and Wellingtons and the only fighters, Hudson and Hurricanes.

At 1.27 a.m. on 2 December 1942, David Jones finally climbed into Wellington HE118 for his first operational sortie over Burma. He was to navigate to the enemy airfield at Akyab and additionally to act as the bomb aimer, his responsibility being to ensure their payload of bombs would inflict as much damage as possible upon the Japanese aircraft and airfield facilities. David recorded a simple logbook entry indicating that the bombs fell in a line of five near the north-east to south-west runway, and that the operation took five hours and ten minutes to complete. Having landed at Fenny, which was their forward operating airfield, they would later return to their main station. Three nights later, he was not so fortunate. Unable to find the target at Taungoo airfield, they consumed more fuel trying to identify their position. Running out of fuel, David dropped the bombs into the sea and managed to locate Dum Dum airfield for an eventual safe landing after having been airborne for just over eight hours. Dum Dum was less than 100 miles east from Digri and relatively close to Calcutta, indicating how perilously close the safety margin with their fuel had been. He redeemed himself to his crew on the last day of the month when they once again successfully navigated to the target of Akyab. The pressure upon navigators was immense as they shouldered the responsibility of ensuring the operation had a chance of success in reaching and returning from any target.

Navigation was terribly difficult for all of the navigators—the pressure of being required to know where the aircraft was at any one time during the long sorties over occupied Burma was immense. When an aircraft is in the air, its flight path over the ground and towards the intended target is determined by its speed and its direction through the air. However, the direction and speed of the wind moving that air affects the navigator's calculations. The skill of any navigator is thus determined by his ability to judge these variants. For example, a five-hour flight, with the wind blowing at just 30 miles per hour, would end up with the aircraft being roughly 150 miles away from where it would have been without the wind. The pilot would always expect the navigator to know where he was. This could be regarded as a simple task when over land and in daylight with perfect conditions. However, at night or over the sea, dead reckoning comes into use, a practice of consistently drawing the course on maps, calculating the distance travelled through the air, and then adding in what effect the wind has had on the aircraft. This process was enhanced by taking Astro readings if the stars were available or partly available to sight.

Astro navigation is a most important skill taught in navigation basic training. It uses the position of the stars to determine the position of the aircraft. At any given time there is a place on Earth directly underneath any star, this is known as the sub-stellar point. The navigator would use the sextant by looking through the eyepiece of the device to locate a defined star; with the device on the side of the instrument, similar to a camera's focus ring, the navigator would adjust the angle of a rotatable prism until the star showing in the eyepiece aligned beside the bubble in the machine, which provided the level. The prism and focus device work together in circular scales, marked off in degrees. From these scales, although it became possible to read the star's altitude, the acceleration of the aircraft and weather turbulence were always likely to deflect from the true vertical and a single reading was most probably inaccurate. For that reason, the bubble sextant also has a mechanical device with a wind-up clock. It was able to take sixty altitude readings over a two-minute period, displayed on a counter. The further away the aircraft was from the sub-stellar point, the lower the angle calculated on the sextant device. It was this reading that calculated where, at any given moment to the particular point, the aircraft was. There were twenty-two primary navigation stars, some only usable in the south and others north of the equator. The navigator must be able to instantly recognise these stars in order to be able to work out his position. In addition to having located the target area, David then took charge of the aircrafts bomb aiming device and instigated the deployment of the bombload onto the target.

The official duties as a navigator in the Royal Air Force were to:

Prepare the flight plan before any flight.
Give the pilot magnetic courses to follow while in the air.
Keep written records of the aircrafts actual or estimated positions and enter in the flight log.
Inform the captain of the aircraft positions on request.
Initiate requests for direction finding bearings from the wireless operator whenever thought necessary.

Additional to the Allied aerial bombing, one of the more robust British military counteroffensive actions in Burma was an attempt to recapture Akyab in late 1942.

Akyab Island formed part of the area known as the Arakan, situated in the western coastal region of Burma and strategically important with its port and airfield. The island would be crucial for any successful Allied offensive in order to penetrate deeper into Japanese-held territory; however, the Allies would only achieve their objective of holding this island much later in the war. In the meantime, the Allied Air Forces from India would consistently attack Akyab, as evidenced in David's flying logbook, which confirmed the bombing of that target as well as Mandalay on five occasions during February 1943.

The Photographic Reconnaissance Unit operating from Dum Dum in India provided significant early aerial photographic cover across Japanese-held territories. The unit was officially named 681 Squadron in January 1943. It had a fairly mixed complement of aircraft, including the two-engined American B-25 Mitchell. These were employed on strategic reconnaissance sorties in Burma, Thailand, Malaya, Singapore, Java, and Sumatra. The aircraft were stripped of extraneous equipment and an extra fuel tank was installed in the fuselage to increase the distance capabilities. Despite the modifications, the B-25 aircraft did not have the speed to outpace Japanese fighters and they were completely unarmed. The crew consisted of a pilot, a second pilot, and a navigator. Volunteer ground-based photographers were required to fly as additional aircrew in the Mitchells to maintain the three large mounted cameras on the floor, about halfway down the fuselage. One camera pointed straight down, while the other two were angled to overlap the images. Further towards the tail was another camera, which captured images at high altitude. In addition, the cameraman was required to keep a lookout for Japanese fighters from the Perspex astrodome. This had replaced the mid-upper gun turret. Fighter aircraft were often encountered and several aircraft from this unit were lost flying sorties to photograph targets on the airfield at Myitkyina, the docks at Rangoon, the airfield at Chiengmai, and the first exposures of the new Burma–Thailand Railway that was being built by thousands of British and Allied prisoners.

The American B-25 aircraft were originally destined for the Dutch Air Force, but events in the Dutch East Indies saw them delivered to India. Four leading aircraftsmen were selected from the volunteers and received the additional flying pay, but they were not provided with the status of air crew as no such trade of cameraman existed. One of these men, Leading Aircraftsman Benjamin Weighell, lost his life with his crew on 13 February 1943, his life now simply commemorated on the Singapore Memorial. Another airman photographer, who had also volunteered, Leading Aircraftsman Alan Fox, was awarded the Distinguished Flying Medal, believed to be one of only three airman photographers who received this decoration. The recommendation, dated 12 October 1943, states:

Leading Aircraftsman Fox has completed fifty-nine operational sorties flying as photographer in B-25 aircraft in this Unit and has experienced anti-aircraft fire six times and fighter opposition seven times. He has shown great keenness and devotion to duty on all operational flights. On numerous occasions when his aircraft has been attacked by enemy fighters Leading Aircraftsman Fox has given invaluable assistance to his pilot by informing him of the position of the enemy aircraft. He has shown great coolness and courage and has set an excellent example to all. I strongly recommend him for the award of the Distinguished Flying Medal.

On 14 March, David Jones returned from attacking the railway sidings at Mandalay (a major target) at around 1 a.m. the following day. No doubt feeling very accomplished, he recorded in his records that the bombload had been dropped directly upon the engine sheds. He was to climb back into the same aircraft, HE131, just a few hours later when his pilot Flight Sergeant Rowlands took off on another short transit sortie with another 99 Squadron Wellington. Both aircraft had been ordered to fly to the advanced landing ground at Agartala, an airfield situated on flat terrain east of Calcutta, to collect ground crew personnel. Once landed, both aircraft were loaded with the men and they took off to return to Digri. The aircraft had only been in the air for a few minutes when tragedy struck—Wellington HE112 colliding with Wellington HE131. The collision was catastrophic and Wellington HE112 plummeted to the ground. By great fortune Wellington HE131 suffered less damage. David and his crew all suffered numerous injuries, but remarkably no fatalities. The entire crew and passengers within the other aircraft were all killed. Pilot Officer Lorne Dobson, from Manitoba, Canada, was the pilot in that ill-fated aircraft and the following men all died alongside him:

> Sergeant William Field (1378559) RAFVR, aged thirty-four.
> Leading Aircraftsman Franklin Thomas (553775) RAF, aged nineteen.
> Leading Aircraftsman Horace Jopson (748808) RAFVR, aged twenty-seven.
> Leading Aircraftsman Frederick Keane (1135398) RAFVR, aged thirty-one.
> Sergeant David McDougle (1131124) RAFVR, aged twenty-one.
> Sergeant Stanley Morris (1177069) RAFVR, aged twenty-two.
> Aircraftsman First Class Arthur Nottingham (1031351) RAFVR, aged thirty-one.
> Leading Aircraftsman John Sweeney (1189895) RAFVR, aged twenty-six.
> Flight Sergeant Clifford Westcott (635886) RAF, aged twenty-one.

David recovered in hospital over several months and returned to 99 Squadron in July 1943; his squadron was at that time at their new operational station in Jessore, Bengal. In his absence, the Squadron had received slightly improved or upgraded Wellingtons, and he joined a crew captained by Sergeant Sharwood-Smith. This pilot was a most confident and capable man, and had developed an early reputation for pressing home his attacks in adverse circumstances. He subsequently received a commission as an officer, completed two tours of duty, and won a Distinguished Flying Cross. Despite having been injured and experiencing the trauma of such a serious accident, the business of operational flying and navigating was immediately reimposed upon David

Jones. He and his new crew would receive briefings to carry out intruder operational patrols off the Arakan coast. These operations were coded as FIRPO, a term used in all briefings and logbook entries. The crew's instructions were to report upon and attack any shipping targets that were identified.

The following month saw another reorganisation of the Allied Far East Forces—the new South East Asia Command was formed. This was a bonded Anglo-American configuration commanded by Admiral Lord Louis Mountbatten. The Air Command South East Asia element was under the control of Air Chief Marshal Sir Richard Peirse. The vision was a focused development of capability between the Royal Air Force and the United States Army Air Force. India, at that time, only had three Bomber Squadrons capable of striking deeper into Japanese-held territories: 99, 215, and 159—the one Liberator B-24-equipped squadron. It had become commonplace for experienced Wellington crews to support the smaller B-24 unit, but, until the supply of more Liberators was resolved, Wellington operations from India would continue. Men like David Jones appeared rather dishevelled wearing various arrays of uniform and headgear, making do and mending what they possessed. The weather conditions caused clothing materials to break down and very quickly appear worn out and tired, conditions far removed from the European theatre of war.

It is prudent to mention Squadron Leader Lucian Ercolani at this point; a stalwart and unshakable character who had been with 99 Squadron since October 1942 and had served alongside David Jones, although they had not crewed together. Ercolani was a young officer who wore the rarely seen medal ribbon of the Distinguished Service Order, a very rare accolade to be awarded to a junior Flying Officer. He had been awarded the medal during his European service in 1941. Even more impressively, he had been recommended for the immediate award of that illustrious medal. During a bombing raid over Germany, the weather prevented the bombing of a main target, so Lucian attempted to drop his bombload over the secondary targets, but they failed to release. His aircraft was then hit by German anti-aircraft fire, setting it on fire. For over two hours he flew the aircraft before ditching in the English Channel. He and his crew then spent fifty-seven hours in a rubber dinghy before being picked up. It had been an extraordinary feat of flying and survival.

Squadron Leader Ercolani experienced trauma over Burma on 6 February 1943, when he was flying his Wellington to attack the railway station at Mandalay. The return journey saw serious mechanical troubles develop leaving just two engines—losing any engines within a Wellington was always likely to be potentially lethal scenario. He managed to reach landfall and successfully landed the damaged aircraft at Fenni, a long way from the Squadrons home base at Digri. There was no such ending for a fellow Wellington crew five days later. Pilot Officer Watson and his crew in HD973 were only on their second operation over Burma, attacking Sagaing Jetty, when they were forced down and landed in Japanese-held territory near Gabgaw. The crew of six survived to become prisoners of war in Rangoon's jail. Watsons' second pilot, Sergeant Jim Manser, was killed in the accidental bombing of that jail by American

Liberators in November 1943. Flying Officer John 'Jack' Wright and the Australians Pilot Officer Gregory Kirwan and Sergeant Malcolm Woods were all liberated from Rangoon jail. The crew's front gunner, Sergeant Ron Haddon, was amongst the men forced-marched from Rangoon jail prior to its liberation. However, he made an escape to freedom and later located the Allied forces. To conclude, exposing the potential dangers experienced by crews on these long-endurance flights, on 2 March, Sergeant Seymour captained his crew to bomb the Sagaing Jetty near Mandalay. Bad weather played its part in their fate on the return; as they reached India, the fuel finally ran out. The crew baled out and suffered various minor injuries as they landed south of Calcutta, while their aircraft eventually plunged down into open countryside.

Squadron Leader Ercolani was promoted to a Flight Commander in September 1943 and received a posting away from 99 Squadron. Before his departure on 17 August, he demonstrated his personal doggedness by being the only pilot from four aircraft to reach and bomb the target of Akyab despite bad weather. Squadron Leader Ercolani gained valuable experience on the B-24 Liberator. It would be this aircraft in which he would develop operational techniques that would be used for 'bridge busting', a duty that became of utmost importance to the Allied military objectives in fighting the Japanese within Burma and Thailand. Ercolani would eventually seek to form his own Liberator crew, selecting men he had knowledge of or those highly recommended to him. One vitally important member of his crew would have been his navigator. That position would eventually be occupied by David Jones, who in the meantime remained operational in the 99 Squadron Wellingtons, unaware of his status and credibility in the mind of Lucian Ercolani.

The vital target of Akyab continued to be attacked by 99 Squadron. On the night of 7 September 1943, unpredictable weather enveloped the target and thick cloud forced the operation to be aborted just as the aircraft arrived over Akyab. One Wellington suffered the failure of an engine, which would prove catastrophic for the crew. Despite dropping their bombs and disposing of all armaments and anything removable from the aircraft in an attempt to lessen the weight, they gradually descended towards the sea. The radio operator issued an emergency wireless distress signal and they eventually ditched into the sea. The bomb aimer and rear gunner were trapped and taken down within the fuselage of the sinking aircraft. Although the three remaining crew managed to secure a lifesaving dinghy, which had automatically inflated, it had suffered damage and the loss of air resulted in it being incapable of holding all three men. The dinghy was kept afloat with the use of hand bellows, and the men took turns hanging onto the side while fully immersed in the water. The following day, 99 Squadron sent five Wellingtons to search for the missing crew; David Jones flew with Flying Officer Bent in Wellington HZ138, but within ten minutes of having taken off the fuel filler caps on both wings unexplainably opened forcing an immediate return to Jessore. That matter was rectified and within twenty minutes they took off again, carrying supplies in the hope of locating the missing crew. Pilot Officer Hamilton in another Wellington did successfully sight the dinghy and initiated a rescue operation that proved successful. Flying Officer Allan, Sergeant Butler, and Sergeant Chopping had been remarkably lucky in surviving that harrowing ditching and, in doing so, became eligible to join the coveted Goldfish Club.

There were a number of clubs during the Second World War that a serving member of the Royal Air Force or Commonwealth aircrew could become eligible to join. The Caterpillar Club, awarded for surviving a life-threatening incident by using the silk parachutes built by Irvin. The Goldfish Club was formed as a result of airmen using equipment designed and manufactured specifically to save lives at sea. The Late Arrivals Club was through sheer determination on the part of the airman to return back to Allied lines on foot, primarily in the Western Desert. Finally, eligibility for the Guinea Pig Club was the most exclusive, an airman having had to be operated on by the legendary plastic surgeon Archibald McIndoe, who was famous for repairing shocking burn injuries. In Southeast Asia, survival odds were always heavily stacked against Allied aviators, partially due to the fact that the Japanese forces adopted fierce retribution on the men who bombed them, often inflicting terrible beatings and decapitation.

On 22 October 1943, David Jones once again navigated his aircraft on an offensive patrol off the Arakan coast, departing from Jessore at 9 a.m. and returning at 5 p.m. On that day, Admiral Lord Louis Mountbatten had visited his station and addressed all the ranks with a speech on the war. Squadron Leader Ercolani later described in his notes that his experience of meeting such an important personality left him with the observation that 'Mountbatten electrified the whole area on his arrival, rather like Nelson hoisting his pennant on HMS *Victory*'.

No doubt Admiral Mountbatten's address would have included material recently released for publication by the Reference Division of the Ministry of Information, a document that provided a good overview of events concerning the war in the air over Burma. It read:

In the face of world-wide commitments, the Royal Air Force has once more proved its ability to take the initiative. Despite the vital necessity for retaining its hard-won mastery of the skies over Western Europe, and in the Middle East, it has been found possible to send what must have been substantial reinforcements to India for use in the air offensive over Burma. Enough publicity has already been given to the immense work of organisation and maintenance involved in sending aircraft and crews overseas in other connections; it may however, be mentioned in passing that conditions, especially weather conditions in this theatre, are particularly trying on both men and machines, thus aggravating the problems already existing. Striking features of the Royal Air Force offensive over Burma are the diversity of the tactics employed—day and night bombing, fighter sweeps, and low-level fighter bomber attacks—and the variety of targets chosen. It has, furthermore, been estimated that whereas the Japanese are now dropping bombs on India by the hundredweight, we are dropped them on Burma by the ton. The cooperation of the Royal Air Force with the United States Army Air Force has been of higher order, and augurs well for the future. The absence of serious opposition over many targets has helped in keeping our losses low, even negligible for long periods at a time; even when attempts have been made to intercept our aircraft or shoot them down, they have met with little or no success.

In Britain, the war was much closer to men and women who suffered under the European conflict, but the government's 'Wings for Victory' campaign conducted in 1943 also brought the Burma war into focus. In particular, the populace was introduced to the American-built B-24 Liberator.

Winston Churchill had the foresight to appoint the Canadian-born newspaper magnate Lord Beaverbrook as his Minister of Aviation Production. Lord Beaverbrook took up the post on 15 May 1940 and was charged with increasing the production of aircraft within all of the United Kingdom-based factories. With war costs escalating, the government urged the public to donate funds specifically to facilitate the purchase of a dedicated or 'named' aircraft. This concept had been successfully used in the First World War and was therefore resurrected by Beaverbrook. The target valuations of £5,000 for a single-engined fighter, £20,000 for a twin-engined aircraft, and £40,000 for a four-engined aircraft were published; these were not the actual costs for the production of those aircraft, but figures chosen to represent proportionate sums. However, they were significantly large sums of money for those times. The government subsequently appointed First World War pilot Wing Commander William Shakespeare, recipient of the Military Cross and Air Force Cross, as the Royal Air Force liaison officer with the National Savings Committee. The movement comprised of Local Savings Committees, large numbers of local associations that were run by volunteers responsible for selling the various national savings products and sending the money to the government. These voluntary organisations were supported by National Committees and regional sub-committees—civil servants employed to assist and advise. The Royal Air Force was to co-operate with the movement, promoting the scheme in supplying men and aircraft to assist in what was to become 'Wings for Victory' week during 5 March and 3 July 1943. Large bomber aircraft were transported into city environments and reconstructed in order to be displayed to the public, creating an impressive spectacle.

Very few people had seen or heard of the Consolidated B-24 Liberator before December 1941. A testimony of its success and popularity can be measured by the fact that the American-built B-24 became one of the specific aircraft that could be purchased within the 'Wings for Victory' week in Great Britain. The Secretary of State for Air had set the sum of £40,000 for each B-24 aircraft. Only the British Sunderland four-engined flying boat was more expensive, at £50,000. These were obviously staggering sums of money, but the savings groups were also able to set targets in terms of specific parts of an aircraft or selected pieces of equipment. Every little nut, bolt, or split pin necessary to the aircraft was seen as important. The published target costs for aircraft parts relative to a four-engined B-24 aircraft were illustrated in posters and other advertisements distributed across towns and villages. It was thought that advising component parts such as a single spark plug at 8*s* (todays value: 40 pence) was likely to encourage the most menial contribution or induce collective contributions during the savings campaign. The following are examples of the range of aircraft components and their respective costs:

| | |
|---|---|
| £2,500 | Single engine |
| £1,500 | Undercarriage |
| £500 | Air gunner turret |
| £400 | Instruments |
| £350 | Propeller |
| £250 | Wireless set |
| £120 | Wheel |
| £100 | Self-sealing fuel tank |
| £100 | Machine gun |
| £100 | Ailerons |
| £60 | Bomb sight |
| £40 | Oil tank |
| £35 | Individual parachute |
| £30 | Pilots control column |
| £10 | Tail wheel |
| 15*s* | Pilots flying goggles |
| 12*s* | Air crew flying helmet |
| 10*s* | Navigation folding lamp |
| 8*s* | Individual spark plug |
| 6*d* | Individual rivets |
| 6*d* | Machine gun bullet |

With specific reference to aircrew flying the B-24 over Burma, the savings campaign itemised the Far East Tropical Kit required for each man. The Khaki-coloured uniform kit for each man could be purchased at a cost of £2 14*s* 4*d*.

The average working family, who were already struggling with strict rationing and being subjected to capital bombing campaigns by the enemy, were encouraged by the government to invest in every way possible. The B-24 Liberator became instantly recognisable to the people in Britain and the conflict in Burma was provided with the recognition it deserved. Mountbatten's plans for the retaking of Burma were beginning to come together, but he knew the Japanese were still ambitious in their campaigns to invade India.

The prime minister of Japan directly supervised the Bureau of Propaganda in Burma via his appointed director. The intent of eradicating any harbouring of Anglo-American influences within the minds of the occupied country was prevalent. The prime minister actively promoted the policy of a strong Burma within a free and prosperous Asia. Japanese aircraft consistently dropped propaganda leaflets across Burma, while on the ground more than 100,000 posters had been displayed advocating the close co-operation and collaboration of working with Japan and the war effort. A treaty of alliance between Japan and Burma was signed by Ba Maw. He had been previously arrested for sedition within Burma on 6 August 1940 and subsequently imprisoned in Mogok jail, eastern Burma. Ba Maw had been released from jail by the occupying Japanese, who provided him with the opportunity to lead a coalition government.

On 1 August 1943, Ba Maw, in his stately position as the Head of Burma, met with the Japanese ambassador in Rangoon, and several treaty alliances were signed between them. Article one agreed to co-operate militarily and politically with developing the Greater East Asia Co-Prosperity Sphere. This facilitated for the additional treaty documents to be signed on the same day with, among others, the Commander in Chief, Burma Theatre Army, Masakazu Kawabe. This secret military agreement had far greater resonation for Burma. Article two of the treaty stated that the Japanese and Burmese governments agree to co-operate closely in establishing and developing the Greater East Asia Co-Prosperity Sphere for the purpose of common prosperity within East Asian countries.

Article one stated:

Japanese forces will, during the prosecution of the Greater East Asia War, possess entire freedom of action in the execution of military operations in Burma. The Burmese government acknowledges the matters stated in the above clause and pledges to provide the Japanese forces with all and every necessary assistance in order to execute the military operation in Burma.

Article two stated:

The Burmese government pledges, in order to maintain joint defence during the prosecution of the Greater East Asia War, to place Burmese forces under the command of the Supreme Commander of the Japanese occupational forces in Burma.

The agreement progressed in detail, requiring the Burmese government to aid the Japanese forces in Burma in commandeering the supply of labour forces. This in itself would be most significant in the ambitious developments of the railway communication plans to progress towards India. This matter would entail massive manpower to construct the bridges and cut through the jungle. Historically, Ba Maw's rule is now most bitterly remembered for this agreement and its use of forced Burmese labour to help the Japanese.

After more than fifty years of British occupation, Ba Maw announced that same day the declaration of independence of Burma with his signature placed upon document number forty-three. On 1 August, he also signed a declaration of war in a lengthy document that concluded with the statement:

> Burma, therefore, declares that she has today entered into a state of war with Britain and the United States of America. She will prosecute the war against these aggressor powers to the end in complete unity of will, purpose and action with Nippon and her Allies.

These political manoeuvres had no effect on the men who were bombing Burma from India, but the stability of Burma was important in respect to the fighting factions and loyalties for or against the Japanese. Back at Jessore, David Jones continued with his own personal war, conscious that he was rapidly approaching the completion of his first tour of operations and he would then be rested. November 1943 had been exceptionally busy for 99 Squadron, with daylight operational hours reaching over 150 and night operational hours close to 550 hours. David Jones' flying logbook that month recorded some fifty-seven hours on bombing sorties, which included the dropping of pathfinder flares and incendiaries, a relatively new strategy in Burma and one that reflected well upon his navigational and bombing skills. He had also spent nearly eight hours in the air searching for a missing crew captained by Flight Sergeant Clement, one that tragically was never to be found.

Following some fraught inter-Allied negotiations at the highest level, the American General Stratemeyer arrived in India in 1943. He had been appointed Commanding General of the United States Army Air Forces and as Air Commander of the Allied Eastern Air Command. He proposed to Air Chief Marshal Peirse (Air Commander Southeast Asia) that the two air arms collaborate to destroy completely the most vital Japanese installations in the Rangoon vicinity. Air Chief Marshal Peirse readily agreed, seeing this as additionally reducing the enemy's potential for sustained attacks on Calcutta, as well as reducing the threat of Japanese fighter operations across a wider front.

The plan to commence bombing Rangoon was set for 25 November. The strength of American B-24 and the smaller B-25 aircraft were to attack in two waves, targeting the locomotive sheds and the nearby airfield, while the maximum strength of Royal Air Force bombers would attack the Mahlwagon railway marshalling yards at night. The American bombers would follow up with an attack on that same important target during the subsequent days. The planned series of operations to the various targets in and around Rangoon was expected to last six days and five nights, an ambitious plan that would engage a significant force of men both on the ground and in the air. Twelve Wellington bombers from 99 Squadron were scheduled to participate in the initial operation, with aircraft HZ553 being navigated to Rangoon by David Jones and flown by Flight Sergeant Shar-Smith.

David Jones departed from his airfield at 10.45 p.m. on 25 November, on the long run to the target in Wellington HZ553. The distance flown by the aircraft, who were detailed to attack Rangoon, was greater than that required for aircraft based in Britain to strike Berlin, but the India-based bombers generally faced less anti-aircraft defences. That said, the Japanese had enforced their defences around Rangoon, making it one of the most heavily fortified areas in all of Southeast Asia. Heavy anti-aircraft guns and batteries of searchlights were concentrated at strategic positions. These were advantageous to the defence of Rangoon, and the larger part of the Japanese fighter strength in Burma was based within easy striking distances to the city. It was a city of great value, possessing a river front with miles of jetties and wharves. Ocean-going steamers berthed and unloaded cargoes directly into huge storage sheds, which were in turn served by multiple railway sidings. The Burma railway then fed into the countries supply structure, enabling the Japanese to distribute its goods with ease. Many railway stations existed in close proximity to the docks, and the main station of Phayre Street, Rangoon, had seven remarkably long platforms.

Any Allied operation to Rangoon therefore met resistance, and they did so with little effective fighter protection due to the distance from India. Conversely, the sortie undertaken with just two engines in a Wellington made it even more dangerous for the crews. Flight Sergeant Colin Lee, later Reverend Lee, was awarded a Distinguished Flying Medal as a result of his actions over Rangoon. The recommendation, which was published as a press release, serves to endorse these dangers:

This airman has proved to be a consistently good and reliable pilot who has taken part in many operational sorties in the Burma theatre of war, penetrating deep into enemy territory on many occasions. In November 1943, while over Rangoon, his aircraft was attacked by enemy fighters and in the ensuing combat badly damaged. Nevertheless, Flight Sergeant Lee with great skill frustrated the attackers, damaging two of the enemy aircraft. Throughout his tour this airman has displayed most praiseworthy courage and determination to complete his mission despite very adverse weather during the Monsoon season in Burma.

The weather on the first combined effort to bomb Rangoon raid proved to be completely incompatible for accurate bombing—heavy accumulative cloud had consolidated over the target area. In the case of David's crew, they targeted a searchlight battery as this was the only identifiable target available to the bomb aimer. Other Wellingtons from 99 Squadron were fleetingly provided the opportunity to go below the cloud base at one point, which enabled the bombing of their primary objective. Other aircraft diverted to attack Akyab, several aircraft later reported being attacked by a single enemy fighter. The American contingent also experienced problems. Tragedy struck early on from take-off when two Liberators collided, killing both crews, and another was shot down by the Japanese anti-aircraft guns. American fighter cover that was to be supplied by long-range fuel tanks also suffered as they were unable to connect up with the bombers as planned. The operation had been far from a resounding success.

The Japanese fighter pilots quickly discovered that the B-24 aircraft lacked adequate defence against frontal attack, and so they developed attack strategies for frontal offensives that were capable of inflicting serious casualties. In October 1943, another mark of Liberator, the B-24J with improved frontal firepower, started to arrive in India. Despite this, on 1 December, these new types also suffered over Rangoon. Inexperience in handling the new turrets was hypothesised as a possible explanation of the inability to deter losses and this became a matter to be urgently addressed in training.

During December 1943, David Jones had another opportunity to display his ability as a competent bomb aimer. The upgraded Wellingtons now with 99 Squadron were capable of carrying a single 4,000-lb 'cookie' blast bomb. The very first one dropped during daylight hours in the Far East theatre fell from a 99 Squadron Wellington, flown by Wing Commander Maddox on 13 December. David's opportunity swiftly followed six days later, when his crew carried another 'cookie' that was to be dropped during their six-hour sortie to the industrial target of Maymyo (present-day Pyin Oo Lwin). As usual, he went to the briefing room where the operation was announced, explaining where the target was and the route in and out of the combat area, followed by the meteorological officer advising on the weather expectations—never an easy job in the Far East. This was followed by the armaments officer, who advised on the particular bombloads being carried. The intelligence officers finally reported and the process was completed ready for the confirmed departure time. David would have then written up his flight plan log, recording the breakdown of the route to be followed, the expected weather conditions, and the plotting of his estimated progress along the predicted flight route. It proved to be an uneventful operation in many respects, other than the first for David dropping such a large single bomb.

The Japanese forces continued to establish strong military positions within occupied Burma and, as the new year of 1944 loomed, they had stockpiles of ammunition, fuel, and the necessary plethora of war supplies to support an invasion into India. Strategic bomb and store dumps were heavily camouflaged. These proved very difficult for the Allies to locate during their photographic reconnaissance operations. Admiral Lord Louis Mountbatten himself had emphasised the need to bolster the numbers of photographic reconnaissance aircraft and establish a far better extraction of intelligence from the recovered images. Group Captain Wise commanded the Easter Air Command photographic reconnaissance force and would have been aware of the joint Army and Royal Air Force work being undertaken at the highly secret Wireless Experimental Centre in New Delhi. This establishment was engaged in breaking the Japanese Army Air Force signals, another significant development of intelligence gathering.

David Jones completed his first tour of duty by attacking railway marshalling yards and oil and petrol storage dumps. The latter were capable of creating huge fireballs and explosions that would have been very satisfying when seen from the air. These targets were the result of the Japanese forces stockpiling ammunition, fuel, and military supplies for their intended offensive against India. The final tour operation for David was on 13 February 1944, with the dropping of a single 'cookie' onto the enemy stronghold of Rathedaung. This operation was undertaken at the request of the Fourteenth Army, who had commenced the targeting of selected venues for these large blast bombs. The Fourteenth Army had been formed in India during 1943 and Lieutenant-General William Slim commanded a multinational force. Men from the Indian Army, British units, as well as significant contributions from West and East African divisions within the British Army. In March 1944, the Japanese launched a substantial offensive across the Chindwin River to cut off the important Imphal–Kohima Road. This action engaged the Allies in ferocious battles, which finally resulted in a defeated Japanese Army withdrawing, an indication of the strength and capability of the Allied Forces now fighting in Burma.

The Japanese Air Force at that time continued to mount offensive sorties and was capable of effectively engaging with the Allied Air Forces, their last noteworthy action taking place throughout May during the Imphal conflict. The Japanese Air Force mounted over 300 sorties that month in the hope of enforcing a victory over the Allies. These offensive Japanese sorties were conducted from the airfields of Shwebo, Meiktila, Magwe, Pyinmana, Mingaladon, Prome, and Taungoo. These were names or variants of names that were well-known and frequently mentioned to the Allied pilots and air crews in numerous briefings as they were being consistently bombed at every opportunity.

Having been commissioned to the rank of Pilot Officer, David Jones departed from 99 Squadron. He had completed over 300 hours of operational flying against the enemy. He was rested and posted onto the Air Command South East Asia Communications Squadron at Willingdon, Delhi, India, charged with the responsibility of navigating across India with high-ranking passengers and dignitaries. He frequently flew with Pilot Officer Ferguson in the Lockheed aircraft LV761, one of three Netherlands East Indies Air Force Lockheed 12A aircraft that had been impressed into service with the Royal Air Force after being flown to India, avoiding the advancing Japanese. He also flew in the unit's Dakota, which was regularly flown by Wing Commander Walter DFC. David was well-respected and recognised as an immensely capable navigator. He was selected to participate in an instructor's course during July and October 1944, however, having sat extensive theory examinations, he failed to attain the required examination levels to become a qualified instructor. These developments set in place his destiny to return to operational duty. David would eventually be personally selected by Wing Commander Ercolani to undertake 'bridge busting' duties with him in the B-24 Liberator.

# 4

# The Fight from India in B-24 Liberators, 1944

On 31 July 1944, 99 Squadron flew one of their last operations in the well-worn Wellington bombers. Ten aircraft attacked the Indaingyi military supply dumps situated in central Burma. One Wellington, captained by Flight Sergeant Baptiste, suffered terrible tearing of the dope-covered fabric that was stretched over the fuselage—when damaged, it was always possible that the Wellington's thick fabric could tear backwards in the slipstream and expose the airframe. In this instance, the damage caused the Wellington to crash-land; fortunately, the crew all survived, but Flight Sergeant Inkley suffered serious lacerations to his legs. This was far from being a successful operation, with only six aircraft actually reaching the target. The next day, the Squadron received news that the long-awaited B-24 Liberators were soon to arrive on station.

On the 4 August 1944, seven Liberators circled and landed at Jessore, east of Calcutta. They had been transferred to 99 Squadron direct from 1673 Heavy Conversion Unit at Kolar, near Bangalore, South India. Flying in one of the B-24s as a wireless operator was Thomas Reynolds, who was only twenty-two years old. He sat in the small compartment situated behind the second pilot's seat. The fuselage panel ahead of him had a small Perspex window, which provided natural light and, on this sortie, a view of his new operational airfield. Naturally apprehensive at what lay ahead, he carried in his kit an item that revealed the harshness of the environment in which he was to serve. He had been issued with an Air Ministry Tropical Combat snakebite kit. Constructed from chromed metal and marked with the manufactures name of Gardner Co. London, one end of the small metal case unscrewed to reveal a small metal blade or lancet; this would be used to cut the site of any snake bite, in order to bleed the venom. The other end also unscrewed to reveal a cavity that contained a small capsule, which was filled with Potassium Permanganate for use on the bite. These snakebite kits were issued as part of the tropical survival kits that were far more extensive than anything issued in the European theatre. Also in his kit bag was his flying logbook, which to date had recorded just one completed operation—dropping propaganda leaflets from a Wellington over France on the 5 February that year. Thomas Reynolds was trained as a wireless operator and air gunner, but would also later operate as a flight engineer.

The larger four-engined bomber aircraft, like the Liberator, required a flight crew member to monitor the engines among other critical flight systems. The position of flight engineer was first published in the Air Ministry Order 190/41. In the Far East, during November 1944, a conference within 231 Group agreed that flight engineers were required within their B-24 Liberators. This was despite the fact that the second pilot had the ability to carry out these duties. Flight training time was very sparse for this new post, and from mid-1943 onwards it was quite normal for these men to qualify for their flying badges without ever having flown any substantial hours in any large aircraft. The piston engines on heavy bombers like the B-24, with their multitude of gauges and indicators, required a great deal of attention throughout the flight. Inattention could result in engine or propeller failure and quite possibly the loss of the aircraft, should prompt corrective action not be taken. Additionally and quite crucially, the flight engineer managed the fuel consumption, creating greater safety for the entire crew that normally consisted of the first and second pilot, navigator, bomb aimer, first wireless operator, second wireless operator/air gunner, flight engineer/air gunner, front gunner, mid-fuselage gunners, rear gunner, and the under-fuselage ball gunner (if fitted).

The Liberator-equipped 159 Squadron appears to have never operated with ball turrets—the fuselage where the turret would have been situated was covered by a fairing, which was most probably a simple aluminium skinning. The Commanding Officer of 159 Squadron, for the second half of 1944, Wing Commander James Blackburn, was instrumental in revolutionising the use of the Liberator in the Far East theatre where the targets were ominously distant from India. He significantly increased the bomb tonnage carried by individual aircraft, not just by reducing weight, an example being the removal of the ball gunner, but most importantly by changing the manner in which the Liberators were flown to and from the target. Those matters were very much within the area of responsibility undertaken by the flight engineer and his pilot. The technique of cruising on what became known as the step entailed climbing above the required altitude and then diving back with an increased speed before levelling out at the nominated cruising altitude. This created more speed and less drag, which generated good fuel efficiency for the stable Pratt & Whitney Twin Wasp engines that were run at a reduced airspeed. These techniques enhanced the Royal Air Force adage 'reduce the revs and boost the boost, you'll have enough petrol to get home to roost'.

The Mk VI model Liberators, known as B-24J types, were most likely to have been occupied by a crew consisting of pilot, second pilot, navigator, bomb aimer, wireless operator, flight engineer, and the compliment of air gunners. Most unusually, the rear gunner was instructed to only occupy his turret once the aircraft was in the air and to extract himself from it before landing. This was to assist with the pitching of the airframe on its tricycle landing wheels. His body weight was required to be centrally balanced within the fuselage. The training of the crew ensured that they were able to fulfil other colleagues' duties in any emergency scenario.

Thomas Reynolds arrived on station at Jessore with just thirty hours of flying experience on the B-24—he could hardly be regarded as experienced. Each new aircraft arrived with a new crew, on some occasions accompanied by up to eleven men, and they arrived on a regular basis. Wing Commander Ercolani returned to 99 Squadron, now exceptionally well-experienced on the B-24. This popular character assumed command on 3 September 1944 and oversaw the Squadrons conversion onto the new heavy bomber. As he did so, the war in Burma saw a change—Allied offensives had seen the Japanese forced back on several fronts, and the B-24s would operate in daylight, closely linked with the Army in its ground campaigns.

Winston Churchill wrote upon his meetings with the United States President Franklin Roosevelt, at the Quebec Conference on the 12 to 16 September 1944:

> For nearly three years we had persisted in the strategy of Germany First. The time has now come for the liberation of Asia, and I was determined that we should play our full and equal part in it. What I feared most at this stage of the war was that the United States would say. We came to your help in Europe and you left us alone to finish off Japan.

An interesting statistic (not known at the time of these meetings) is that the Japanese aircraft production had peaked in the summer of 1944, but it declined thereafter. This created the situation of losses not being replaced, the sole reason why Japanese fighters became a lesser threat to the Liberator bombers in 1945 than they had previously experienced.

The conference also revisited the lend-lease agreements relative to supplying the B-24 aircraft. It was confirmed that the arrangement would continue as long as the war in the Pacific was still being waged. The existing governance was the January 1944 Arnold-Courtney Agreement with Air Chief Marshal Courtney and Major-General Giles, who represented General Arnold as signatories. The B-24 aircraft destined for the Southeast Asia theatre were all supplied from the United States within the generic agreement that was consistently reviewed. Gradually, 99 Squadron's strength increased. Crews ferried the new Liberators in from the Heavy Conversion Unit until some fifteen B-24s were on station, the officers' and sergeants' messes were thronging with men from across the entire Commonwealth. However, the ground crews were mostly absent, receiving training and instruction on the new Liberators at 352 Maintenance Unit.

Thomas Reynolds crewed up with the New Zealander, Pilot Officer Johnny Haycock, but this was a partnership that nearly faltered immediately. No. 215 Squadron was also operating from Jessore at this time, and they had recently accepted sixteen new

Liberator aircraft, which arrived at intervals during the month. Twelve 215 Squadron crews had returned from their conversion course at 1673 Heavy Conversion Unit at Kolar. Six further crews remained completing their course of instruction where the dangers associated with warfare were exposed once again to Liberator crews. Pilot Officer Clemments died of injuries received from contact with a rotating airscrew at Kolar. This accident may well be explained by the fact that the standing Liberator on its undercarriage presents the propellers closer to the ground than conventional tail-wheel-supported aircraft.

Flying Officer Brodie, an experienced Canadian Pilot, arrived at Jessore in July 1944. He had been posted from 355 Squadron to serve in 215 Squadron. On 9 September 1944, he was required to give evidence at a Court of Inquiry in Allahabad, in northern India. Johnny Haycock was requested to fly the witness to Allahabad in the Squadron's Harvard trainer. They took off from Jessore shortly before 9 a.m. and, after the legal proceedings, they commenced the return journey. The weather closed in and conditions caused them to lose course, the situation worsened and a lack of fuel forced drastic action. Flying Officer Brodie baled out from a rather low altitude, but landed without any injury. Johnny Haycock remained with the Harvard and crash-landed south of Calcutta. It took several hours to reach the crash site and transport him to the hospital in Calcutta. He had suffered extensive superficial head and facial injuries in an accident that he was lucky to have survived. Five weeks later, he was discharged from the hospital to rejoin the Squadron. Johnny commenced training on the Liberator with his new crew, rejoining with the recently acquainted Thomas Reynolds.

The facilities at Jessore were at bursting point following such an influx of personnel, and news was reported that 99 Squadron, equipped with their new aircraft, would imminently move to the new operating station at Dhubalia, some 70 miles west of their current location. As always, transportation across India was problematical, the journey would involve a river crossing and several complicated rail timetable arrangements. Eventually, the entire strength of over 300 ground personnel arrived on station at Dhubalia, with twenty complete air crews.

The transition onto B-24 Liberators engaged the entire Squadron between October and November 1944, with a training program that included daylight formation flying and bombing exercises. The bombing ranges catered for low-level bombing practice, but newly qualified bomb aimers arriving in India had little, if any, experience on the Mk XIV bombsites in use with 231 Group. Wing Commander Ercolani was demanding excellent standards, well aware of the work that would soon be forthcoming for his newly trained Squadron. The B-24 was a far more versatile aircraft than the Wellington. The tricycle undercarriage provided the crews with excellent vision for both landings and take-off and the ground crews also enjoyed a very stable and level aircraft to work upon as it sat on the ground. The crew accessed the aircraft through the nose wheel opening, the entrance hatchway built into either the bottom of the rear fuselage section or through the bomb bay doors. In the air, the two main wheels retracted outwards and swung into large wheel wells within the wing—a very different configuration to the normally seen backwards or forwards mechanism—and rested in nacelles beneath the wings. The forward nose wheel retracted into the fuselage and, once engaged in the forward fuselage, locked down, slightly forward of the two twin doors that opened inwardly. Those two doors acted as emergency exits for the forward crew members, who were able to activate them by a quick release mechanism within the fuselage. The advanced design feature, with the high-lift wing, created minimum drag to give the aircraft a heavy load capacity over a greater distance. The B-24 had rather unique corrugated sheeting bomb doors, with both sets operated on rollers opening outwards and upwards upon a central beam running along and up the lower fuselage. A small bulkhead structure divided the bomb compartment, creating two bomb bays. It was in that location where the emergency crank handles were situated. These enabled the crew to open the doors in the event of any hydraulic failures in the air. Once again, this B-24 feature created an easy environment for the ground crews when loading and arming bombs in the twin bomb bays, which measured nearly 18 feet in length. The most common bombload deployed was ten 500-lb bombs or five 1,000-lb bombs. Fuses were installed in the bombs once they were loaded on the aircraft. The individual bomb shackle that carried the bomb had three securing points, the end two held the bomb by releasable hooks and the third held the arming wire. The arming wire was a long wire that was inserted into the fuse and, when the bomb was released, it pulled out of the fuse as the bomb dropped. This allowed a very small arming vane on the nose fuse to rotate and arm the bomb. This design allowed the bomb to be free and clear of the aircraft before it was even armed. The fuselage, unlike the Wellington, was of conventional all-metal stressed-skin construction. Taking off fully laden in a Liberator required the pilot to hold the aircraft on the brakes while applying full power to the engines, the noise was immense and the airframe shook and rattled as the physical forces were applied. The pilot would look at all the instruments with the flaps fully down and then set the fuel mixture at 'Full Rich', while ensuring the props were in fine pitch. He would open the throttles wide, cutting in the turbo supercharges, watch the Pratt & Witney engines go to warm, and off with the brakes. Then, with the brakes released, the aircraft responded to the full power of all four engines, slowly hauling the full weight of the B-24 down the runway until sufficient lift on the wing gently lifted the aircraft off the ground—inevitably, every inch of the runway was required.

Operationally, the crews were exposed to significantly longer periods in the air, with operations regularly conducted in excess of fourteen hours. In November 1944, experimental 'caffeine tablets' were issued to Far East air crews to assist with maintaining the capability of enduring such extraordinary lengthy flights. These tablets originated from research carried out by the Flying Personnel Research Committee. They established that a German pilot, captured early in the war, had been in possession of a small amount of tablets that, following analysis, showed them to be sugar with a small quantity of amphetamine substance. The research into these tablets, which included experiments at the Medical Research Council based at Cambridge University, subsequently led the Air Ministry to issue 'Benzedrine' tablets during the war. These small tablets were used to help with serious fatigue frequently experienced by bomber crew personnel. Benzedrine was by no means mandatory and the responsibility to take it rested with each and every individual. Benzedrine, which was a trade name for amphetamine, was also incorporated into the escape packs carried by individual airmen. Evidence exists in a number of post-war evader reports to confirm that Benzedrine tablets helped some men to escape from dire situations, and they were recognised as being of great assistance in securing freedom. The survival aids carried by airmen included matches, magnetised razor blades, a small compass, a heliograph signal mirror, Benzedrine tablets, water-purifying tablets, a rubber water bottle, needle and thread, and fishing twine.

The hot climate naturally induced the Far East crew members to consume more water than their counter parts in the European theatre of war. The humidity at times was very difficult to deal with and was naturally very debilitating. The B-24 crew would urinate before taking off, creating a commonly seen routine of men practising their last ritual for good luck. The official toilet within the aircraft looked like a waste bin and was known as the 'Elsan', which was fixed to the floor of the aircraft's fuselage. It was positioned towards the rear of the aircraft and the rear gunner was effectively the closest crewman to this rather crude and undesirable facility. The Elsan was nothing more than a large can with a lid, which had a clip device to secure the top onto its base. In the air, it would have been an unpleasant experience to use. Despite the fuselage wind deflectors fitted at the waist gunner positions, the wind would stream down the fuselage and clearly clothing needed to be removed to use these basic facilities. An added burden for the rear gunner was caused by the close proximity to the Elsan as they had to endure the unpleasant smell and spillages that frequently occurred. Equally unpleasant was the duty of the ground crew who had to empty and clean the facility. Any unsecure or faulty lid attached to an Elsan was always likely to allow its contents to spew out—during manoeuvres conducted in battle, it was highly likely that the entire content would be expelled in some way or another. It was commonplace for the air crews to endure significant discomfort in order to avoid using the toilet. The men also had the option to use the 'relief tube', a simple device that was situated at the front end of the bomb bay. This device would naturally only be used in stable flight as it required the user to hold onto the racking structure around him while passing his fluids. Flying at height on oxygen with a distended bladder could become very painful.

In the aircraft fuselage, thermos containers were carried with hot water to make tea and pre-packed K-rations were carried for meals. Three types were frequently encountered, but the breakfast pack in a blue-grey-coloured box was always desired as it contained cheese and bacon. These rations were effective and greatly valued by the crew during their exceptionally long and arduous sorties.

Overall, the Liberator was a very sturdy platform in the air from which to bomb. It was capable of sustaining severe battle damage, but, like many aircraft, it was dependent upon an effective hydraulic system that operated the landing gear, wheel braking, flaps, and bomb bay doors. That system was driven by the number three engine and supplemented by an emergency auxiliary electrical pump, as well as a hand pump. The B-24 crews gained great satisfaction from knowing that there were self-sealing fuel tanks on board (twelve in total). All were interconnected within the wings and were regarded as being of excellent design and very capable of operating effectively when pierced.

November 1944 saw a number of major changes in high command. Air Chief Marshal Peirse handed over his command to Air Marshal Guy Garrod. Eastern Air Command assumed day-to-day operational control of all Royal Air Force B-24 Liberator Squadrons. No. 99 Squadron, based at Dhubalia, fell under the command of number 231 Group, as opposed to 221 Group. No. 231 Group Eastern Air Command itself comprised of three wings. The Liberator was equipping 355 and 356 Squadrons in 184 Wing and 159 Squadron in 185 Wing. The newly equipped 99 Squadron remained within 175 Wing, and 231 Group itself was commanded by the Strategic Air Force. It was also in November 1944 that the Burma railway planning headquarters and the Special Railway Bridging Unit suffered from Allied bombing. Several engineers were killed, resulting in the units occupying a less conspicuous location away from the important construction site at Kanchanaburi. The Japanese also sought to deploy camouflage methods on this venue, which would increasingly become a significant target to the Allied Liberator heavy bombers.

On 3 December 1944, twelve Liberator crews were led by Wing Commander Ercolani to attack the railway station at Nong Pladuk. This was the first operation against the Burma–Thailand Railway for 99 Squadron. Johnny Haycock's crew were not tasked with this operation deep into Thailand, but two of his air gunners were required to replace two gunners who the Medical Officer had removed from flying due to sickness. Johnny Haycock's gunners, Flight Sergeants H. Pickup and G. E. Tudor temporarily joined Flying Officer Jones and his second pilot, New Zealander Pilot Officer E. P. Parcell, in their Liberator KG973.

The twelve Liberators took off safely and gradually gained height to form up. The aircraft would have been loosely gathered and commenced the route according to their flight plan. After some five hours into the sortie and near to Tavoy Point, on the Burma coastline, two Liberators (KG973 and EW286) collided in the air, instantly causing a massive fireball explosion. Fortune played its part as no other aircraft suffered any damaging consequences of the explosion, but tragically the two air gunners from Johnny Haycock's crew were amongst the casualties. The remaining ten Liberators continued with the operation and, fourteen hours after having left Dhubalia, they returned safely. Undoubtedly, they would have all been engaged in the enquiry concerning the collision and its apparent unnecessary loss of life. The sight of friends seen falling to the sea and the exploding debris of the two Liberators would have been traumatic.

The Singapore Memorial records details for those men who have no known graves from within Liberators KG973 and EW286. It had been an ominous start to the campaign against the Burma–Thailand Railway.

KG973 casualties:

Flying Officer G. E. Jones, Flight Sergeant G. E. Tudor, Flying Officer R. C. O'Neill, Flight Sergeant A. H. Brameld, Flight Sergeant J. E. J. Farrow, Flight Sergeant J. F. Grimshaw, Sergeant J. R. Milligan, Pilot Officer E. P. Parcell, Flight Sergeant H. Pickup, Sergeant W. J. D. Pugh, Flight Sergeant S. R. Smith.

EW286 casualties:

Flying Officer S. D. Booth, Flight Sergeant B. W. Corrigal, Sergeant F. R. Cragg, Pilot Officer N. D. Harrison, Sergeant W. M. Mann, Sergeant P. McNerney, Sergeant D. K. Moss-Vernon, Sergeant G. W. Richards, Sergeant R. Robertson, Flight Sergeant R. E. S. Sanger, Flight Sergeant M. Schonberg.

The New Zealand Plt Off. Erroll Philip Parcell continues to be remembered at his former university in Canterbury Lincoln, New Zealand. A scholarship exists commemorating his life, with direct connections to his farming background.

The same day on which that tragic accident occurred, a conference was held at the Headquarters of 231 Group. The navigation officers from the respective Squadrons led by the Canadian Group Radar Officer Flight Lieutenant Huestis discussed and planned for the assessing and accuracy testing of 'Loran', the abbreviation for the long-range radio navigation aide transmitted from land-based stations. This equipment was to eventually arrive on stations in early 1945 where it proved to be an asset, but not the answer to the unique difficult requirements of navigating over such vast distances in the Far East.

Seven days after that disastrous collision in the sky, Flight Sergeant Thomas Reynolds and his captain, Johnny Haycock, with his two replacement air gunners, accompanied eleven other Liberators on another long run to Thailand. Wing Commander Ercolani led them on an exceptionally low bombing run in order to destroy locomotive sheds. At a height of just over 100 feet, they bombed and strafed the target area. Low-level bombing sorties would soon become a speciality for these crews, but in the meantime they were all part of a learning process. For this operation, the commander's Liberator sustained widespread damage from debris thrown up by the explosions, insufficient to be of great concern in relation to remaining in the air, but nonetheless something that was very much undesirable. This problem was resolved by bombs being fitted with delay action fuses, enabling the aircraft to avoid blast and bomb fragmentation damage.

Thomas Reynolds' flying logbook recorded a remarkable daylight sortie entered on the 13 December. This was his third long trek into Thailand, specifically attacking the Burma–Thailand railway line and, in particular, the first specific bridge busting target at a place called Hninpale. The sortie commenced at 7.40 a.m. and they would not return until after 5 p.m. Johnny Haycock reached an altitude of approximately 2,500 feet in Liberator EW255 when a Japanese Oscar fighter attacked them. In a rare uncoordinated encounter, the attacking Oscar was shot down by his crew's defensive guns, especially the waist gunner's position manned by Thomas Reynolds. The Nakajima Ki-43 fighter was known to the Allies as an 'Oscar' and by the Japanese as 'Hayabusa'. The Ki-43 was the most important Japanese Army fighter and, like its naval counterpart, the Zero-Sen, the Oscar was powered by a Nakajima Ha-115 14-cylinder radial engine, which had two-speed supercharging. The engine rotated a three-bladed constant speed metal propeller and was enclosed by a large diameter cowling; this feature instantly made the fighter recognisable and it was always flown aggressively by their pilots—very few air gunners had opportunities to submit successful combat reports against Ki-43 fighter pilots. Two months later, Thomas Reynolds proudly pasted a published news cutting about the incident in his flying logbook.

*Evening Post*, Issue 49, 27 February 1945, page 6
New Zealand AIRMAN SAVES HIS CREW (RNZAF Official News Service.)
CALCUTTA, February 25.... By skilful piloting during a bombing raid on enemy objectives in the Rangoon area, a New Zealand pilot not only saved his Liberator and crew, but also accounted for a Japanese fighter. He is Flying Officer John Haycock, of Nelson.

He made a swift but quite unorthodox manoeuvre with the aircraft so that the waist gunner caught the enemy in his sights and fifty rounds of accurate gunnery did the rest, but not before the Liberator was swishing through shrubs only eleven feet off the ground. Mushrooming smoke and steam, the enemy aircraft disappeared into the broad waters of the Irrawaddy. Flying Officer Haycock arrived in India early last year. After a short course at the jungle training school, he was posted to his present squadron and has made many long trips over enemy-occupied territory, including Siam, attacking communications and installations.

The Japanese Oscar had achieved the accolade of attaining great air superiority over Burma and China during the early campaign. The relatively slow British Blenheim and Buffalo were to some extent easily shot down by the Japanese pilots in their superior fighter aircraft; however, the B-24 Liberator was a very different aircraft to destroy in the air. Rarely could a single Oscar shoot down a B-24. They generally needed to attack in unison in order to achieve success. On 1 December 1943, five B-24 bombers from the American Seventh Bomber Group were shot down by Japanese Oscars during a daylight operation to Rangoon and this was by no means an exception. The Japanese fighter pilots acting together were very capable and exceptionally committed in attacking the Allied aircraft. The evolution of armament within the B-24 was progressive; initially, the B-24D had a single machine gun in the nose, a Martin A-3 Dorsal Turret fitted with twin machine guns, and a Consolidated A-6 rear gunner turret, also with twin guns. Heavy machine guns would be added in the nose in addition to the two waist-mounted machine guns positioned in the fuselage. The heavy duty machine guns were fired electrically by solenoids and another electrical system fed the ammunition into the gun breeches. A hydraulic system operated the turret manoeuvrability, as well as the gun elevation and depressions. The air gunners aimed their weapons using a reflector type gunsight.

The Japanese fighter attack tactics dictated that the nose compartments of the B-24 needed yet more capability, which led to the installation of the heavy duty front-mounted power-operated nose gunner turrets. These aircraft subsequently became identified as B-24J models, but the addition of the front turret did reduce performance in the air (a fact that several pilots expressed a negative opinion upon). It must be said that the addition of the front power-operated gunner turret completely changed the appearance of the B-24 aircraft. Additionally, navigators suffered with impaired visibility due to the installation of the turret, and the nose section of the aircraft became very restricted. The dorsal upper turret was normally manned by the flight engineer—it was positioned immediately behind the pilot and readily accessible. An electrically operated turret that was renowned for its reliability and ease of operation, the operator sat with his feet resting on footrests as the turret swiftly turned in full rotation. The control handles allowed the operators hands to depress the two safety switches, which activated the turret. To move the turret, the handles were turned—to the right to go right and to the left to go left. Pressing down on the handles raised the guns. Pulling up on them lowered them. The slightest movement on the wrists regulated the turning, raising, or lowering motions. The index finger on both handles accessed the triggers.

Thomas Reynolds and the rear gunner Flight Sergeant Woodrow had their joint kill of the Oscar confirmed by other 99 Squadron air crews who witnessed the unusual attack from the starboard rear quarter. Johnny Haycock and his crew flew onto the target, reduced height to just 100 feet, and attacked their target, dropping their bombload, which added to the destruction of the bridge. Very rarely could a B-24 wireless operator or air gunner write a logbook entry recording an enemy aircraft shot down and a bridge destroyed on an operation conducted at the close of 1944.

At this period of time, 99 Squadron had a high contingent of Royal Air Force personnel within its flight crews. Several men arrived from the Commonwealth Air Forces, and among them was Colin Woolford, aged twenty-eight from Melbourne, Australia. He had volunteered for the Royal Australian Air Force in late 1942 and trained in the United Kingdom before flying in Liberators at the Heavy Conversion Unit in India. As a fellow navigator, Colin Woolford welcomed the assistance of men like David Jones, whose operational experience was invaluable.

Wing Commander Ercolani called for more training as the final days of the year approached. He wanted to develop further the Squadrons expertise in difficult low-level bombing, with simulated attacks on railway bridges. The importance of fuel management on long-range operations, deep into Thailand, remained prevalent, an imposition also endured by the second pilot as he had the fuel and oil pressure gauges positioned immediately in front of him on the flight deck. Thomas Reynolds had received some training as a flight engineer, but had been primarily engaged as an air gunner and second wireless operator. Unbeknown to him at that time, plans were in place for him to become Johnny Haycock's primary flight engineer in the New Year.

After the excitement and jubilation of the shooting down of the Japanese fighter, Johnny Haycock's crew had a less eventful and much shorter sortie on the 23 December. During this sortie, they bombed the Japanese supply dumps at Tangup, dropping their 8,000-lb bombload onto the target at over 6,000 feet—this was to be the last operation for 99 Squadron in 1944. All twelve Liberators returned safely, hoping that they would be able to celebrate Christmas with a planned football match and special meal.

The men serving in the Far East Liberator Squadrons were made aware that they were to imminently receive a newly designed flying suit. The instances of disease spread by mosquito bites and the unique weather conditions had led to the design of the 'Beadon Suit'. Constructed of a green-coloured cotton material, it was both lightweight and shower proof. Only the head and hands were exposed when worn and the suit had numerous pockets sewn into the material, all of which were to hold various escape and survival aids. This would simply become known as a coverall to those whose chose to wear one and the wide-fitting belt would normally been seen holding a Kukri or similar hunting knife.

# 5

# The Thailand–Burma Japanese Railway Network

Having occupied Burma, the Japanese sought to build a railway to connect their Southeast Asian territories and to facilitate the movement of troops and supplies for the planned conquest of India. They looked for a southern route into Burma from Thailand and embarked on a line from Ban Pong, Thailand, to Thanbyuzayat, Burma. This linking railway would connect into the pre-existing railway structure, but it would cross treacherous territory that separated the two countries. In Tokyo, the Japanese Imperial General Headquarters issued direct instructions to the Southern Japanese Forces on 20 June 1942.

The Southern Army Railway Corps, Railway Regiments, were to construct the Burma–Thailand Railway according to the precise orders issued. These orders contained seven specific objectives:

Construction: The objective of railroad construction is to insure the land supply route to Burma and to develop a commercial transportation route between Burma and Thailand.

Course of Construction: The railway shall extend from Nonprodock [Nong Pladuk], Thailand to Thanbyuzayat, Burma for the length of 400 Km. [248.5 miles.]

Transportation Capacity: One way daily transportation capacity is estimated at about 3,000 tons.

Period of Construction: The anticipated completion date shall be the end of 1943.

Materials Essential for Construction: Mainly materials available in the areas. Other necessary materials shall be provided by the Government.

Construction Expense: Yen 700 million

Construction Forces: Mainly the following: One Railroad Superintendent Headquarters. Two Railway Regiments. One Railway Supply Depot and auxiliary units. Labour Forces for Construction. Labourers in the areas and Prisoners of War.

The Japanese Labour Service Corps were to be engaged throughout Southern Burma. This official authority initially consisted of 2,000 members divided into sections or squads. The corps was to select young and able Burmese from every district throughout Burma and allocating one doctor to every 1,000 labourers. The corps were to be assisted by Commanders of the Japanese defence troops and members of the Japanese Military Railway Unit. The Japanese railway engineers, known as *gunzokos*, were a unique branch of the army that specialised in the operation and construction of railways—they comprised primarily from the employees of the Japanese National Railways. Two Japanese Railway Regiments had been formed in 1938 and 1941, with 5,000 conscripted employees from the Japanese National Railway supporting them. Identified as the Special JNR Group, this combination of railway expertise would be engaged in the construction of the proposed railway.

The majority of smaller bridges and viaducts were constructed from local wood, all of which would be harvested from the adjacent jungle. The river banks in the majority of instances were of dense undergrowth, with trees averaging some 20 metres in height. Occasionally, hard rock cliff faces erupted, almost purposely creating obstacles where huge structures like the Arrow Hill Viaduct were required to be built. These and similar planned constructions would eventually carry the railway alongside its route parallel to the north river bank.

As the Japanese conquered much of Southeast Asia, they captured tens of thousands of British military personnel. Some 30,000 of these prisoners of war later worked on the Burma–Thailand Railway, and more than one in five of them died in terrible circumstances. The Dutch formed the second largest contingent of Allied prisoners of war on the railway. Estimates vary, but the number who worked on the railway was deemed to be as high as 18,000. These men were from the 42,000 Dutch military and naval personnel and 100,000 Dutch civilians, all of whom were captured when the Japanese conquered the Netherlands East Indies territories in early 1942.

The creation and defence of what the Japanese called the Greater East Asian Co-Prosperity Sphere required millions of labourers who came from every Japanese-controlled territory, and, while some worked voluntarily, most were subject to some form of coercion. In 1943, the Japanese recruited an estimated 200,000 Asian labourers to supplement their 60,000 prisoner of war workforce. These labourers were ruthlessly exploited by the Japanese. It is impossible to calculate any reliable statistics, but in all probability up to 90,000 Asian labourers died on the railway.

Despite their large numbers and their terrible suffering, the post-war history of the Second World War has been neglectful to these victims. There are few memorials to their suffering, primarily due to the fact that they were not military personnel, and they were not interred in the extensive Commonwealth War Graves Commission cemeteries at Chungkai, Kanchanaburi, and Thanbyuzayat—all of which have strong associations with casualties from the railway. Given that almost no records exist of where any were buried, the plight of these poor people is often completely unrecognised. Many of the ill and frail men simply crept into the jungle to die. Many victims of cholera were cremated, while others were hastily buried in shallow unmarked graves. A number of privately maintained memorials to these labourers who were pressed into serving Japan can now be found in Kanchanaburi, near the bridge on the River Kwai.

The Japanese Labour Service Corps provided each district authority with funding to facilitate some monetary allowance for the conscripted members. They also initiated the design and construction of a badge to be given to each member, no doubt a concept thought to promote Burmese industrial spirit and to promote native co-operation with the Japanese forces. In effect, the Japanese enlisted these Burmese men into a Labour Corps, also known as Heiho Tat, which was essentially a part of the Japanese Army.

The Burmese government, in the form of Ba Maw, the first Premier of Independent Burma and the leader of the wartime government that ruled with the occupying Japanese from 1942 to 1945, supported the manpower initiative. Ba Maw's ministers travelled to the southern districts of the country to drum up enthusiasm by painting a very rosy picture of this employment opportunity. Between July 1942 and January 1943 they had enrolled 87,000 Burmese labourers for railway work. The Thailand government and its national railways engaged with the Japanese, assisting in the railways progression within Thailand. The Japanese utilised an entire labour force of Allied prisoners of war, taken in the campaigns across Southeast Asia. Additionally, they brought enforced labour from Malaya and the Dutch East Indies, men who toiled alongside the Labour Corps conscripts from Thailand and Burma. From June 1942 onwards, large groups of Allied prisoners were transported periodically to Thailand and Burma from the three main locations of Java, Sumatra, and Borneo. They were transported in packed train carriages in sweltering conditions, with very little concern for the most basic of human requirements. Many Korean soldiers were conscripted for guard duties throughout Burma and Thailand. Controlled by the Japanese Army, these men would become particularly renowned for their brutality towards the prisoners of war.

In Thailand, the railway construction site was initially based in close proximity to Bangkok. The works were to commence at both ends of the proposed line. Two independent workforces, one in Thailand and the other in Burma, worked inward towards each other on what was officially called 'The Thailand to Burma Rail Link' (Taimen Rensetsu Tetsudo). The Japanese construction plan dictated that the track would be regulated to prepared ground of between 4 to 5 metres in width and the sleeper ratio was to be fifteen within any given 10 metre length.

The Japanese provided their railway engineers with comprehensive topographical photographs. These were as detailed as possible and once collated and compiled created significant continuous lengths of images. These plotted the route upon the geographical terrain; however, the monumental task would become more apparent when assessed on the ground. Detailed reconnaissance planning undertaken by the

Japanese meant that much of that work was undertaken from the Mae Khloung and Khwae Noi Rivers.

The manual workforce to build the railway was organised into groups of between 2,000 and 12,000 men. Two groups operated in Burma, while four were in Thailand. Another 10,000 prisoners of war were administered directly by Japanese forces in Malaya and it is estimated that the Japanese Army itself engaged some 12,000 to 13,000 men. Primitive tools and huge manpower would be required to move monumental tonnage of building materials and build huge numbers of bridge and viaduct constructions, designed and overseen by the specialist No. 4 Railway Bridging Unit. When the first prisoners of war arrived, their initial task was the construction of three major work camps at Kanchanaburi (abbreviated as Kamburi), Ban Pong in Thailand, and Thanbyuzayat in Burma. Some 3,000 prisoners of war were transported to Ban Pong, a position close to where the new railway line would branch out from the Singapore to Bangkok line and begin its journey to Burma.

With the intention to join the two countries railways together, the new railway would follow the Mae Khloung River to Tamakan, where the river divides into two tributaries. The proposal was for the railway to follow the north-west tributary, the Khwae Noi (Kwai) and thence to Three Pagoda Pass in Burma. The railway would continue following the Zami and other small river ways to Thanbyuzayat. The Japanese Railway Regiments were also responsible for constructing a comprehensive telegraph line alongside the railway line. The telegraph line was to be built with four pairings of wires, utilising both copper and galvanised cables, and this frequently ran along access roads built in close proximity to the railway.

Many thousands of railway labourers would eventually pass through the camp at Ban Pong as it functioned as a transit camp for the huge railway construction project. The prisoners' basic huts all tended to be built 8 metres wide and of significant length, each with a long sloping bamboo roof that ran down almost to the ground. With just an opening at both ends, this made the huts dark and dismal places, where the men slept on split bamboo upon slightly elevated bed platforms. During monsoon periods, these huts were engulfed in water, frequently sweeping in foul matter and making them nothing more than infection ridden pits.

Transportation to the railway construction for Allied prisoners of war was inevitably by rail from the south, while many others were shipped up the Malay Peninsula into the Gulf of Martaban. An example of the hardship endured by those men can be illustrated by the events on 15 January 1943. The steamer *Nissan Kisen* was carrying Japanese troops along with 965 Dutch prisoners of war destined to be employed on the railway. In the holds were railroad rails, tools, and equipment to be utilised on the railroad construction. American B-24 bombers attacked the small convoy and sank the steamer, resulting in the death of approximately forty Allied prisoners of war who were killed in the attack. The Japanese information bureau calculated in their post-war statistics that nearly 11,000 Allied prisoners of war were lost during ship passages. Some ships simply sank without a single survivor—entire crews, troops, and prisoners, having been secured deep in the ships holds, died in terrifying circumstances. In 1944, the large Japanese steamer *Junyo Mary* was sunk while carrying many Allied prisoners of war and civilian labourers—the combined loss of life was 5,640. Many of these casualties would have been sick or simply exhausted from previous hard labour work and the small numbers of fit survivors recovered or rescued were simply returned to work, in this instance upon the Sumatra railroad.

Prisoners transported by rail into Burma were inevitably loaded into conventional goods trucks in Singapore. The journey was likely to take five days and nights and, once the doors were shut, little fresh air passed through each truck. The men had insufficient space to lie down. In many cases, upwards of 1,000 men at a time were transited in trains. In such confined and inhumanly hot conditions, many men died. Those casualties were simply pushed out onto the line at any of the infrequent stops for fuel or meagre food. Dysentery had created terrible conditions within the trucks. The stops for collecting wood fuel for the locomotive became opportunities to try and clean up, but it would not be until Ban Pong was reached that any effective personal cleaning could take place. Ban Pong transit camp had an adjacent stream, which became the human washing pit, but it was no more than an overnight respite as the prisoners were inevitably marched away the following evening. These men marched for several nights, with several dying along the way, but eventually they would reach their allocated work site, which in many instances was the construction of a bridge.

The Thailand route progressed well for the first 50 kilometres (Nong Pladuk to Kanchanaburi), but this was flat terrain with ample accessibility. It proved to be a different story progressing along the river Mae Khloung, which would need bridging as would the valley with its tributary. The Kwai could then itself be followed by the north-bound railway. The dry season only lasted between November and March, and that time period alone allowed for engineering works to be unhindered by the monsoon weather.

The Japanese engineers decided to build the railway around the edge of the rivers ravine, in places cutting through the rock, in addition to constructing viaducts that progressed northwards—the Kwai followed the mountain ridge, with steep sides that could be described as ravines. In places, the railway would need to be gouged out of the rock, as well as bridged, in order to progress into the awaiting jungle that lay ahead of them. The jungle itself would be just as problematical, but also resourceful in providing the huge hardwood trees required for the bridges. Trees cut from the jungle were manoeuvred by elephants to the Kwai and then floated down the river to the lower reaches construction sites. This was the main commodity in constructing the required 688 bridges, many of which were small where it crossed small rivers and streams. Seven bridges of significance were to be built with concrete and steel: the Mae Khloung Bridge at Tamarkan—so frequently called 'The Bridge on the River Kwai'— as well as bridges that crossed the tributaries of the Kwai called the Zami, Apalon, Mezali, Winyaw, Khonkhan, and Myettaw rivers.

The Japanese Railway Regiments intended to transport significant amounts of railway materials up the line from Malaya. A 200 mile stretch of functioning line was removed from the east-coast railway between Mentakab and Kuala Krai, as well as other areas where it was deemed acceptable to do so. The main lines running from Singapore to Kuala Lumpur and Bangkok remained intact. Malaya not only supplied nearly 300 miles of track to construct the Burma–Thailand Railway, it also became the provider of locomotives and rolling stock. The Japanese also robbed the railway line for the Burma railhead by ripping up the twin track line from Rangoon to Taungoo, another example of the many hugely labour intensive processes that were taking place with the construction of the railway.

Jungle clearing was a heavy task in which prisoners of war were provided with the most simple of tools. The two-man-handled saws were blunt and many trees needed to be cut to create an opening before any would fall as they were interwoven with thick creeper. The only machinery as such was the elephants that proved very capable in tree root extractions, the conditions were dangerous and debilitating for the prisoners who were provided with little food. There was one job that was always desirable and associated to working with the elephants, the hooker who followed behind the elephant to hook the chains onto the logs.

Embankments were the most common type of engineering task along the railway. They could range from small earth movements, the levelling of local undulating terrain, to momentous movements of soil and rock, creating massive artificial hills rising out of the jungle. These immense structures were necessary to maintain a gentle gradient along the railway, designed to allow the steam trains to climb or descend slopes. As a rule, the larger the earthwork, in respect of its height, the wider the base work was to support the construction, and Japanese engineers saw that rough frameworks were made to illustrate the dimensions of the embankments. The local geography frequently acted against the ability to resource heavy rock and appropriate earthwork materials, prisoners, and labourers were forced to move materials over long distances. Weak men then carried their individual loads up the steep banks to the top where it was deposited and stamped down, a daily process that was endless.

British prisoners of war from Singapore directed by Japanese engineers of 9th Railway Regiment commenced work on two bridges at Mae Khloung in September 1942. Slightly downstream from the primary bridge was to be a wooden bridge to take light rail traffic, while the main steel and concrete bridge was being constructed. The main bridge required extensive excavation of the river bed to a depth of 8 metres to support the concrete piers. That work commenced on 1 October 1942 and required a Gatmel dredger to bore into the river bed. The wooden bridge construction progressed swiftly. Prisoners used simple pile drivers, which operated with ropes and weights to drive the wood deep into the river bed. In places where the river bed was more substantial, long timber piles were driven into the ground using a heavy weight suspended by a rope from a timber scaffold. A group of prisoners below pulled the weight up to the desired height, after which it was dropped onto the pile. The weight would then be lifted up again and the process continued until the pile was driven far enough into the ground. Crossbeams steadied the piles, which allowed the bridge to take shape quickly. Once the temporary bridge foundations were laid, the pre-cut timber sections were assembled at the construction site. Bamboo scaffolding was created and the heavy beams were lifted up using ropes and pulleys.

The permanent bridge over the Mae Khloung was to span some 300 metres, with intermittent concrete supports. Each of the eleven spans measured some 20 metres across. It was an ambitious project by the Japanese engineers and work on bridge building was dangerous, especially for men who were already weak and ill. The risk of falling off the structures was always present, particularly as they were inevitably carrying heavy loads on timber that was wet and slippery. Boots or other footwear was in short supply, so many men were forced to work barefoot. The prisoners were exerting great energy in the labouring and the Japanese always had high expectations of daily accomplishment. These men were fed on poor-quality rice and little else, which caused consistent malnourishment, leading to debilitating diarrhoea and vulnerability to various tropical diseases. Prisoners were often carrying deep ulcers and other skin conditions that were initiated by simple scratches, minor cuts, and abrasions. In some cases, tropical ulcers continued to develop until they reached bone matter. Mosquito bites were also capable of breaking down the skin tissue, but, of course, the major danger was that of malaria, which became commonplace amongst the men. The mosquitoes were also responsible for spreading dengue fever, making their victims weak and incapable of carrying out any real physical work. Prisoners were always likely to receive punishment by those who drove the human workforce so hard. Little, if any, compassion was ever shown in relation to illness. The Japanese assumption towards prisoners who became sick was that it arose from a lack of determination to remain fit for work and as such they needed less food. These conditions and influences were so terrible, they became the reason why so many died and were simply buried adjacent to the working sites along the River Kwai.

Latrines for the prisoners were often inappropriately placed, creating contamination sources where flies simply commuted between human excrement and food being cooked in simple cook huts. In all probability, the chances for these men to catch dysentery was high, and the resulting dehydration was capable of taking their lives. A lack of vitamins in their diet would be likely to manifest into what was called beriberi, inducing red-raw skin tissue in mouths, tongues, and throats. Beriberi caused the men to suffer gross swelling of the limbs and stomach. Prisoners' minor injuries frequently developed lesions, which soon turned into tropical ulcers that, as often as not, became gangrenous and resulted in hundreds of men having limbs amputated as a last resort. These dangerous operations were frequently undertaken by the few trained medics who had fallen into Japanese captivity at Singapore, men who were responsible for remarkable work in trying to save countless lives. There were base hospitals within the main camps of Chungkai, Tamarkan, Nong Pladuk, and Thanbyuzayat. Only desperately sick men were ever moved from the sub-camps to these, but the system was far from being efficient as they had little equipment or medicines.

The Kanchanaburi temporary wooden bridge was finally completed by January 1943. Kanchanaburi would soon be a name entered in many Allied air crew flying logbooks and it was to be the location which epitomised the Bridge on the River Kwai. The work camp at Kanchanaburi was exceptionally large. While the primary bridge was still being constructed at Mae Khloung, the smaller wooden bridge crossing allowed light train traffic to cross and then run along the east bank of the Kwai onto the major labour works at Chungkai. At that location, the prisoners were cutting through rock to build two very large viaducts. The Japanese Commanding Officer of the overseeing Railway Construction Unit, Major-General Shimoda, was placed under severe pressure to complete the railway by instructions from Tokyo, who had set unrealistic expectations. On 26 January 1943, Major-General Shimoda took to the air to survey the progress of the railway. His aircraft crashed into the deep jungle forest, Shimoda and nine others were killed. While a search party managed to locate two survivors, they in turn died from their injuries shortly afterwards.

With the concrete bridge piers at Mae Khloung completed by March 1943, the steel trusses that had been removed from the railway at Java had arrived at the site. Japanese surveyors calculated the amount of work needed to meet Tokyo's demands for the completion of the railway. The bridging works alone would need to meet 10 metres of progress each day and immense amounts of groundwork would need to be completed, none of which was achievable with the work force being deployed. To increase productivity, the transit camp at Ban Pong soon witnessed relentless numbers of additional men being squeezed into an ever-increasingly squalid environment, which was simply killing men and reducing others into an inhumane existence. Vast numbers of labourers and prisoners of war were marched on foot across vast distances simply to reach their work stations.

North of Kanchanaburi, the significant multiple trestle bridges that followed the curve of the sheer limestone cliff which rose from the banks of the Khwae Noi River at Wampo had been completed. The steel bridge at Mae Khloung was eventually completed in April 1943 and steam locomotives ran across the river Kwai and along the railway which at that time terminated at a location known as Wan Yai. An additional ten thousand prisoners of war had been transported from Singapore by mid-1943; these men became known as 'D', 'F', and 'H' Forces, which were deployed to work on the mid-railway construction sites.

In June 1943, the monsoon rains arrived. The prisoners clothing rotted and footwear simply fell apart on their feet. More worryingly, the latrines overflowed, spewing the foul contents. The rotting bodies of the dead and diseased lay in shallow graves and the rain brought their decomposition to the surface, spilling into the occupied shelters and communal areas occupied by the prisoners. The monsoon period created conditions that made everything more difficult, tangibly reducing productivity on the railway, which induced horrific beatings of the men. However, more alarmingly, the mass of men living in the most basic way, combined with the consistent dampness, saw breakouts of cholera—an epidemic that was likely to kill at a ratio of one in two men. Swiftly and within a day, a man would display terrible diarrhoea, vomiting, cramps, and abdominal pains, which could lose him his life. By example, the infamous Hellfire Pass, where prisoners were chiselling by hand through enormous rock, recorded seventy-two men who died within a nine-day outbreak of the disease. The meagre medical staff administered strict discipline in deploying all means possible to deal with cholera. However, in the segregated native labour camps, no such discipline existed. The squalor and flies simply exacerbated the situation, resulting in terrifying circumstances of death for many hundreds of men. Large communal burying pits were dug for the victims who never survived. The Japanese were very fearful of cholera and additionally they induced immediate pyres to incinerate the corpses.

The work of the medics was exemplary. By example, Private Arthur Pitman (captured in Singapore) was transported into Thailand and worked tirelessly with prisoner of war cholera victims. His work was later evidenced in a recommendation published in *The London Gazette* in January 1947, awarding him the British Empire Medal:

> This Private was a prisoner of war in Thailand. During the cholera epidemic in the summer of 1943, he did marvellous work. He nursed hundreds of cholera cases quite fearlessly, washed, fed, and cleansed them without any regard for his own safety, in the most indescribable filthy conditions. Mere words cannot do justice to the work he carried out or the fine example he set, and by his personal care many lives were saved.

The Japanese Railway Regiment based at Thanbyuzayat was in charge of constructing the Songkurai Railway Bridge, the northernmost Thailand sector of railway line that proved very difficult to progress. Many men worked in the dangerous fast-flowing waters all day and the Japanese had secured lighting to enable working at night. The pressure upon the prisoners and labourers to build the railway was relentless and, in many instances, the Japanese guards applied brutal force to those deemed not working hard enough. To the north was the Hintock Bridge, a 400-yard-long and 80-foot-high structure built of non-hardwood tree stock, which had also created significant problems as it had collapsed three times due to the inferior wood, killing several prisoners.

Disease and death was never conquered, but the sheer number of human labourers did actually complete the railway. Both tracks progressed towards each other at Konkoita in late September 1943. The track finally linked up in the thick jungle at Konkoita. The cost in human lives was to be incalculable, but it would continue to claim lives, with thousands of the native labour force perishing in the days, weeks, and months that lay ahead. When finally completed in October 1943, the railway consisted of a complex railroad infrastructure capable of supporting multiple Japanese train movements on a daily basis. Japan supplied a total of forty-five locomotives, with Burma providing eighty-five, Malaya thirty, Java nine, and Thailand supplying just four. The Japanese type C56 locomotives operated with a maximum axel load of approximately 10 tons. Although built to a common standard, many of the wooden bridges needed to be crossed by these engines at dead slow speeds.

The headquarters of the Railway Administering Department was based in Bangkok and was commanded by Major-General Ishida. It was from here that the operation of the railway was controlled and the complicated timetables were written. The railway had some sixty-three primarily named stations along its length—the railway then broke down into several operating sections. Some were small, with nothing other than a passing track or loop built to simply allow constant use of the main single line. Others combined large stations with workshops, store depots, and repair facilities. Each railway section had their own communication centre constructed at the end of their section. In order to maximise the use of the locomotives working on the line, turning triangles were constructed at some of the larger stations. Railway passing loops were frequently built and extended to significant lengths, and railway spurs were built at an estimated 10-mile interval. These spurs ran for some 500 metres into thick jungle, providing camouflaged protection for locomotives and rolling stock.

Kanchanaburi was a significant location for the railway, with complex stores and locomotive repair capabilities. The locomotives that operated on the railway had been sourced from Japan and the territory it had occupied, including Malaya and Burma. The locally impressed locomotives were fuelled by wood-burning engines and were less powerful than the coal-burning Japanese trains. However, with the plentiful supply of wood, these engines became steady workhorses for the Burma–Thailand Railway, allocated to the more gentle sections of the railway. They operated a shuttle service, passing their rolling stock onto the more powerful coal trains when the railway reached more difficult terrain. Some sections of track, due to the incline, required a locomotive at each end to both pull and push the laden trains.

The Allied Air Headquarters in India sought to gather as much information as possible on the railway after its completion. They instigated comprehensive photographic reconnaissance sorties to obtain images of the entire network, the first of which was completed the day following the Japanese official opening ceremony, on 24 October 1943. The subsequent detailed report, which covered the northernmost 86 miles, gave evidence of the extensive and detailed bridge works.

On 17 November 1944, the Secretary of State for War Sir James Grigg announced to the House of Commons a statement concerning British prisoners of war associated with the building of the Burma–Thailand Railway:

> I think the House would wish to hear a brief statement about ex-prisoners of war who have just returned from Siam [Thailand]. As the House was told on 31 October, some 150 survivors from a sunk Japanese transport carrying United Kingdom and Australian prisoners of war from Singapore to Japan were rescued by United States

Naval Forces in September. The survivors from the United Kingdom have now reached this country. The result of preliminary examinations of the men gives at last a first-hand account of the way our men were treated in the Southern areas of the Far East; and there is now no longer any doubt about the policy which was pursued by the Japanese military authorities towards prisoners of war in these areas, which include Burma, Siam, Malaya and the East Indies. I should make it clear at once that this information does not relate to Hong Kong, Formosa, Occupied China, Korea or Japan, where we believe present conditions to be relatively tolerable. Nor does it refer to civilian internees.

The great majority of prisoners in Singapore and Java appear to have been moved, early in 1942, to Burma or Siam [Thailand]. The Australians were sent by sea to Burma, crowded into ships' holds which had been horizontally sub-divided so that ceilings were no more than 4 feet high. The prisoners from the United Kingdom were sent by rail to Siam so crowded into trucks that they could not even lie down during the journey. They were then marched some 80 miles. This and subsequent movement in Burma or Siam appears to have been on foot, regardless of distance, weather, or the prisoners' state of health. The United Kingdom prisoners were then set to work on the construction of a railway through primitive, disease-infested jungle passing over the mountain range between Siam and Burma to meet the Burmese end of the railway, on the construction of which Australians were engaged in similar country. The conditions under which all these men lived and worked were terrible, even for natives of the country who were also forcibly employed on the same work.

Such accommodation as was provided gave little or no protection against tropical rains or blazing sun; worn out clothing was not replaced; soon many lacked clothing, boots and head covering; the only food provided was a pannikin of rice and about half a pint or less of watery stew three times a day. But the work had to go on without respite, whatever the cost in human suffering or life. The inevitable result was an appalling death-rate, the lowest estimate of deaths being one in five. When the railway was finished about October, 1943, those not needed for maintenance work were moved to camps in Siam out of the jungle, and here conditions are less intolerable. From these camps, the fittest were later sent to Singapore en route to Japan. The rescued men were on a ship, which left Singapore early in September, 1944. There were probably 1,300 United Kingdom and Australian prisoners of war on board. After she was sunk, the Japanese deliberately picked up all Japanese survivors, but left the prisoners to their fate, and I fear the great majority of them were drowned. We have asked the Protecting Power to make the strongest possible protest.

I am sure that I speak for the whole House and for all the British people in expressing admiration for the way in which the United States submarine crews risked their own safety to rescue men from the sea, and our very deep gratitude to those crews and to the United States authorities for the care and attention given to them at every stage. Thanks to them nearly all the rescued men are recovering from their terrible experiences. There is one redeeming feature in the whole story. All the rescued men tell of the amazing way in which the morale of the prisoners has remained high, despite the worst the Japanese could do. In particular, tribute is paid to the medical officers who were captured with them and who have achieved little short of miracles in looking after the sick and injured despite lack of essential medicines, instruments, and hospital equipment. All that we have learnt from these men reveals that our prisoners have been true to the highest traditions of our race. To the relatives and friends of all the prisoners concerned, our deepest sympathy goes out. It is a matter of profound regret to me that these disclosures have to be made; but we are convinced that it is necessary that the Japanese should know that we know how they have been behaving, and that we intend to hold them responsible. Here I would add that we are collecting from the survivors every scrap of information they can give about other men, and this information will be passed on to the next-of-kin concerned as quickly as possible

However, the tide of war had changed for the Japanese and the Burma–Thailand Railway would never support the anticipated growth of its Asian expansion nor its intended invasion of India. It did, however, contribute to the military actions of the Japanese in fighting the Allied advances in Burma, but the railway fell ridiculously short of what it had been planned for. The railway was an important supply route for the Japanese, who utilised the returning movements of rolling stock carrying materials for shipment back to Japan. In addition to supplies for the Imperial Japanese Army, trains carried materials for the maintenance of the railway and supplies for the labourers who continued to work along the route. The Japanese fitted railway wheels to standard diesel-fuelled trucks to enable small mobile units to be used for transporting small maintenance teams to inspect general maintenance sites. The Allied bombing campaign against the railway added significantly to the maintenance work required along the entire length of its construction. Bridges were a particular target of Allied bombers, particularly the robustly constructed steel bridges. In the case of the bridge on the River Kwai, a significantly high number of prisoners in the nearby Tha Markam camp were available for repairs and maintenance upon both bridges.

Kanchanaburi became the site where prisoners of war were held prior to their eventual return to prisoner of war camps in Singapore. Little, if anything, was facilitated for the native workforce who had built the railway. Approximately 10,000 of the strongest prisoners were selected for work in Japan, while others would be held in various camps to act as a maintenance and repair force. East of Kanchanaburi was the Ban Pong station that linked the railroad to Bangkok and south of that was the Nong Pladuk halt. This was an area of railroad sidings to enable travel south to Singapore or westwards onto the Thailand to Burma railroad. In close proximity were two large prisoner of war camps, with an estimated combined capacity to hold around 12,000 men. One of the camps was situated close to the Japanese shunting yards and workshops that facilitated the Burma railroad link. Japanese ammunition dumps and other war supplies were stored in the vicinity and an anti-aircraft flak battery was sited between both camps. It would have been obvious to the Japanese that any Allied aerial bombing on this important target would inevitably cause casualties within the camp. Many prisoner of war camps were situated in similar areas of high vulnerability, and the Japanese forbade any type of air raid slit trenches or similar protection to be dug. In the event of an Allied air strike, the men had no choice but to remain in their bamboo huts.

The Burma–Thailand Railway consumed a workforce during its construction of over 61,000 Allied prisoners of war. An estimated 12,399 of those men had died by the end of the war. These Allied prisoner of war casualties were, however, in the shadow of the number of deaths sustained by the native labour forces. The Japanese kept no records appertaining to these men and only a few individual graves now exist as most of these casualties were buried or incinerated in mass graves. In order to build the Burma–Thailand Railway, 300,000 men were drawn from military prisoner of war camps and from numerous cultures and races. Once completed, it then became one of the most significant targets to destroy by the Allied Air Forces in 1945.

The Inter-Service Target Section working within the Allied Strategic Bomber Force continued to issue target intelligence from its headquarters within Eastern Air Command. The bombing strategy intelligence was issued by General George Edward Stratemeyer, Air Commander, Eastern Air Command. On 12 February 1945, he submitted a report on the Burma–Thailand Railroad. Recent intelligence reveals:

A bypass has been completed for the Kanchanaburi bridge (Bridge No. 277 new No. Q-654).

Waterborne traffic on the Meklong River has increased.

Railway spurs and jetties have been constructed on either side of the Meklong River at Kanchanaburi.

In view of the above it is believed that destruction of Bridge No. Q-654 will have comparatively little adverse effect upon traffic on the Burma–Thailand Railroad. A search for an alternative target has revealed that bypasses and river jetty facilities have not been developed at Bridges Q-633 (1,680 ft) and Q-577 (1,120 ft). Destruction of either of these would implement more effective interdiction of the Burma–Thailand Railroad than is likely to result from further attacks on Bridge Q-654.

The Burma–Thailand portion of the railway between Thanbyuzayat and Banpong is a single track meter gauge line 245 miles long with adequate passing loops. There are no tunnels but many steep grades with 285 bridges or viaducts over 400 ft. It was built between January and November 1943 by 24,000 British and Australian prisoners and 10,000 Chinese coolies. Complete cover shows 45 locos, 900 Rolling stock including 15 trains.

Since this line contains so many excellent targets for breaking or blocking the line it is suggested that all day effort be devoted to interrupting suitable stretches of the line Banpong to Thanbyuzayat rather than between Thanbyuzayat and

Pegu, or Banpong and Bangkok. Further, if this is done in the hilly jungle country on either side of the frontier, the enemy will have the maximum obstacle to using motor road alternatives which in any case may be put out by monsoon, further the reinforcements will be held up as far as possible from Burma proper.

It is most important to interrupt the line in as many points as possible, spaced out over a considerable stretch rather than a too localised effort, this will cause the maximum delay in repair work particularly in the hill portions of the route. Interruption can be obtained by bridge and viaduct busting, creating of landslides, or spike bombing of the track. It is suggested that a proportion of spiking is always carried out to ensure some definite breaks in the line. Breaches in the line and broken bridges near the two end junctions will be in flat country with good road nearby and parallel to the railway, this will enable rapid repair and easy short-circuiting by the use of motor transport.

There are a few profitable targets for a normal night attack, on the Pegu–Bangkok Railway where congestion has resulted in the stations and yards. They are, in order of priority:

Moulmein. The Salween crossing has never been bridged, this plus our mining effort has caused considerable delay in ferrying to Martaban with presumably increased congestion at Moulmein. Normally 150 Rolling Stock and a few locos, troops awaiting transhipment.

Mergui, Tavoy, Moulmein–Martaban, Sittang River Ferry at Mokpalin, Port Blair, Bangkok, Go Sichang and Sittahib is of the first priority. In addition certain other channels in the Irrawaddy Delta may need blocking.

Interruption of the Burma–Thailand Railway is next in order of priority, if this is unserviceable the Bangkok–Lampang line must be attacked.

Continue mining operations to deny the use of as many Burma and Thailand ports as possible.

Obtain visual or photographic definite confirmation of the state of the Burma–Thailand Railway. If unserviceable, hammer the Bangkok–Lampang Railway, but switch all efforts over to the former should it become serviceable. The effort available is not sufficient to interrupt both railways for a continuous period.

The remarkable powers of the Jap railway engineer with a plentiful supply of British, Australian, Indian and Chinese slave labour will enable him to repair the results of the worst hammering within a week. Attacks will need, therefore, to be repeated at frequent but regular intervals.

By Command of Major-General Stratemeyer.

It should be noted that various bridges were identified by a simple numbering system, which at some time changed to a letter-coded system. It is thought that this was administered by Air Command Headquarters India:

Reference 'Q' relates to Burma–Thailand.

Reference 'A' also Burma–Thailand.

Reference 'TF' relates to Banpong–Singapore.

Reference 'M' relates to Myingyan–Paleik.

Reference 'H' Moulmein–Bangkok.

Three numerical references appear to be Moulmein–Ye.

Two numerical references appear to be Bangkok–Chiengmai.

The Bridge Q-654 was the wooden secondary bridge constructed at Kanchanaburi. This bridge was bombed on 13 February 1945 and remained out of commission at the end of March 1945.

The reference to spike bombing was the development of bombs that were fitted with spikes on the nose section of the bomb. This spike enabled the bomb to dig into the ground instead of bouncing off as happened frequently—the cause primarily being due to the low trajectory that it struck the target, being dropped from very low altitudes. The bombs needed to be delayed in order to allow the B-24s time to fly away from the target before exploding. Had they not done so, the explosions and shockwaves would undoubtedly have caused damage to the aircraft.

Photo reconnaissance work was invaluable, providing intelligence on the vulnerable points and bridges. Additionally, they were able to monitor the Japanese defences of light and heavy anti-aircraft guns, which were positioned to capitalise on the anticipated low-level bombing runs adopted by the Liberator crews. The Japanese were extremely proficient at camouflage techniques and the deployment of anti-aircraft guns was taken very seriously. The Inter-Service Target Section reports were invaluable to the crews. One such report upon Kanchanaburi advised that the target was approximately 1,004 statute miles from the airfield at Digri. The construction camp appeared quite active, with an effective marshalling yard that normally held a large amount of rolling stock. It also had a workshop facility capable of holding up to twelve locomotives. The reconnaissance identified the probable prisoner of war camp, noting that the anti-aircraft defences consisted of four heavy guns with a possibility of enemy fighter interception, considering that Bangkok was less than 100 miles to the east.

The Mae Khloung metre gauge railway network was constructed to run towards and across the river we now know as the River Kwai. In January 1942, the military forces within Thailand assumed control over the Mae Khloung Railway network that ran from Bangkok into central Thailand. Prime Minister Lang Pipul collaborated with the Japanese, embracing their objective of ruling over the entire South Pacific. He officially declared war against the Allies on 25 January 1942 and in October 1942 he sought and took dictatorial control of Thailand, becoming a loyal puppet of Japan.

Thailand had an effective railway infrastructure that eventually became a target for Allied heavy bombers, in particular the B-24 Liberators. Allied bombing disrupted significant lengths of railway line and the substantial rail workshops at Makkasan were consistently targeted. These operations affected the repair and rebuild capability to the railway, which, when combined with destroying the principal signalling centres and station yards, created great incapacity for the railway to function effectively. The railway had nearly 200 steam locomotives deployed within its rail structure. The greatest potential loss to the Japanese forces in Thailand was the destruction by bombing of several substantial steel bridges. Three bridges in particular caused dramatic disruption to the railway infrastructure and, as a result of the Liberator operations against them, they were unable to be repaired properly until hostilities had ceased.

# 6

# Rama VI Bridge across the Menam Chao Phraya

The Rama VI Bridge connected Bangkok with the southern line, a primary connection bridge that consisted of five spans totalling over 400 metres and had a beam of 8 metres, allowing medium-sized ships to pass beneath it. It was designed to be a rail link between the eastern bank of the Chao Phraya River and the western bank, connecting the railway system of Bangkok with the west and south of the country. The Rama VI, described as a through-type steel cantilever rail over River Bridge, was eventually completely destroyed by Allied aircraft on 7 February 1945.

## Surat Bridge across the Menam Tapi

This bridge was built on the southern line, south of Bangkok, and consisted of three spans totalling 200 metres. The bombing destruction of the River Bridge near Surat left the railway line to the border isolated from the rest of the network. A temporary station was created on the Bangkok side of the bridge, where various cargos were barged across the river to the railway line on the other side of the river. The bridge was only brought back into use in 1953.

## Bandara Bridge across the Menam Nan

The railway bridge at Bandara, also known as the Poramintara Bridge, spanned the Nan River. Built on the northern line, north of Bangkok, it was another three-span construction, totalling nearly 300 metres in length. Constructed as a cantilever bridge, it opened for service on 7 December 1909. The Poramintara Bridge was bombed and destroyed by the Allies on the 24 and 25 April 1944. The bridge was eventually reconstructed in 1953.

The Japanese Battalion Railway Regiments were subsequently ordered to build the Pekanbaru–Kra Isthmus railway link in order to connect Chumphon to the Malay railway line. The Kra Isthmus link was a relatively short connection between the east and west coastlines and was completed in December 1943. The Kra Isthmus Railway would figure in Allied operational raids, severing the supply line from Malaya.

Sumatra, an island rich in coal and oil, represented a vital energy resource for the Japanese. The construction of the Pekanbaru rail link, also described as simply the Pekanbaru or the Sumatra Railway, was important to the Japanese. The plan had been to create a 138-mile rail connection between the town of Pekanbaru and an existing rail line, which ran to the city of Padang on the Indian Ocean coastline. The Japanese had desired for the Sumatra Railway, once completed, to provide a direct link between east and west Sumatra. By joining the new railway with the old, and constructing a new secondary line to connect the railway to the Sumatran coal mines, the Japanese planned to transport fuel and troops by rail for shipping from Padang to Singapore. From May to September 1944, the Japanese deployed many thousands of native workers and Allied prisoners of war to work on the railway, the majority of which had been captured on Java. They consisted of men from the Royal Dutch Indies' Army and the British and Australian Army, Navy, and Air Force. The Pekanbaru Railroad had fourteen labour camp sites along its track length. Many of the prisoners of war who were made to work on this railroad were older than those selected for the Burma–Thailand Railway. Shocking conditions prevailed upon these men and the labourers, ill-treatment and diseases took the lives of several thousands of them, with the majority being the pressed native force labourers.

Work initially started on the line at the large port at Pekanbaru, and the railway headed south-westerly with impressive bridges built across the two Kampar Rivers and another crossing the Indragiril River, near the Moeara coalfields. These railway bridges were built in an identical fashion to the Burma–Thailand Railway, as were the very deep cuttings and high embankments.

The Pekanbaru Railway was completed on 15 August 1945, ironically on the day that marked the end of the Second World War in Asia. The railway was never used to profit the Japanese war effort—all of the endured suffering was, in effect, for nothing. Very swiftly, the railroad materials were purloined for other purposes, leaving the jungle to retake its territory and the swampy conditions to consume everything left behind. Japan had ordered the building of this railway as an integral part to their vision of superiority across Southeast Asia. The Pekanbaru Railway is yet another example where post-war analyses will never know just how many men lost their lives while creating that Japanese vision—in particular, the thousands of enforced labourers from across the Japanese-occupied territories that had been sent there. A monument to this railway is located at the National Memorial Arboretum in Staffordshire, England. It is a simple, but poignant memorial dedicated to all those who lost their lives in that swamp-infested territory.

The Rangoon–Myitkyina Railway, known as the Burma Railway, served central and northern Burma. It provided the main northern track from Mandalay to Myitkyina in the north and Rangoon in the south. In 1942, the Japanese removed approximately 300 miles of track from this railway for the construction of the Burma–Thailand Railway. Much of that track was from subsidiary spur lines around Mandalay. Lateral spurs branched off to serve various parts of the central Burmese basin. Sufficient track remained for the route to be operational for their military purposes. However, during their occupancy of Burma and Thailand, this railway was to become a source of regular track pillaging. The railway ended up operating in four large, but isolated sections. One vitally important line was north-east to Lashio and a short track also ran from Mandalay northward to the small mining town of Madaya. The heaviest railway traffic, however, progressed west and north on the loop to Yeu and direct to Myitkyina.

This railway network provided a great many targets to the Allied Liberator bombing campaign. Rangoon, Thanbyuzayat, Pegu, Henzada (present-day Hinthada), Pyinmana, Thazi, Letpadan, Paleik, Mandalay, Ywataung, and Naba were significant railroad junctions. Rolling stock was frequently identified at such locations. Prome, Bassein, Moulmein, Martaban, Myingyan, Mandalay, Monywa, Katha, Mogaung, and Myitkyina were locations where rail and river traffic systems merged, all of which were centrally targeted for aerial reconnaissance. Frequently, these names would appear in operational orders as targets attacked by the Allied heavy bombers from the airfields in India.

The railways across central Burma offered numerous bridge targets: Ava Bridge across the Irrawaddy, near Mandalay, and the Sittang River Bridge on the Pegu–Moulmein track (which had been demolished by the British in their withdrawal to India). On the Rangoon–Mandalay railway line, the Pazundaung Bridge (south of Pegu) and the Myitnge Bridge (over which all goods from the south fed into Mandalay) were important targets, as was the Mu River Bridge on the Yeu branch. On the Lashio line, the impressive Gokteik viaduct spanned a vast gorge. These four bridges—Pazundaung, Myitnge, Mu, and Gokteik—would receive attention from many operational bombing sorties, primarily by the United States Army Air Force, in attempts to destroy them.

The heavy bombers of the RAF were not the only aircraft that sought out targets of opportunity along the Burma railways. Many sorties were carried out by RAF Beaufighters, who purposely sought to attack rail freight and locomotives at every opportunity. These strafing attacks frequently inflicted enough damage on a locomotive boiler for it to require upwards of a month to repair, while other attacks had the ability to inflict complete destruction. On 19 April 1944, the British War Correspondent Bill Duff experienced a sortie in a Beaufighter, after having sought permission from Air Marshal Sir John Baldwin to be taken into the air and report upon the experience for the services newspaper of South East Asia Command, which was printed and distributed from Calcutta. His published report read:

In less than five minutes after my arrival I was scheduled to go on a strafe next morning at 06.30 hours.… so there we were Flying Officer J. C. Van Nes a Canadian Pilot and Flying Officer J. T. Matthews from Sale in Manchester. They seemed an ideal team—pilot all fire and dash, navigator patient, careful and controlled. Just how ideal the team was I was to learn within the hour, and to marvel at throughout the remainder of our nine hundred mile, four hour trip. We were steadily dropping down until the tree tops were a bare two hundred feet below us. In front lay the silver ribbon of the Irrawaddy. I looked idly round and the bullet proof doors between the two cabins, which had silently closed a second or two before reminding me sharply that we were not out for pleasure. Suddenly through the intercom came Matts voice, 'This is it,' he said and Van swung the huge machine into a tight right hand turn at two hundred miles per hour, when you are not expecting it, is quite a thing…over another bend of the river the country was changing. Cover was becoming denser, trees still sparse in trunk and foliage, more closely ranked. Again, 'This is it,' over the intercom, another sharp swing and we were following the single track railway that leads north to Swebo and its termination at Myitkyina, the life line for the Japanese in northern Burma.

The purpose of our patrol was a photo recce of certain features along the line, with, of course secondary intention to shoot up anything Jap that moved. But said Van apologetically before we started, 'I'm afraid this will be a rather dull party. The Japs know we have this line taped and they are moving on it only at night. We may not see a thing or fire a shot.'

Just how dull the party was is shown by the facts and the photographs that established them. We, I mean Van and Matt destroyed four Jap Locos, three of them under steam and damaged two more, exploded an oil tanker and turned a perfectly good and amazingly well camouflaged water tower into a gigantic colander. A dull party indeed—and we used one thousand rounds of twenty millimetre ammo and three thousand three hundred rounds of point 'three o three' ammo in doing it. So you can take it that the property that was busted was well and truly busted. The Jap is an industrious and crafty blighter. He builds little bashas for his locos and hides them among the trees so you need an eagle eye to find them. Unfortunately for the Jap, both Van and Matt have just that kind of eye. For me, I could have stooged up and down the line for a month and seen nothing, except of course the grand big loco obligingly left with its coaches uncoupled and dispersed smack on the track. Even I saw that, but its makers never will again. We gave it three attacks and it vomited forth everything it had in the way of steam, water and oil. As we pulled out of the third attack more steeply than ever before Van turned his head and asked, 'Are you all right?' Thinking he meant had the steep dive to fifty feet minus and the sharp pull out unnerved me, I called back, 'Yes thanks.' Then he pointed to the centre of the windscreen. A beautiful star-shaped scar marked the spot where a Jap machine gunner with incredible accuracy had scored a bull. Van patted the Perspex lovingly with his gloved hand and laughed, 'I like that stuff a lot,' he said. And that goes for me too.

The oil tanker had been earlier in the proceedings—our first strike in fact, and a satisfying one. By some miracle Van had spotted it under a roof of thatch, and down we went. From my stance in the well [fuselage] the view was a grandstand one, practically through the gun sight. Beneath my feet there sounded the staccato, angry rumble of the cannon. Through the cockpit floor came the acrid but stimulating fumes of cordite. A brilliant flash of flames marked the end of the tanker as its gas content ignited, blew it to no good at all.

As we stooged on along the line Matt was busy in his office with map and camera. Every strike we made was recorded by the big camera in the nose. Every feature that had to be reconnoitred, and everything new and likely to interest the intelligence officer was recorded.... Van had found a newly made railway spur over which the Jap had actually placed sandbags as it crept between the tall trees. At the end of the spur what should there be but another loco with its little summer house. It's an ex loco now. It was about this time that a heavy clang shook the aircraft. 'We've been hit I thought,' though there was no sign of flak. 'A Vulture,' said Van after a moment as nothing appeared amiss. Back at base we found the Vulture was a bullet that had penetrated the cannon panel, pierced an ammo chute, missing everything vital and done little damage. This was not the Japs lucky day. Another wide sweep and the sun settled down to shine on our port side instead of the starboard. Our outward patrol was over and course was set for base. Back along the line we flew, always at fighting height, always on the alert for targets.... As we climbed to meet the hills I felt the fresh breeze again behind me. The bulletproof doors were open and Matt, whom I had not seen, it seemed for ages, was grinning at me over his reports and maps.... Back to ten thousand feet what a machine 'Y' for Yorkie is. I felt then as I feel now tremendous affection for her. She drove like a luxury train all that morning. Everything she was asked to do she did perfectly. Jap flak she took in her strife. As I gazed contently at those pale blue spinners I thought of the men responsible for the Beaus' perfection, the ground crew who mended her. Not for them the joys of Jap strafing, not for them the serene beauty of the heavens at ten thousand feet, nor the throat catching thrill of tree tops at fifty feet. Never for them the headlines but always for them the honour and glory, don't forget these men ever. Their pilots honour them and so must we, 'Y' for Yorkie was doing them proud, as they have done her.

Base was chattering away to Matt over the radio giving a fix. Van grinned turned up a thumb as we heard a bearing. We were precisely where we should have been as we came down from the mountains, just another ordinary everyday miracle of precise navigation. This said Van, 'Is a piece of cake.' Ahead of us twenty miles away lay the home strip.... I looked around the cockpit for the last time as we were touching down. I climbed down clutching a battered map that Matt had politely lent me.... I would be awfully glad if he would let me have the map when he had done with it. It will remind me down to my extreme old age of two very grand chaps and a superb machine. And of course I shall be able to shoot a horrid line down Fleet Street on the strength of it.

Bill Duff's report was published and circulated to thousands of Allied troops who read the popular circulation, but his expectations of returning to Fleet Street with his treasured map never materialised. Shortly after his article's publication, the same newspaper printed the following account:

SEAC Scribe Dies in Crash.
CALCUTTA—William George Duff, Royal Air Force, assistant editor of South East Asia Command, daily newspaper for the British troops, was killed this week in the crash of an American Liberator bomber, about three hundred and thirty miles north of Bangkok. Duff was aboard the plane as a war correspondent, to report on a low-level bombing mission. The aircraft was on its second run over the target when two engines went out in flames, apparently from ground machine-gun fire. The plane crashed into a hillside with eleven men aboard.

   Their target had been the Railway Bridge at Kaeng Luang on the Thailand northern line. The Kaeng Luang Bridge was a large three-span, steel truss construction of some one hundred and seventy four meters in length. It crosses the Mae Nam Yom or Yom River in the north of Thailand. The Allies saw Thailand's Northern railway Line as an important target and Bill Duff was on board the B-24 Liberator to record the events of 'bridge busting' in Burma. He was a member of the Royal Air Force Volunteer Reserve, Aircraftman 1st Class Press Officer (1721871). He served as a war correspondent to the British South East Asia Command newspaper and was flying as an observer on a B-24J aircraft assigned to the United States Tenth Air Force. They were part of a twelve-plane formation that departed Madhaiganj in India to attack the bridge. Immediately after successfully bombing the target from about three hundred feet, the B-24 was hit by anti-aircraft fire on the left wing, which caught fire. The B-24 lost altitude and crashed twenty five miles southwest of Bhre, Thailand, with no survivors.

In most unusual circumstances this British Royal Air Force aircraftsman now lies in the American Jefferson Barracks National Cemetery, having been recovered alongside the American servicemen who died with him. The United States of America adopted a policy of recovering its casualties to home soil at every opportunity. It is appropriate in many respects that he was jointly recovered and remained with the men who died alongside him in the Liberator that plunged into ground in Thailand.

# 7

# The Fight from India in B-24 Liberators, 1945

For the Liberator crews in India, 1945 commenced with unpredictable and abnormal weather conditions. An incessantly and ominously deep depression produced very poor flying conditions, which prevented the capability to mount effective operations across the entire central belt of Burma. Despite those prevailing conditions, 99 Squadron continued as best possible to function effectively. The Fourteenth Army had launched a successful offensive down the Arakan Coast, followed by a major advance deep into central Burma, pushing the Japanese forces into areas of retreat. The men of 99 Squadron became fully engaged in strategic bombing, in an attempt to prevent the Japanese efforts of supplying troop and material reinforcements from reaching the fighting fronts. No. 99 Squadron hoped to accomplish this by bombing the Burma–Thailand Railway, with the objective to keep that and other railway lines closed. To achieve success, among the targets were the bridges that spanned the rivers and, in particular, the bridge on the River Kwai. Wing Commander Ercolani, Flight Sergeant Thomas Reynolds, and Pilot Officer David Jones were at this time all operational together at Dhubalia, and these men all became engaged in these important operations.

Wing Commander Ercolani was in command of an acknowledged and effective squadron, part of the Allied Strategic Bomber Force, commanded by Air Commodore Mellersh. He would be working closely with the Allied ground offensive operations, attempting to reach deep into Burma. As soon as he arrived at Dhubalia, Wing Commander Ercolani requisitioned David Jones to fly as his regular navigator. Thomas Reynolds was still within Johnny Haycock's crew, flying as his regular second wireless operator/air gunner. The Squadron strength of operational crews was by this time twenty in number, and ahead of them was a consistent requirement to maintain operational efficiency against the 5,000 miles of railway track across Burma—in particular, the Burma–Thailand Railway link. The Royal Air Force intelligence staff had worked hard on gathering as much evidence as possible on the known and probable prisoner of war camps situated along that railway line. Annotated photographs were distributed to the squadrons and each wing of the group had access to an impressive scale model of the railway, built to the highest detail possible. Of concern was the fact that the Japanese had not marked any hospital or prisoner of war camp facility, making it very difficult, if not impossible, for those camps to be differentiated. In an effort to work with the most up-to-date and efficient intelligence, it became policy for all operations against that railway to be directly cleared by Eastern Air Command Headquarters. This was primarily to avoid endangering the lives of Allied prisoners of war if at all possible. The Japanese, however, were not reticent in placing anti-aircraft guns in relatively close proximity to labour camps and it was inevitable that, despite the best planning, accidental deaths of the men constructing the railway and bridges were always likely to occur.

Efforts to gather the best evidence of bridge construction and structural detail were obtained from British Mosquito aircraft that were fitted with a long-lens camera facing forward, but installed at a slight angle. This equipment provided excellent images of the potential targets and additionally provided the pilots with a photographic view, which included a horizon. This factor was of great value to them, particularly when flying at low levels. Whenever the weather permitted, photo reconnaissance work took place along the lengths of the Burma–Thailand, Bangkok–Chiengmai, Pegu–Thanbyuzayat, and Rangoon railways. These reconnaissance sorties were constantly identifying new works and updating bridge status reports.

David Jones immediately commenced his additional tour of duty by flying on 1 January 1945. He acted as the navigator for Flying Officer Kemp and his crew on his first operation to bomb the railway bridge at Thanbyuzayat, one of the northernmost positions on the Burma link of the Burma–Thailand Railway. No doubt David would have been apprehensive as, although he had made a good impression upon the Squadrons navigation leader, he was an unknown commodity to this crew. He now sat alone at a small table facing backwards in the front section of the Liberator KG976. In front of him were his compass indicators and other navigational instruments. At the rear of the navigator's compartment was an entrance to crawl through; this actually passed under the flight deck, passing the front wheel storage area to access the bomb bay and flight deck. David completed his inaugural operation with a resounding success and they landed safely after their twelve hours in the air. The remaining eleven Liberators of 99 Squadron also achieved similar results. The Squadron had attacked two bridges that day, however, not all returned safely. Warrant Officer McCredie's Liberator had been struck by flak, two engines were lost and a fire broke out on the beam deck. Warrant Officer Bassett, one of the air gunners, did well to deal with the flames and remarkably the crew managed to reach India and accomplish a forced-landing at the substantial all-weather Cox's Bazar airfield. The same could not be said for Flight Lieutenant White's Liberator, KH360, which was shot down into the sea while opportunely strafing Japanese merchant shipping on the return to base.

The B-24 aircraft was always likely to break apart when ditching in the sea. The fragile bomb bay doors collapsed instantaneously on impact and water forcibly surged into the fuselage, creating little time for the crew to escape. Among the life-saving devices fitted to the Liberator were two five-man life rafts. These were stowed in compartments above the wing fuselage section and could be manually opened from within or outside of the aircraft. Activating the release mechanism saw the life rafts catapulted clear of the airframe and into the water. This was a most innovative design feature of the B-24 Liberator and no doubt responsible for saving many lives. In the case of Flight Lieutenant White's ditching, he and seven of his crew were taken down to a watery grave within the Liberator. The three men who escaped into the life rafts eventually became prisoners of war.

The dangers of low-level sorties flown along the Japanese railways in Burma and Thailand can be well described by a remarkable incident that same day in the B-24 Liberator flown by Squadron Leader Clive Beadon of 215 Squadron. The following is the official 'Command Recommendation' for his award:

> An aircraft of the above squadron was carrying out a sortie against locomotives and bridges on the Moulmein–Bangkok Railway at 16.00 hours on 1 January 1945. At milestone 37, the aircraft received a direct hit at the extreme rear of the fuselage, immediately in front of the rear turret, from a concealed Bofors gun site. At the point of entry, the fuselage sustained a hole two feet square, and the burst killed the rear gunner, tore away the turret doors, and riddled the fuselage in that area, removed the top turret, damaged the elevators, and started a large fire, which eventually so weakened the structure that the turret almost fell off.
>
> Sergeants Bennett and Hindson who were manning the beam guns were knocked down by the blast, but immediately, and without thought of the exploding ammunition, went into the flames and endeavoured to rescue the rear-gunner. Finding that he was dead, they set about extinguishing the fire. This proved to be extremely difficult and dangerous as ammunition was exploding, and hydraulic oil, the gunner's parachute and equipment and feed belts were all well alight. These two were joined by Sergeant Morgan and Warrant Officer Cobbe, the latter sustaining burns to the hands while endeavouring to sever the ammunition belts. All extinguishers were used and then bottles of tea and water all exhausted, with the fire still unsubdued. The captain, Squadron Leader Beadon, having the aircraft under control in spite of the extreme nose heaviness due to the damaged elevators, recalled the second pilot to take over and came back to assess the general damage.
>
> With the assistance of the ball-gunner he removed the rear-gunner, whose clothing was still alight, and made every effort to extinguish the flames from the hydraulic oil pipes. The parachute was thrown out of the aircraft, as well as other burning material. Eventually after three hours, the flames were extinguished and the transfer of fuel from the bomb-bay tank successfully accomplished, and the return journey of over one thousand miles continued.

It is considered that the aircrew named above showed courage and coolness in the face of extreme personal danger in attempting the removal of the rear-gunner, and in subduing the fire. At no time was there any shirking of duty, signs of panic as the fire remained uncontrolled, or doubt shown that they would eventually reach base. This confidence in their captain reflects greatly to his credit, and the manner in which he has trained them.

The 215 Squadron records later advise that the entire crew mentioned in the attempted rescue of their Rear Gunner Sergeant Harding all received a Command Mention. This incident provides further evidence of the capabilities of the B-24 Liberator to maintain flight, despite sustaining massive damage to the integrity of its airframe.

Two day after this incident, on 3 January 1945, another 215 Squadron Liberator, KH214, was lost on operations while attacking bridges on the Burma–Thailand Railway. KH214 was struck by defensive light flak and crashed at a location called Tisen. Nobody survived the crash and the remains of the casualties, which comprised of six Canadian, three British, one New Zealander, and one Burmese National, were buried in a nearby bomb crater. The Canadian Pilot of KH214, Flight Lieutenant Brodie, had been the man who had parachuted out from the stricken Harvard being flown by Johnny Haycock the previous September. The Liberators rear gunner had been Flight Lieutenant Sao, a Burmese man who had been in England when war was declared. His parents were connected to the Royal Circle in Burma, making him a prince. Sao volunteered to serve in the Royal Air Force and qualified as a wireless operator/air gunner. He was a member of a unique minority of Burmese men who undertook aerial operations against the Japanese over his home country.

Returning to events within 99 Squadron, the newly arrived Australian navigator, Colin Woolford, took the opportunity to commence his war by navigating his new crew to targets on the Burma–Thailand Railway. Successfully completing operations on 3 and 5 January, he settled in exceptionally well among his colonial friends. The pressure upon these men was colossal, especially for the navigators. Colin Woolford would also perform a similar duty on the 9 January, witnessing the experienced David Jones and Wing Commander Ercolani fly to the specific railway cutting identified as Milestone 54 at Tadein. He led the force of fifteen Liberators that took off at 4.06 a.m. and bombed the railway side cuttings effectively, with all aircraft returning safely nearly thirteen hours later. Milestone 54 was a relatively large target, which also featured a long road cutting. The swathe of jungle cuttings made it easy to recognise from the air, providing the light and weather conditions were favourable.

Another incident over Milestone 54 engaged a crew from 215 Squadron. The Liberator, piloted by Plt Off. Neville, had an inexperienced second pilot who, while over the target, adjusted the engine throttles without loosening the control knob. These levers sat within a bank of three similar sets. To the far left of the second pilot were the turbo boost levers, then the throttle levers and the mixture levers, which were closest to him. He tugged on the four throttle levers, cutting power to the four engines. The aircraft was being targeted by anti-aircraft fire at that time and thinking that the engines had been hit, the crew immediately received an emergency 'prepare to bale out' message. This would have been a frightening message for the ball turret gunner to receive encased down below the aircraft. Occupying that position was Flight Sergeant Hubert Reekes. His only escape was to be pumped up by the hydraulic system into the belly of the fuselage assisted by a beam gunner, who would take up his position to extract the ball gunner who would then gather his parachute and go to the beam escape hatch. While standing at the escape hatch, Reekes received a thumb's up signal from another crew member. However, this message was supposed to indicate that the pilot had restarted the engines and all was well. The ball gunner thinking it was the indication to jump went out backwards and fell into the sky. His parachute operated safely and he was seen to fall into the trees not far from the railway line. Landing without injury, he made contact with some Burmese natives who, despite being given the assurances of a reward, responded to the intimidation of the Japanese to hand over any fallen airmen. His crew survived the experience and returned to base to report his absence. Reekes faced capture and interrogation at the hands of the Japanese, no doubt finding it difficult to explain his isolated capture. He was eventually imprisoned in the Rangoon jail.

Two days later, on 11 January 1945, Thomas Reynolds flew with his Kiwi pilot Haycock and eleven other Liberators to bomb a bridge at Phitsanulok, situated near one of the oldest cities in Thailand. He simply wrote in his logbook: 'bridge busting, Height 300 feet, bomb load 5,000 pounds'. Having dropped the bombload, Johnny Haycock turned his aircraft away from the railway to view the damage to the embankment and the northern end of the bridge structure. As he did so, his crew sighted a goods train stationary within a siding partially hidden by the jungle canopy; the air gunners were able to open fire and strafed the entire length of the train, including the locomotive that burst into steam as it blew up. The Liberator crews became adept at recognising the extensive embankments built by the prisoners of war and these were in themselves targets to destroy. In many instances, they represented many hundreds of hours of construction work to complete.

Flight Lieutenant Barrett of 159 Squadron was provided with a rare opportunity on 18 January. The Squadron was participating in a mainland bombing operation upon the railway siding at Martaban. While making for the target independently, he sighted a lone cargo vessel off the coast of Burma, which he estimated to be approximately 200 feet long. The wireless operation transmitted a message seeking authority to attack this target in preference to continuing to Martaban. Permission was granted and a bombing run was calculated to run from stern to bow. The attack was an immense success as one bomb struck the stern and another the bow. Due to the accuracy of the bomb aimer, the crew witnessed a glaring and bright green-coloured explosion that engulfed the target, which simply disappeared. The debriefing reports concluded that the vessel had been transporting munitions or chemicals associated with munitions. The cause of the vivid green explosion had resulted from the catastrophic explosion caused by the two bombs so accurately striking the target. This action and his service on 159 Squadron saw Francis Barrett awarded the Distinguished Flying Cross, with *The London Gazette* publishing the award on 19 October 1945 (see Appendix VI).

The remaining weeks in January saw Thomas Reynolds embark on several daylight operations: flying to Mandalay and bombing Japanese troops, attacking Meiktila Airfield, Ramree Island, Kangaw, and the ancient capital of Amarapura (where they destroyed a military supply dump). As they bombed this target, the crew had the satisfaction to see the important bridge that spanned the Irrawaddy River and connected the two mainlands together had been demolished. The Mandalay operation engaged the entire strength of 99 Squadron, who flew in formation and achieved impressive results in advance of the Fourteenth Army's advance into the city. The attack on Meiktila airfield was also successful, but once again the Wing Commander's Liberator appeared to have been singled out to receive damage from the Japanese anti-aircraft guns.

David Jones shared in those same operations flying with the Wing Commander and witnessed a horrendous collision in the air between two Liberators on a raid to Ramree Island, which took place on 21 January. Both aircraft were captained by warrant officer pilots—Warrant Officer Sayer of the Royal Air Force and Warrant Officer Biccard of the Royal Australian Air Force. These men were killed, along with their entire crews. One of the crew members was the previously mentioned Australian navigator Colin Woolford, who had completed just six operational sorties on 99 Squadron before losing his life. The Liberators had been tasked with dropping air-burst bombs upon the beachhead areas. Wing Commander Ercolani would later comment upon this tragic incident as it had been closely witnessed by him and his crew as they flew alongside the fated aircraft. This incident proved to be something that he dwelt upon and is reflected in his personal notes, which are now held at the IWM. Document 15352:

> … there was our formation training, our first daylight ops when we weren't quite sure what the opposition was going to be—those two awful collisions, especially the last one which happened right alongside us—both aircraft with twelve thousand pounds of bombs—nothing left but the enormous red ball of fire in the sky which left a great cloud of black smoke. That was the pre-invasion bombing of Ramree….

Vice Admiral Sir Arthur Power later described the important Allied amphibious landings on Ramree Island and the ensuing six weeks of fighting that additionally secured the northernmost stronghold Kyaukpyu:

> The disadvantages to the Japanese lay in the indescribable horrors of the mangrove swamps…. It proved to be beyond even their endurance to exist for more than a few days. Prisoners taken out of the mangroves were found to be semi-dehydrated and in very low physical condition…. Because of the losses suffered by the enemy troops,

and the manner in which many died, the Battle of Ramree has been associated with reports of Japanese soldiers being eaten by saltwater crocodiles in the mangrove swamps.

The two 99 Squadron crews (consisting of nineteen men from the Royal Air Force, three from the Royal Australian Air Force, and one from the South African Air Force) that perished on the Ramree operation, are all commemorated in one collective grave in the Maynamati Cemetery.

The Ramree operation also threw up an unexpected scenario for the 356 Squadron Liberators. They had engaged in attacking the Japanese troops and defences at a position identified as Black Hill. Bombing in formation and at around 2,500 feet, huge quantities of smoke and debris, including bomb shrapnel, was thrown into the air. Flight Sergeant McNulty, a flight engineer in the Liberator EW153 'H', captained by Flight Sergeant Toovey, was exceptionally lucky to survive when a large lump of bomb sliced through the fuselage of their Liberator. McNulty was thrown up to the roof of the fuselage and, from there, head first onto the ball turret encasement where he remained for some moments temporarily stunned, his helmet and oxygen mask having been torn away. When he recovered, he noticed that a fire had started in the floor of the fuselage. The fire was intensified by damaged and bursting oxygen bottles. There was a large hole in the fuselage and ammunition from the waist guns was exploding, causing further damage. He opened a fire extinguisher, but it did not extinguish the blaze, so he made his way forward, informed the captain quickly of what had happened, and obtained a second fire extinguisher. This second extinguisher also failed to stop the fire. Flight Sergeant McNulty then removed his flying suit and proceeded to smother the fire until it went out, meanwhile kicking the burnt remains of oxygen bottles, flying suit, and gloves through the holes in the fuselage. The rear gunner Don Hughes slid his turret door open to see the catwalk that provided access through the Liberator's fuselage to be twisted up into the air. Despite the damage, the pilot remarkably managed to reach Chittagong where he successfully landed. The B-24 was immediately written-off for scrap after having been so badly damaged. The crew were later returned to Salbani airfield where the station medical officer, Flight Lieutenant McDougall, treated McNulty for his burn injuries. Flight Sergeant McNulty was later recommended for, and immediately awarded, a Distinguished Flying Medal for his gallantry in saving the crew and aircraft.

Returning to 99 Squadron, the Wing Commander additionally fitted in a final operation with his Squadron on 31 January, joining other squadrons that were attacking the Japanese headquarters at Kyaukse, south of Mandalay. Once again, David Jones precisely navigated and led the twelve Liberators from his squadron to the target. Bombing photographs taken on the operation gave evidence of a very successful and well-concentrated result against what had been an important target. The cameras carried on the B-24 bombers were of utmost importance—instructions were that each camera was tested on the ground before take-off. The test exposures were always removed from the camera equipment, a precaution to avoid any images from the home station falling into enemy hands. In the air, the fixed camera images were taken in sequence to allow vertical overlapping in order to gather important detail. Any additional handheld images taken from the waist gunner positions enhanced the opportunity to gather other intelligence.

On 3 February 1945, Wing Commander Ercolani briefed twelve Liberator crews on what was to be the furthest formation attack for 99 Squadron at that point of the war. The flight training he had instigated in relation to establishing fuel efficiency would be put to scrutiny. The operation was to attack the railway marshalling yards at Chumphon or, as was recorded in David Jones's flying logbook, Chum Phon. This operation would involve a round trip of more than 2,600 miles, taking more than fifteen hours to complete and return to base. It is difficult to imagine how much concentration would be required and the level of intensity imposed upon the navigation accuracy. The flight engineers would record the engine gauges every hour, note the engine manifold pressure, oil pressure, and fuel consumption. These individual detailed logs would eventually be scrutinised by the squadron engineering officer for comparison of performance and fuel efficiency. The bombing force witnessed positive results against the railway yards and, upon leaving the target area, several rear gunners reported seeing several fires burning with some ferocity. The rear gunners assisted their navigators by reporting on the wind drift whenever such fixed-point observations were available. The endless miles across the Bay of Bengal also provided white wave caps for wind observations, which were fed back to the navigator.

Flying Officer Haycock and his crew were not among the participating crews to the above operation, but they did participate in operations to bomb troop concentrations at Madeya and the supply dumps at Yenangyaung, situated east of the Irrawaddy River. Over this target, they were subjected to unexpectedly and accurate heavy anti-aircraft fire. The supply dumps were undoubtedly storing oil taken from the Burma Oil fields. These selected targets took priority over the anticipated bridge busting sorties and once again Rangoon appeared on the target sheets.

Thomas Reynolds and David Jones were in the air together with their respective pilots on 11 February, once again *en route* to bomb Rangoon with a heavy force. The Wing Commander of 99 Squadron led his force of twelve Liberators alongside the Liberators from similarly equipped RAF squadrons—American units and fighter escorts were also jointly deployed. Heavy anti-aircraft fire and Japanese fighters engaged with the bombers over Rangoon. A total of seven B-24 Liberators from 99 Squadron were damaged in this operation. At the end of the operation, Thomas Reynolds recorded in his flying logbook, 'One fighter destroyed'. Unfortunately, the Squadron records fail to provide any additional information, but suffice to say that his log entry was checked and endorsed by his 'B' Flight Commanding Officer, Squadron Leader Stroud.

In comparison to the huge bomber streams attacking targets in Germany, this operation against Rangoon was limited, yet it engaged 143 heavy bombers that, in itself, were significant numbers for the aerial campaign in Burma. Both high explosive and incendiary bombs were dropped on the targeted large supply store in Rangoon, causing many secondary explosions and fires that created a smoke pale some 11,000 feet high. The Japanese had accumulated multiple stores of varying quantities in and around Rangoon. The reconnaissance photographic images ultimately enabled the heavily camouflaged dumps to be identified and allocated as individual targets. This was a great success for the heavy bombers that had participated.

On 15 February, it fell to Squadron Leader Stroud to lead eight Liberators, including Johnny Haycocks' aircraft, to attack the Japanese headquarters at Nyaunglebin, a target in central Burma that appeared to the crews to have been successful, having destroyed or seriously damaged the target area as briefed. Thomas Reynolds' noted in his log that they had carried a bomb load of 11,000 pounds and the operation took six hours and twenty minutes to complete. Identical bombloads were carried to targets, noted in his logbook as Sangaingnyo, Kaunghmudaw, and Myingyan, all of which were Army close support operations within the central belt of Burma.

David Jones continued to spend time with the Wing Commander, perfecting bombing techniques alongside participating in the operations to a supply dump on 22 February and to Myingyan, another supply dump, on 24 February. For Thomas Reynolds, the month was rounded off with a return to attack the railway tracks at Korat, Thailand. Johnny Haycock took off amongst twelve Liberators at 10.30 a.m., and it would be thirteen hours and ten minutes before they would safely return. Once again, a target associated to the railway infrastructure was bombed with precision, but the reduced load of 4,500 lb carried reflected the distance they had flown on that particular operation.

No. 99 Squadron's monthly operational record during February 1945 confirms a total of 1,223 hours of flying, with over 1 million pounds of bombs dropped onto enemy targets. The majority of operations were in support of the Allied Army campaign. These figures are impressive and were only achievable by consistently having both serviceable aircraft and competent crews, supported by huge ground staffing. It was around this time that the RAF addressed the situation of how long aircrews in Southeast Asia were to serve operationally before being rested or at least assigned to training duty. The previously agreed timescale of 300 operational hours flying was astonishingly increased to 400 hours, or one complete year of operational flying duty, whichever status was achieved first.

The matters of bridge destruction remained a high priority, despite the incessant requirements to support the ground forces. These bridge busting operations were exceptionally demanding sorties that required pilots to undertake training in order to effectively complete. The bridges around Kanchanaburi and Thanbyuzayat were to receive constant bombing. Photographic intelligence exposed that the Japanese had constructed a bypass at Kanchanaburi and railway spurs with jetties under construction either side of the Meklong River. The Strategic Air Force, 231 Group Command, had placed bridge busting at the top of its target priorities. Railway bridges between Moulmein and Bangkok on the Burma–Thailand Railway were all equally as important. The B-24 pilots were expected to fly their large four-engined bombers in the same way as smaller fighter bombers, engaging in exceptionally low-level sorties on difficult to hit targets.

In February 1945, bridges along the Bangkok–Singapore railway line were subjected to numerous attacks. The Chumphon Railway Bridge was bombed by nine aircraft on 6 February and again by five aircraft on 11 February. The substantial bridge at Rajburi was also attacked by eight aircraft on 11 February. To actually demolish these difficult targets was exceptionally difficult, but these operations saw various bridge spans displaced or partially destroyed, rendering the bridges inoperable until repaired. Heavily protected bridges required resources to be specifically tasked in order to destroy the defences, normally anti-aircraft batteries. Each bridge tended to be unique in relation to its construction and the surrounding geography. Sorties to attack the countless bridges engaged differing numbers of Liberators, in some instances just one aircraft, while other sorties engaged strength of fourteen or more from two squadrons upwards. As an example, twenty-five Liberators were deployed to attack a single, but substantial and well-defended bridge on 5 February. Then, two days later, attacks were mounted upon five independent bridges by a lesser number of aircraft, with just one bridge confirmed as demolished and, on 9 February, twelve Liberators were sent to bomb a specific viaduct bridge that was damaged, but not destroyed. On 13 February, the bridge at Thanbyuzayat was destroyed by a force of just eight Liberators, while two days later fifteen Liberators were ordered to the three most northerly bridges identified on the same railway. The remaining days in February saw a further ten bridges in the area of Thanbyuzayat attacked by the various Liberator squadrons, it had been a consolidated period of differing tactics deployed in the fight to restrict the Japanese movement of troops and supplies.

The Bangkok to Chiengmai line was attacked on three occasions during February 1945, while the Pegu to Ye line also received attention, targeting five bridges. At the end of the month, forty-three Liberators converged upon the railway station and yards at Korat, the important junction and sidings on the railway line east of Bangkok, Thailand. This daylight operation proved to have been successful and February 1945 closed having set the pace for ongoing operational sorties against the Japanese railway network. Bridges, however, would always remain on the monthly operations listings of all heavy bombers operating from India—they never lost any importance in the Allied offensive against the Japanese in Burma and Thailand.

The Liberator crews were also aware of the importance the strategically placed water towers were to the Japanese railway infrastructure. These towers or tanks supplied water for the locomotives and were inevitably exceptionally well camouflaged. If spotted, the air gunners would always blast them, hopefully rendering the towers useless, if not totally destroyed. These quite remarkable low-level strafing attacks were undertaken in Liberators that were simply not designed for such work, a testimony to the way in which they were flown. The Allied fighter bomber crews flying in the agile Beaufighter aircraft also specialised in seeking out these vulnerable targets during their free-ranging fighter patrols. They capitalised on the performance of an aircraft, which was highly suited to such low-level sorties of destruction. On 20 February 1945, Wing Commander Ercolani attended a conference in Salbani. The Air Officer Commanding, Air Commodore Mellersh, discussed standardising briefing procedures and bombing methods with all of the squadron commanders.

The 'Pathfinder' attack against the railway system at Bangkok saw Wing Commander Ercolani receive a Mention in Despatches, no doubt in recognition for his work in improving the accuracy of his squadron's work. This reward also endorsed the trust he had imparted in his navigator, David Jones. He had consistently navigated as the lead aircraft on a great many operations, where many aircraft were in the air for upwards of fourteen hours. His work as navigator deserved to be acknowledged, tropical storms frequently required course changes and plotting of dead-reckoning position when taking sun shots were not possible. Although not documented alongside his Wing Commander, David Jones would eventually be recognised.

March 1945 commenced for 99 Squadron with a major night bombing attack upon the Bangkok railway sheds and goods yard. Nos 215, 159, 355, and 356 Liberator Squadrons within the Strategic Air Force participated. No. 99 Squadron dispatched twelve Liberators at around 6.30 p.m. on 2 March. They were to embark on marking the target with flares in order for the large force of bombers to drop their loads as effectively as possible. At a low altitude of just 500 feet, the markers were placed and the main force bombed them accurately. Aircraft from 215 Squadron later reported witnessing a large blue secondary explosion from the target area. Encouragingly, this would have been interpreted as indicating a large explosion of munitions or similar. Thomas Reynolds, in Johnny Haycock's Liberator, witnessed some significant anti-aircraft defences and the presence of enemy fighter activity. Their aircraft was later forced to make an emergency landing at Cox's Bazar, the result of a fuel leak. The aircraft was repaired and at 8 a.m. the following day, and the crew finally returned to base safely. The fuel leak problem may have affected their availability to fly on the next operation, however, having missed the briefing, they were unable to participate in the raid to Bangkok on 4 March. Wing Commander Ercolani led that operation and acted as a master bomber, controlling the actual bombing by the participating B-24s from 215, 355, 356, and 99 Squadron. Bangkok Railway Station played an important part in the Japanese rail transport structure, so this bombing force sought to inflict as much damage as possible by concentrating its forces with accuracy. Nominated Liberators from the participating squadrons also carried markers, which could be additionally dropped on the orders of the master bomber. Warrant Officer Collier of 356 Squadron was the nominated marker from his squadron and, at an exceptionally low altitude of approximately 450 feet, he bombed the target, striking what must have been an ammunition train. The violent explosion and blast force damaged his aircraft, forcing him to endure a fraught passage back to base, which he successfully achieved. Subsequent photographic reconnaissance revealed damage to the target and adjacent areas, at least twenty direct hits being obtained on the main line and sidings, and forty to fifty rolling stock was derailed or damaged.

Master bombers and pathfinder marking techniques were used in the European Air War, engaging the permanent Number 8 Group Pathfinders within Bomber Command. These principles were to some extent belatedly deployed in Southeast Asia and men like Wing Commander Ercolani drove the principle forward. The European Pathfinders were well-established, their tour of duty consisted of forty-five operations, only five less than what was frequently accepted as two tours of duty within Bomber Command. A Pathfinder badge was initially awarded to its crews on a temporary basis and then permanently awarded with a certificate. None of these special procedures were adopted or recognised in the Far East.

Three nights later, on 7 March, Thomas Reynolds, flying in Johnny Haycock's Liberator, formed up in the air within a force of twenty-two Liberators to attack the railway sidings at Martaban. The target was within the rather complex waterways inland from the Gulf area; once again, as the B-24s commenced their attack, the Japanese anti-aircraft gunners put up a strong defence, damaging one of 99 Squadron's Liberators. Overall, the operation was successful and all of the participating aircraft returned safely. That statement could not be echoed for the operation to bomb Rangoon four days later, on the morning of 11 March. This was another large force of aircraft comprised from within the Strategic Air Force bomber strength. Wing Commander Ercolani's expertise was required to lead the operation, with his trusted navigator mastering the route. Long-range P-51 American fighters were to escort the bombers, who anticipated once again to be confronted by a heavily defended target. No. 99 Squadron mustered twelve aircraft for this operation and nine aircraft were immediately damaged on their initial bombing runs by the anti-aircraft flak. Johnny Haycock was in his favoured Liberator EW178, which he would always choose to fly whenever available. This aircraft carried the identification letter 'X' and was known to the crew as *X-Ray*. Johnny Haycock had just completed his bombing run, releasing the load directly on target, when they sustained a strike by flak that caused one engine to immediately burst into flames. The following news clipping from Thomas Reynold's logbook explains further:

*Evening Post*, Issue 81, 6 April 1945, page 4
RETURNED TO BASE
NELSON PILOT'S FEAT [RNZAF Official News Service].
BURMA FRONT, April 4. Flying Officer Johnny Haycock, of Richmond, Nelson, has 'made it' again. With his Liberator bomber completely collandered, his rudder controls shot away, his elevator controls almost destroyed, and his rear-gunner seriously wounded, he brought his aircraft staggering over the mountains and paddy fields of Burma to a successful landing at base. While the Eastern Air Command was staging an attack on Rangoon, Flying Officer Haycock's squadron ran into devastating flak. Hit just at the end of the bombing run, his machine lost

speed rapidly as Haycock momentarily lost control. Flak was still coming up. As the Liberator lumbered out of range, the crew took stock of the situation. In addition to the damage to the rudder and elevator controls, both servometers [power regulators] were shot away and the control wires were shattered. As Haycock struggled to keep the aircraft flying, the flight engineer working desperately and managed to tie the elevator and rudder controls with string, thus giving the pilot just sufficient control to keep the aircraft in the air. Four hours later he made a shaky but safe landing at base. The rear gunner is recovering but with 159 holes in it, the aircraft was so badly damaged that it was consigned to the scrap heap.

Not mentioned in the article was the fact that this aircraft retained the under-fuselage ball-turret gunner's turret. The claustrophobic little bubble, which sat beneath the aircraft, was occupied by Flight Sergeant Kyle Ball and it had also been damaged. The damage was such that it was encasing him inside, making it impossible for him to escape. The ball gunner had witnessed the traumatic situation that engulfed the aircraft and felt the dramatic loss of height as the aircraft plummeted downwards, with Liberator EW178 barely under control; the ball gunner could see the bomb bay doors jammed open and the outbreaks of fire in the rear fuselage. Several gaping holes were present in the fuselage and no doubt Flight Sergeant Kyle Ball assumed the worst in the most distressing way possible. The first and second pilots fought hard in the cockpit, successfully extinguishing the engine fire, but experiencing serious problems in controlling the flight of the Liberator. Then, at a relatively low height, Johnny Haycock ordered that efforts should be made to release both the ball and rear gunners. Two men, Thomas Reynolds and the flight engineer, negotiated their way to the rear fuselage, extinguished the fires, and commenced to rescue the trapped ball gunner. The rear gunner Flight Sergeant Woodrow, who had no doubt shared in the shooting down of the recent Japanese fighter with Thomas Reynolds, had to be extracted from the turret partially conscious with dreadful injuries to his upper legs and suffering significant blood loss through a main artery, which was spurting blood with great vigour. His life was saved with a tourniquet and morphine injections and, quite remarkably, his crew managed to manhandle him through the damaged fuselage, which was no more than a 10-inch walkway through the bomb bays. That route, with the bomb-bay doors still in the open position, was very perilous—the narrow walkway was a simple construction that was fitted with guide rails, which supported the bombload, but was otherwise essentially open to the elements. The wind would have torn through that area adding to the dangers. As stability of the aircraft took over, two further crew members joined in the rescue, assisting in moving the rear gunner towards the flight deck to gather some warmth. Another 99 Squadron Liberator shadowed the damaged and barely stable aircraft back to Dhubalia. It was a comforting sight for the crew, who additionally suffered another engine failure just before reaching the airfield. Remarkably, the rear gunner survived, as did the whole crew, despite a precarious landing where a burst tyre caused the aircraft to swing violently on the runway. The rear gunner's turret had fallen away from the fuselage completely by that time, emphasising to the crew how lucky they had been.

The emergency repairs undertaken to Haycock's controls had directly led to the crew's survival. The flight engineer had remained in the rear damaged fuselage, where he saw the rudder cables to be distressed and damage. This was no doubt one of the primary reasons why the Liberator was so difficult to control in the air. The flight engineer appears to have used the cords from a parachute, which he tore apart and tied together in order to repair the damage. This incident is a classic example of innovative quick thinking on the part of a flight engineer. Despite the serious injuries to the crew's rear gunner, he endured a rapid recovery and quite astonishingly rejoined Johnny Haycock's crew to complete his tour of duty.

Another rear gunner worthy of note from 99 Squadron, and a fellow New Zealander with Johnny Haycock, was Warrant Officer Stewart. Originally from Scotland, he was probably one of the oldest air gunners of any crew flying over Burma. Aged nearly thirty-eight, he was almost double the age of the average volunteering air gunner. He had immediately volunteered to serve early in the war, but had been rejected by the Army because he had two fingers missing on one hand. The Royal New Zealand Air Force then excused him because he was also married. The policy on married men was later changed and, in April 1942, he enlisted in the Air Force. In the knowledge that the training of air gunners was the quickest way to get into the air, he elected for air gunnery, trained in Canada, and finally arrived in India in August 1943. His missing fingers were no handicap to his abilities as an air gunner and he successfully flew on many operations within Liberators over Burma and Thailand.

Wing Commander Ercolani always chose to fly in Liberator KH218 when with 99 Squadron and so it became known as the CO's aircraft. On 17 March 1945, he once more led an attack in that aircraft, with the target once again being Rangoon. This city, regarded to be of utmost importance to the Allied advance, needed to receive a sustained aerial bombing offensive. It was a combined heavy bomber raid, with the Royal Air Force and United States Army Air Force participating and providing Allied fighter protection. The entire operation went according to plan and was later interpreted as having been most successful. This operation also marked the Wing Commander's last offensive action with 99 Squadron. He would later receive special instruction from Command to lead another Liberator Squadron on more defined duties. His dependable Liberator KH218 would later be transferred onto 356 Squadron where it served until ditching in the Andaman Sea on 18 August 1945. The crew within KH218 broadcasted a 'Mayday' message stating that they were ditching and gave their position. A subsequent and extensive search conducted upon the coordinates given found no trace of the aircraft or any of its crew.

The men on 99 Squadron would continue mounting sorties against the retreating Japanese. They had been fighting with their accustomed tenacity, but the battle for Central Burma had been nearly won. Mandalay had been recaptured and the Allied sights fell firmly upon the consistently bombed prize of Rangoon. That primary supply port, which directly fed Burma and the railway infrastructure, had almost been completely destroyed, as had the constant sorties targeted against the railways—a point emphasised on 22 March 1945, when 99 Squadron Liberators destroyed a number of locomotives seen operating on the Burma–Thailand Railway. On 27 March, Thomas Reynolds, flying in Johnny Haycock's replacement Liberator, once more endured a gruelling fourteen-hour flight to bomb Bangkok. The replacement aircraft carried the identification letter 'S' and his logbook simply noted that the anti-aircraft defences were 'meagre'. However, rather unexpectedly while approaching the target, the Japanese Naval ships on the Bangkok River also fired upon the B-24s, two of which received damage from that unexpected quarter. The Liberators had taken off at 7.45 a.m. and reached the target area at around 3.50 p.m. The air raid warnings across Bangkok had sounded and 141 Allied prisoners of war were being held at the National Warehouse on the quay at Bangkok. These men were allowed to shelter as the bomber force arrived overhead.

As with many of the operations where prisoners of war were being utilised in target areas, the crews hoped that they had not inflicted any casualties on those poor individuals. Sadly in this instance, like many others, that was not to be the case. Twelve prisoners of war had been killed, six wounded, and two missing and believed killed. Also engaged on the attack against Bangkok was Flight Lieutenant Birley from the contingent of Liberators provided by 355 Squadron. This was to be his final operation, having completed his tour of duty as a navigator, which had included a fateful operation to Mandalay marshalling yards on 1 May 1944. Returning over the Bay of Bengal, his Liberator suffered fuel starvation. He successfully navigated to reach mainland India on two engines before the aircraft lost power completely. At a height of between 3,000 and 4,000 feet, the entire crew baled out, leaving the Liberator to eventually plunge to earth. There were four exits to jump from within a Liberator, through the nose wheel hatch, the forward bomb bay, the rear bomb bay, and the rear entry hatch. The guidance was for all crew to face forwards in all of these locations and simply roll out headfirst. Regardless of circumstance, baling out was traumatic. In this case, all of the parachutes deployed safely. No injuries were sustained on landing and by ingenious means the entire crew returned to their base on bullock carts and trains, arriving back on station within two days of their departure. These men successfully applied to the secretary of the Caterpillar Club and eventually received their tiny gold badge and membership card.

On 28 March 1945, the Liberator carrying the letter 'Y' identification code was allocated to Thomas Reynolds' crew. This aircraft had been air tested and assessed, indicating it to have most probably been a newly supplied aircraft. That particular Liberator consequently became Haycock's regular aircraft. His crew flew in it to attack the Japanese headquarters in Rangoon the following day. Unsurprisingly, Thomas Reynolds noted in his logbook that Rangoon was still being heavily defended by anti-aircraft guns on that operation. It had been estimated that over 500 supply dumps had been wholly or partially destroyed by the consistent heavy bomber operations across Rangoon. The Japanese headquarters in the city itself was a very specific target, which was spectacularly destroyed and only during post-war analysis did it become known that some 400 Japanese, including many officers, were killed in that one operation (*The Fight is Won*, 1954).

Operational flying for 99 Squadron during March had been relentless. The various crews had been in the air, offensively attacking the enemy for 1,377 hours. No. 231 Group activity, specifically relative to bombing bridges, discloses that the Burma–Thailand Railway was attacked on ten occasions during that month. On each of those operations, between two and seven bridges were attacked, damaged, or destroyed, and repeated attacks were made on targets that had suffered little or no damage. The Pegu railway line itself was bombed during five days, with fourteen bridges targeted. Ten bridges were targeted on the Bangkok–Singapore Railway. These are impressive statistics when consideration is given to the additional concentration of attacks upon Japanese supply dumps and major targets like Rangoon that were also taking place. Additionally, the United States Army Air Force was also operating B-24s and their Seventh Bombardment Group, part of 231 Group, was also actively bombing the Japanese railway infrastructure. The Chief Intelligence Section of the RAF published consistent secret intelligence summary reports from within the Eastern Air Command of Southeast Asia. This information was overseen by Major-General Stratemeyer and Air Marshal Sir Coryton, who had become his deputy on 4 December 1944. The report was published on 30 March 1945:

> The Ban Lum Sum Bridge
> The Burma–Thailand Railway might be characterised as a railroad of bridges. In its distance of 244 miles, it has a total of 688 bridges or 2.8 bridges per mile. The longest bridge in the entire system is the bridge at Ban Lum Sum, a bridge that is 1,680 feet long. The destruction of a bridge of such a size and representing a great many man hours of construction cannot help but have a serious effect in the volume of traffic the Japanese are able to carry on this supply line. This bridge was attacked by twenty-two B-24s on 24 March. The bombing was good, the photographs show 700 feet of track and concrete embankments destroyed in five separate places, five breaks in the viaduct from 60 to 325 feet in length, and river banks and concrete bases blown into the river.

The Strategic Air Force, 231 Heavy Bomber Group, consisted of the following squadrons equipped with B-24 Liberators:

No. 99 Squadron, operating from Dhubalia. 175 Wing.
Nos 355 and 356 Squadrons, operating from Salbani. 184 Wing.
Nos 159 and 215 Squadrons, operating from Digri. 185 Wing.
No. 357 Squadron, operating from Jessore, Special Duties.
United States Army Air Force, Seventh Bomber Group Squadrons, operating from Calcutta.

Digri, Salbani, and Dhubalia were airfields where 159 Squadron operated from at one time or another between 1942 and 1945. These airfields were relatively close together, Dhubalia situated north of Calcutta, Digri and Salbani to the west of Calcutta on the main line of the Bengal–Nagpur Railway. A siding ran into the heavy bomber stations, from which the supplies and engineering requirements were delivered. Each station was adjacent to the north–south rail line coming up from Kharagpur, approximately 70 miles from Calcutta.

Aircraft fuel was initially supplied on the rail link by petrol bowser carriages. This was a slow time consuming process that was also inherently dangerous. A direct fuel line was eventually constructed supplying the airfields from a central supply in Calcutta. The station fuel store pumps were far superior, supplying a continuous supply of fuel with no logistical problems. The 159 Squadron motor transport officer, Flying Officer Drew no doubt being the most relieved person of all after the fuel came on line.

To get to Digri or Salbani from Calcutta, the rather unreliable rail service involved a change of trains in Kharagpur and then a journey due north for some miles. Salbani was roughly 20 miles from Kharagpur, and Digri another 12 miles north. Dhubalia was more isolated to the north of Calcutta and any ground transit to that station from Digri or Salbani was very problematical.

In the Far East theatre of war, large identification symbols were applied to the tail and rudder fins of Liberators. This was to assist with immediate squadron recognition, particularly in the air. On the top half of the rear rudder fin of 99 Squadron's Liberators, a large white circle was applied. No. 215 Squadron's aircraft had their tail rudders painted black, with two horizontal bars, one above and towards the rear of the tail markings and the other below and again towards the rear. No. 355 Squadron had vertical black and white stripes painted upon the rudders, which made them boldly recognisable. However, 356 Squadron held the claim of them all, with two large white crosses painted across the entire rudder surface. No. 159 Squadron was devoid of any symbols, probably testimony to them having been the original Liberator-equipped squadron in the Far East theatre of war. Another area of aerial recognition for the Liberators was the adoption of fuselage roundel and tail markings in the South East Asia Command colours of dark and light blue. This identification completely removed the possibility of any confusion with the Japanese red-circle markings.

Two war artists, Frank Wootton and Thomas Hennell, were in India in 1945. Both men had been assigned the responsibility of capturing life drawings on the operational airfields. Frank Wootton was a serving member of the Royal Air Force and not technically an official war artist, while Thomas Hennell had been appointed by the government as an official war artist in 1943. These men captured on canvas and paper various aspects of the war in India and Burma. Frank Wootton in particular painted several Liberator scenes at Salbani. A number of his works illustrated examples of the impressively large sun pens, which had been constructed on the airfields to provide shade from the intense heat. The incessant sun had the capability to make the interior and exterior metal surfaces of Liberators agonisingly hot. Ground crews needed protection while working on these aircraft and such was the size of these pens that a Liberator was capable of being completely shaded by them. The roof consisted of several large half-oval hoop shapes, which were designed to fall front to back. The pens were open on three sides with supporting stanchions that were substantial in order to cope with the prevailing winds. The two open sides were frequently mounded with earth to add protection to the aircraft, and these combined factors enabled the aircraft to be maintained during the intense midday heat. These rather unique constructions featured predominantly and incidentally in several paintings. Later, in 1945, Thomas Hennell was captured by Indonesian terrorists in Batavia. He was reported missing, later presumed killed.

Other artists also used the B-24 Liberator as their canvas on a personal level. The high contingent of Canadian air crew serving in India brought with them a tradition of applying artwork of various types onto their aircraft. The Liberator, with its deep fuselage, became an ideal subject to hold such works. In several examples, great skill was displayed by the men who applied this artwork. Naturally, the female form featured predominantly and 159 Squadron had several bold, but tasteful examples. *Lady X*, *Yvonne Yippee*, and *Canadian Cutie* were classic examples. These illustrations were mainly applied on the front cockpit area and collectively this is now known as nose art.

The replication of small-scale concentrated formation bombing by Wing Commander Ercolani was praised by the Far East Heavy Bomber Group. The results achieved directly influenced the agreement to train and develop further the principles of 'Master Bombers' within No. 231 Group. The Liberator-equipped 159 Squadron, which had been recognised for their outstanding work in precisely dropping sea mines in ports and estuaries, were identified for this role. Those particular mine-planting duties could not be better illustrated than by the immediate award of the Distinguished Flying Medal to Flight Sergeant Frank Bailey. He, on the night of 22 March 1945, was serving as a bomb aimer. The published recommendation of his award read:

> He in company with the remainder of his crew was detailed to lay mines in the Bangkok area. As the last mine was laid, the aircraft was hit by an explosive shell which exploded in the nose compartment, seriously wounding the Navigator whose right leg and arm were practically severed by the explosion. Flight Sergeant Bailey rendered immediate first aid, applying tourniquets, and did a most excellent job in an attempt to stop the serious loss of blood from these large wounds. However, all his efforts were unavailing in saving the life of the navigator and the medical authorities have given the highest praise for his first aid rendered. At the same time Flight Sergeant Bailey rendered invaluable assistance to the captain of the aircraft in helping him navigate back to base.
>
> *The London Gazette*, 22 May 1945

The Canadian navigator inflicted by those awful injuries was Pilot Officer Nelson Ortom. The efforts to save his life came to an end three hours after their Liberator had landed safely at Digri. He succumbed to his wounds and now lies in the Ranchi War Cemetery (*They Shall Grow Not Old*, a book of remembrance, 1992).

An incident that took place on board a Liberator, flown by Warrant Officer Newman of 356 Squadron, during an attack on a railway bridge is also deserving of mention. Two bridges on the Moulmein Railway were targeted by ten Liberators on 29 March 1945, just seven days after the 159 Squadron epic mine-laying incident. Eight of the ten participating 356 Squadron aircraft suffered damage from light anti-aircraft defences. Casualties were sustained in several aircraft. In Warrant Officer Newman's case, his navigator suffered terrible injuries. During their bombing, he was struck and fell forwards onto the bomb aimer. The ball turret gunner, Flight Sergeant Falkenstein, had been killed while encased in his confined space. No doubt he had been attempting to supress the enemy fire being thrown up from their camouflaged positions. The navigator Flight Lieutenant Cressy-Marcks later died of his injuries. Despite these events, their bombs were dropped on a road sighted during their manoeuvres away from the railway bridge. The remaining Liberators continued to attack the bridges, ensuring on at least two low passes each that damage was inflicted; one bridge, identified as H148, was demolished, while the other was badly damaged.

The Japanese ingeniously devised a dual-drive vehicle that to some extent combatted the consistent breaches upon their railway. No doubt photo reconnaissance identified this vehicle, which was known as a Loco-truck. A small diesel-driven engine fitted with both rail and tyres that could be removed from the rails and driven overland past the obstruction. These machines merely enabled small loads or maintenance access. In essence, they became part of the relentless efforts of the Japanese to deal with the bombing offensive upon their railway structure. The continuous distribution of aerial leaflets dropped on almost every raid undertaken by the Liberator squadrons also impacted upon the Japanese railway. Many leaflets were dropped providing advanced notice that bombing attacks could be expected on certain areas. The native railway workers were known to be absent from work in response to these distributions, adding to the dysfunction of the network.

No. 159 Squadron was to be commanded by Wing Commander Ercolani. He was required to enhance and provide additional training for operating on very low-level bridge busting and pathfinder methods. These were two very differing disciplines. In particular, the bomb aimers skill to drop munitions and markers accurately from various heights, using the on board aiming devices. While on exceptionally low altitudes, no devices other than improvised aiming points and sightings using selected points from the forward fuselage were available. Using instinct and experience, many crews adopted the rows of rivets along the top of the forward fuselage as bomb sights for these bridge busting operations. Methods were reminiscent of the famous 617 Squadron Dam Busters, who developed a unique sighting device used within their Lancaster cockpits to drop the bouncing bombs onto the waterways in order to destroy the dams in Germany.

The personnel within 159 Squadron were very experienced in attacking railway targets and had reaped success in many diverse sorties. The British Boulton Paul Type E rear gunner's turrets were fitted to several of the unit's Liberators. It proved to be one of the most successful turrets designed and produced during the Second World War and was easily converted into the Liberator fuselage. This popular turret maintenance on station proved to be uncomplicated for the ground crews. The turret used individual pumps, operated by an electrical supply feed to power the controls. The British four-gun turret was rounder in design and created a more moulded profile than the more frequently seen American A6 turrets.

Wing Commander Ercolani penned a most positive picture of 159 Squadron when he compiled his first resume of work within the unit's operational record book:

> … The number of operational and training sorties carried out demanded of all personnel very considerable effort, and serviceability figures gives ample evidence that this requirement was not found lacking. Damage to aircraft in the main from small arms and light machine gun fire from railway targets attacked at low level was more than in the previous month and on the attack against Bridges Q27 and Q28 on the Burma to Thailand Railway on 8 March 1945. No less than seven aircraft out of twelve received damage severe enough in the case of two aircraft for them to be declared complete write offs … these were exceptionally dangerous sorties to be undertaken by large heavy bombers.

Sadly, the new Wing Commander also had the unenviable task to write to the families of an almost entirely Canadian crew lost that month. On 15 March 1945, the seven Canadian and one British crew member were flying in Liberator KH256, attacking a bridge at Moulmein. They failed to return and no trace was ever found. The crew were officially regarded as missing, particulars unknown. Those families will have gained greatly from the personal letters because officialdom would have followed and thence afterwards their only solace was to know that the names of their loved ones were inscribed on the Singapore War Memorial.

Better news was that the Squadron's expertise in mine laying had brought good results. Unexpected information from a clandestine source advised that their work had been responsible for the sinking of two large merchant ships. Both were sunk in the Bangkok River, one being a prized Japanese tanker. It was rare to receive such positive information upon these hazardous operations and so the news would have been enthusiastically received, enhancing the morale across the entire squadron. Sergeant Frank Holden, the bomb aimer within Flight Sergeant Brown's crew, was particularly pleased. He had been responsible for dropping dummy sea mines in the Rangoon River on 22 February 1945. At just 200 feet, their Liberator KH366 was closely targeted by light machine-gun fire, which the rear gunner was able to silence effectively. The overtly dropping of dummy mines was undertaken to induce enemy shipping to divert into other waters, where operational mines lurked ready to detonate.

# 8

# 159 Squadron: Pathfinding Bridge Busters

Lucian Ercolani, David Jones, and Thomas Reynolds all experienced an interwoven period of service in the Allied aerial offensive over Burma and Thailand, primarily while serving with 99 Squadron. Their ranks will have separated them to some extent on the ground, but in the air these men were equals bound by experience, friendship, and professional ability. The next level of operational experience would call upon all of those skills.

Wing Commander Ercolani personally selected five experienced crews from within the strength of 99 Squadron to accompany him on his posting to command 159 Squadron. Without question, David Jones continued to act as the Wing Commander's navigator. He had implicit confidence in David's abilities and Thomas Reynolds would act as the flight engineer, remaining in the crew of Johnny Haycock. Flying Officer Haycock himself was regarded as a pilot of exceptional ability and at that time held the responsibility of being the Squadron's engineering officer, in effect being responsible for all flight engineers. It is quite possible this position would have had some significance in the role changes that had taken place, in particular, the duties for Thomas Reynolds.

Flight engineers on Liberators were responsible for the deployment of the small auxiliary power units, which needed to be started simultaneously with the engine start-up procedures by the pilots. It was a small capacity two-stroke petrol engine that powered an electrical generator. The small engine was situated under the flight deck and was started electrically to initially supply power to the essential electrical circuits. Once the aircrafts engines reached sufficient power to energise their own individual four generators, the auxiliary unit was shut down. In the air, the flight engineer became ultimately responsible for the aircrafts engine performance, monitoring fuel mixture and consumption. Calculations were recorded during the flight, regardless of the fuel gauges and when the aircraft landed the ground crews would always dip the fuel tanks. The engineers' calculations were in many instances calculated against the amount of fuel still within the tanks and it was a matter of pride to be as accurate as possible. These duties all led to efficiency in fuel and engine management, which was essential in the Far East where operations were being conducted over such vast distances. Individual aircraft figures were calculated to carry just enough fuel for a safe return to maximise a bombload. For that reason, many crews desired to fly what they would describe as their own aircraft, knowing its capabilities and characteristics.

During the long flights deep into Thailand from India, flight engineers would transfer fuel from the outer wing tanks to the inner tanks. This procedure required using an electrically powered pump, which necessitated a safety isolation process, transferring the fuel and then re-isolating parts of the electrical fuel circuit. Working with the pilot, the fluid movements caused an imbalance to the aircraft that would always need to be trimmed. There were twelve self-sealing fuel tanks, often called fuel cells, built into the central wing section. Each engine was primarily fed by dedicated tanks and that power unit was capable of pumping its own individual fuel supply while in the air. Likewise, each engine had its own independent oil supply system, each unit holding some 56 gallons of circulating oil.

The Strategic Air Force had embarked on consistent long-range operations to disrupt the Japanese communication structure, but this had not been achieved without a heavy price. During the period from January 1944 to April 1945, sixty-three heavy bomber crews had been lost—thirty-four from the Royal Air Force and twenty-nine from the United States Army Air Force. The British Commander of the Fourteenth Army, General Slim, made it known that the Army Air Force Co-operation played a significant part in the Allied advances in Burma. The American Seventh Bombardment Group had, during April, sent their B-24 bombers to attack the Burma–Thailand Railway infrastructure, supporting the many operations conducted on the same target by the Royal Air Force's 231 Group. No. 159 Squadron would participate in many low-level bombing operations to destroy the bridges associated with the Japanese railway infrastructure in Burma and beyond.

On 8 April 1945, Thomas Reynolds sat at his flight station monitoring the aircrafts performance as it departed Dhubalia. He and his crew were to join 159 Squadron at Digri; at the same time, five crews from Digri embarked on the reciprocal journey to join the depleted 99 Squadron strength. This redistribution of air crew personnel took place in all of the Liberator squadrons. Just two days after their departure at Dhubalia, a most intense and forceful cyclone struck the airfield. The exceptional conditions caused damage to almost every structure across the open airfield. A fire broke out in the Officers' Mess and the strong winds carried and spread the fire in an uncontrollable manner, which caused total devastation. The squadron records state that officers' kit and possessions were all destroyed, including their flying logbooks.

Flying Officer Johnny Haycock and his newly appointed flight engineer Thomas Reynolds immediately commenced training, with an ambition to increase the crew's bombing accuracy. Wing Commander Ercolani made it obvious that he had set the standards of accuracy to be within a 25-yard circle of any target and anything outside of 50 yards would be frowned upon. During April 1945, many bombing and aiming calibration exercises were flown by the crews. The bombing ranges were well-managed and provided accurate results to assess the crew's abilities. A club was formed, known as the Pickle Barrel Club. Sergeant Frank Holden became the first bomb aimer to join the club following his superb his accuracy in dropping bombs into the 'Pickle Barrel'. He had achieved the best accuracy from the entire group's results and proudly recorded his achievement in his record book, which was endorsed by Wing Commander Ercolani.

No. 159 Squadron would also conduct low-level sorties that would include planting aerial sea mines into precision locations from low heights. The newly arrived personnel had joined a selection of handpicked crews from across the group's squadron strength. It entailed newly appointed flight commanders and respective leaders to all of the air crew positions. A new and specialised Bombsite Section was formed to intensify the bomb aimers' capabilities. The Wing Commander made everyone aware that 159 Squadron's work was to become the finest possible, and very much better than anything they had previously experienced. No one was left in doubt about his determination to create an elite pathfinder squadron, which would participate in some of the longest Far East raids undertaken in the war.

The foundations of 159 Squadron abilities had been set by the previous commanding officer, Wing Commander Blackburn, and Ercolani took on that mantle with great vigour. He appointed his 'B' Flight Commander to be Flight Lieutenant Tommy Watson, a Canadian fighter pilot who had converted onto Liberators and tended to fly them in the manner of his old fighter days. He was an instantly recognisable character, with a large scar down the left side of his face and nearly always consuming a cigar (or the remnants of one). The 'A' Flight Commander was another Canadian, Squadron Leader Freddie Stroud. The Wing Commander had selected him from 99 Squadron. Both Flight Commanders individually spoke to their air crew personnel in order to gather as much knowledge as possible about their experience and abilities. Although Flight Commanders preferred to fly in what could be termed as their aircraft, no ownership of aircraft officially took place. Aircraft were simply assigned according to serviceability. Some pilots in particular liked or disliked specific characteristics of certain airframes and this became the basis of most preferences. Wing Commander Ercolani for instance referred to his B-24 aircraft as his old 'M' for mother as it carried the recognition letter of 'M' on its fuselage.

For Thomas Reynolds, life as a flight engineer did not present too much of a challenge. He now sat on the flight deck area confronted with very different duties and able to communicate directly with his pilot. The pilot had no access to the fuel transfer or electrical generator systems. On the rear bulkhead of the flight engineer's position were the electrical controls for the engine-driven generators attached to each of the four engines. Thomas was responsible for monitoring the generators during flight and he was to some extent fortunate in that he had his own independent oxygen supply, provided by two bottles beneath his seat. That said, the oxygen system was in many cases stripped from Liberators to lessen weight as this restricted the height at which those aircraft were able to operate. The fuselage of the Liberator was effectively divided into five compartments, comprising of the nose section, nose wheel, flight deck, bomb bay, and rear. Movement from the nose and flight deck was by means of a passageway through the nose wheel compartment, which required manoeuvring around the nose wheel gear.

On 18 April 1945, Johnny Haycock flew with Thomas Reynolds on his first sortie with 159 Squadron, a fifteen-hour operation to drop mines at the most southerly location, off Victoria Point. The laying of mines was a tactic designed to hamper and destroy Japanese shipping. No. 159 Squadron had become very efficient, performing these operations in the Malacca Straits and the South China Sea. In the important waterways of Rangoon, the Pak Chan River (north-east of Victoria Point) and other primary waterways, like the Bangkok River and Goh Sichang Harbour, had also been in receipt of mines. In 1945, new acoustic mines (activated by noise or vibrations through the water) were being dropped into the enemy's waterways. The supply of mines into Southeast Asia had been improved and these flexible variant mines, which became available in greater quantities, augmented the consistently deployed standard magnetic mines. Despite the need for consistent training in Ercolani's new rather loosely termed pathfinder squadron, his crews still undertook many mine-laying operations. These mines were inevitably dropped from a relatively low altitude to ensure safe delivery into the water, but more importantly they were dropped precisely on very specific target areas. An example of the Squadron's high workload is shown by the statistics of nearly 200 mines being dropped by 231 Group during May 1945. This intensity of work exhausted the supply of acoustic mines and saw a return to the magnetic type. No. 159 Squadron alone went on to lay 1,178 sea mines during 1945.

The first pathfinder operation for 159 Squadron actually took place on 27 April 1945, but Thomas Reynolds would not be engaged in that operation. He undertook the duties of flight engineer in his Liberator to Bangkok harbour, where, at an altitude of just 400 feet, sea mines were parachuted into the water. The crews that were not on the battle orders to fly on the first pathfinder sortie to Rangoon would have no doubt been disappointed. The Rangoon-bound 159 Squadron's Liberators departed at 3.44 p.m., with the Wing Commander flying in the Liberator KH352. No. 159 Squadron was to pave the way and mark the target for 99, 355, and 356 Liberator Squadrons. David Jones navigated the master bomber aircraft to arrive over the target precisely thirty minutes prior to the main force. They carried six red target indicator bombs, which were dropped unerringly on the target and preceded a most accurate result from the main bombing strength. Both Flight Commanders participated in this inaugural sortie, which witnessed the sighting of two Japanese fighters, both of which, for unknown reasons, did not attack. Having mentioned the presence of the Japanese fighters, it would be an appropriate time to mention that sitting in the rear of the Wing Commander's Liberator manning the tail gunners position was a second tour gunner called Fred Smith. Known to all as Smithy, he had previously served with 159 Squadron, joined 99 Squadron for his second tour, and selected to rejoin 159 Squadron as part of the Wing Commander's crew. It would have been very difficult to have found a more experience rear gunner, and he would eventually be rewarded with a Distinguished Flying Cross for his service.

As Ercolani's Liberator spent some seventy-five minutes directly over the target area, this obviously exposed the aircraft to an extended period of time whereby enemy anti-aircraft could specifically target their aircraft—no doubt Smithy got used to the additional dangers of being over targets for such extended periods of time. He would have been scanning the sky consistently, manipulating his turret and looking for the faint shape that had the capability of rapidly turning into an approaching fighter intent on destroying them. It was always of some comfort for the rear gunner to know that his waist gunners were relatively close to his position. The B-24 rear gunners never occupied their turrets when taking off or landing. This was due to the characteristics of the required weight balance due to the landing wheel configuration. Fred Smith would eventually be rewarded with a Distinguished Flying Cross medal in March 1946.

The morale on 159 Squadron rose swiftly and the indications of having created an excellently skilled selection of air crews was obvious for all to see. In May, the final Allied plans were implemented in the taking of Rangoon. On 1 May 1945, troops were to be dropped by parachute at Elephant Point, an area that oversaw and commanded the territorial entrance to Rangoon Harbour. Prior to the drop, 159 Squadron were to bomb the Japanese gun positions defending that vital position. Wing Commander Ercolani personally undertook that role, while other aircraft partook in more general pre-invasion bombing across Rangoon. Thomas Reynolds recorded that his operation commenced at 7 a.m., while David Jones had departed at 4.05 a.m. The Squadron had mustered fourteen aircraft that day, but only half that number, led by the Wing Commander, actually attacked the gun positions on the Rangoon River at 12.48 a.m. the following day. After a fierce fight, Allied troops took Elephant Point and at 7 a.m., the first landings to take Rangoon had taken place. The precision bombing undertaken by Wing Commander Ercolani and his men was described in their records as dropping no more than 500 or 600 yards in front of the landings. In fact, by the time the Allies reached central Rangoon, they found the capital to have been evacuated. Despite orders from Japan to stand, the Commanding Officer had authorised a withdrawal, something completely unthinkable in respect of the previously displayed Japanese mentality of military honour. The Japanese forces around Rangoon had undertaken a swift withdrawal through Pegu to the east, in order to be able to retreat into Thailand.

There was another man previously connected to 99 Squadron who had served in Liberators as a member of the Crown Film Production Unit. Flight Lieutenant Woodcock was a navigator cameraman, who filmed many operations over Burma and Thailand; on 2 May 1945, he was to film the landings at Rangoon. His pilot was a New Zealander, John Buchanan, who was in charge of their Mosquito that, at 7.35 a.m., flew low along the river towards Rangoon to capture in camera the attack on barges and gun positions. Tragically, their Mosquito was hit by gunfire and crashed in flames. Both men died and were later recovered from the wreckage. They now lay side by side in the Rangoon War Cemetery. Many of the actual films recorded by Flight Lieutenant Woodcock survive to this day in the collection of the IWM in London.

One particular B-24 Liberator deserves especial mention; KH210, from 355 Squadron, was engaged in the operation upon the Japanese gun positions in Rangoon on 2 May 1945, when it was forced to ditch into the sea off Bengal after suffering an engine fire. The aircraft was piloted by Squadron Leader G. A. De Souza who had taken off from Salbani, India, at 12.51 a.m., bound for the target area. Among De Souza's crew was Wing Commander James Brindley Nicolson. He was the officer in charge of Royal Air Force training in Southeast Asia and was on this operation as an observer. Nicolson was famously the only man to have won the Victoria Cross in Fighter Command during the Battle of Britain.

On their outward transit, making towards the target, the number one engine caught fire and was quickly feathered and shut down. The bombs were jettisoned and the navigator plotted the aircrafts return course for Salbani. The wireless operator sent the information relative to their position including height, speed, and course. The rather unpleasant reputation that the Liberator had on ditching into the sea was probably foremost in several minds. However, shortly after the return course was set, the aircraft rolled to starboard, the automatic pilot was disengaged, and normal flying was momentarily regained by the highly experienced pilot and his Australian second pilot, Flight Sergeant Michael Henry Pullen. Using their combined strength on the controls, they regained stability, but the tendency remained for the B-24 to roll. To combat the roll, they throttled back on the three good engines to keep the aircraft level, but that lack of power resulted in a steady and gradual loss of height. When the lack of height became critical, the crew were ordered to prepare for ditching into the sea, but once more the roll condition presented itself and by that time they were at such a low altitude that the Liberator struck the water. Only two men survived to be rescued, the Australian second pilot and the front gunner Sergeant Eric Kightley. One deceased crew members body (Flight Sergeant Samuel Doherty, the second wireless operator) was recovered from the sea. The remaining nine men were never located, despite a search conducted over several days. A court of enquiry found that there was no clear evidence of the cause of the handling problems experienced by the pilots. One theory was that an engine or both engines on the starboard side were cutting intermittently. When an outboard engine failed, the wing on that side of the aircraft would drop suddenly. If the pilot immediately brought the trim tab up on the other wing to arrest the drop and applied full rudder tab to maintain directional stability a loss of control in normal circumstances could be averted. However, the trim tabs designed for fine adjustments were only able to be brought into full countering by several rotations or revolutions of the wheel, implementing those revolutions was likely to create a time delay. This problem was assessed and a modification later took place where an override emergency adjustment was provided to the Liberator controls.

It took the Allied forces two weeks to undertake emergency repairs at Rangoon harbour and to sweep the water for mines. By mid-May, much-needed supplies were at last being unloaded from the docks and this was all achieved before the onset of the monsoon season. The prize of taking Rangoon was fundamental in the Allied offensive strategy. Once fully secured, the conquest of Singapore was required to open up the sea routes to Indochina, and the East Indies would become of utmost importance. No. 159 Squadron received excellent news direct from the infamous jail in Rangoon. Several men from the Squadron who had been recorded missing on operations had in fact been prisoners of war and held in the jail. Among them were Sergeant Norman Davis, Flight Sergeant L. G. Roper, Flight Sergeant Donald Lomas, Flight Sergeant Jack Harris, Pilot Officer Johannes Lentz, Flying Officer Allan Jeffery, Squadron Leader James Bradley, and Sergeant Sid Hill, all of whom had survived the horrors of that awful place. Regrettably, Pilot Officer John Westermark, Warrant Officer John King, and Flight Sergeant Harry Richardson had all died within its filthy walls.

The Canadian rear gunner Flight Sergeant Harry Richardson had been shot down by Japanese fighters in his Liberator, BZ978, on 6 October 1944. His crew, which included three Australians, had been carrying out a low-level dawn attacks on the Bangkok–Lampang railway line where locomotives had been their primary target. It was on one of these missions that their Liberator ditched in the Bay of Bengal. Four crew members never escaped from the ditching, one was known to have been killed in the aerial attack and three men, including Richardson, had suffered injuries. Only Richardson, Hill, and Roper had escaped in the dinghy, which was fleetingly seen, but then lost on two occasions during the air-sea search that ensued after their ditching (See Appendix report). These men were later captured and placed in Rangoon jail, but Harry Richardson later succumbed to his injuries on 28 October 1944. Flight Sergeant Richardson's remains were in all probability buried in the Cantonment Cemetery after his death. This was where the majority of men who had died in Rangoon jail were laid to rest. Records were kept, but many graves were mislaid and many men were buried so close together that the post-war work by the Graves Commission were unable to accurately identify over sixty of them. These graves are marked as 'buried near this spot' and additionally they are commemorated by name on the Singapore War Memorial.

Several men from 99 Squadron were also held within Rangoon jail, among them were Sergeant Charles Thomson, Sergeant Charles Garner, and Sergeant Eric Hardisty—all crew from Liberator KH360. These men had attacked the Burma Railway on 1 January 1945 and, during their return sortie, sighted and attacked four small shipping vessels. Sweeping low over the target, they sustained serious damage from the vessels defensive guns and the Liberator eventually ditched in the sea near Kalegauk Island. Only these three men survived the ditching, which took place some 5 miles away from mainland Burma.

Meanwhile, 159 Squadron continued to receive battle orders and operational briefings. On 7 May, Thomas Reynolds was faced with another long, almost fifteen-hour sortie to drop mines at Chumphon, one of the most southern provinces on the Gulf of Thailand. He was not alone as eleven other aircraft had been briefed to do similar jobs at Mergui, Kissernaing, Pak Chan River, Bangkok, and Prachuap Khiri Khan. Great importance was still being placed upon the offensive mining of enemy shipping lanes. The dangers of low-level mining were once again illustrated, when the aircraft flown by Flying Officer Dowding was struck and badly damaged by light flak during his efforts undertaken at Mergui. Flight Lieutenant Williams in his Liberator also received the attention of flak over Bangkok. The following day, news was received of the unconditional surrender of Germany. However, the Far Eastern Forces faced a very different enemy. The Japanese had vowed to defend to the last man as a matter of honour. The Allied invasion of Japanese-held territories, which she had herself occupied some three years previously, would continue at immeasurable costs in human lives. The reconquest of Malaya and Singapore became the primary objectives for the British and Commonwealth forces, but no one underestimated the struggle required to fight such resolute forces and surge through the mainland and advance onto Singapore itself.

The Psychological Warfare Division of South East Asia Command capitalised upon the fall of Rangoon by immediately printing propaganda to be dropped by the Royal Air Force on their regular operational flights. One particular leaflet illustrated the 'One Rupee' Japanese banknote. This currency had been printed by the Japanese especially for Burma. The Allied propaganda leaflet advised the reader to look at their money. The translated text read:

> Burmese Rangoon is liberated. The Japanese are finished in Burma and the peace returns to your country. Here is a word of advice about money. British money is good money. British Burma banknotes are good. India small coin and India notes are good. British military administration notes are good. But beware of Japanese imitations made to look like good money. Remember all forms of Japanese currency. The Japanese rupee, the military yen and the military dollar are bad. Possession of such money is not against the law, but the last of the Japanese who issued this money and promised to back it cannot do so as they are being thrown out of Burma. British money is good money. Japanese money is worthless.

Back at Digri with 159 Squadron, the crews received briefings on important low-level bridge busting operations in Thailand. The training to take out these targets had gone well and expectations were high for exemplary results to be achieved. On 13 May, the target of Ban Tak Kam, also seen recorded in logbooks as Ban Tah Kam Bridge, appeared on the battle orders. These targets were over 1,200 miles away from Digri, challenging for the navigators like David Jones and for the eventual bomb aimers who were ultimately responsible to accurately drop the bombloads. The first bombs that fell did not achieve any success, but then all the additional training on bomb site calibration reaped results. The technique of diving in and turning onto the target and levelling out only as the bombs release point was reached at around 500 feet proved very effective. The twelve Liberators had achieved an excellent result and Wing Commander Ercolani witnessed the Ban Tak Nam Bridge collapse. The two supports upon the river bed were totally destroyed, while the central span had toppled onto its side and broke up in the waters. Thomas Reynolds himself entered within his flying logbook that they dropped their bombload at a height of just 100 feet, truly remarkable when you consider the size of the Liberator heavy bomber. He had taken off at 7 a.m. on 13 May, while the Wing Commander had departed at 6.10 a.m., no doubt timings reflecting upon his role of 'Master Bomber' overseeing the entire operation. Two aircraft returned to Digri with damage inflicted from light ammunition, but fortunately no injuries were sustained to any crew members. After the primary bombing, both the Wing Commander and Johnny Haycock took exceptionally low-level strafing runs targeting the Japanese rolling stock in the Ban Tak Kam sidings. They had been accompanied on their low-level shooting exploits by two further Liberators flown by Flight Lieutenant Williams and Pilot Officer Hughes. Interestingly, Flight Lieutenant Williams records in his flying logbook 'Dive Bombing', a term far removed from what would be expected of a large four-engined bomber. Their joint prize had been a locomotive pulling three passenger carriages and numerous open flat carriages loaded with military trucks and armoured cars. This particular raid was to receive a letter of congratulation from the Officer Commanding 231 Group, Air Commodore Mellersh. It had been a resounding success.

The second bridge busting operation engaged thirteen 159 Squadron Liberators. Flying Officer Johnny Haycock's crew was on this occasion not to be observed by their Commanding Officer as his crew did not appear on the orders listing the participating crews. Two bridges identified as TF102 and TF104 were to be targeted on the Chumphon–Singapore railway. At 5.40 a.m. on 17 May, Wing Commander Ercolani departed for his consecutive operation against specific bridges, however, this one was not to be so rewarding. While low over the target, he thought he had observed some light anti-aircraft or machine-gun fire coming from the target. The number two engine oil pressure immediately started to drop, causing some concern, and as they left the Arakan coast the engine seized completely. Unfortunately, the number three engine then suffered from fuel starvation, making the situation immediately perilous. David Jones instantly calculated a navigation route to reach the nearest landfall and then the nearest airfield that was on the island at Akyab. Quite remarkably, they reached the safety of that aerodrome at 6.40 p.m., completing what had been a most harrowing experience. David wrote in his flying logbook that the bridge had not been destroyed. That was indeed very true, it was left still standing, but possibly suffering from twisting out of alignment. The second bridge was also left standing, but with some damage to the railway tracks. Cameras had been deployed on all of the participating Liberators, including the oblique handheld type. Over the target, one camera being used from the waist gunner's position was struck by a bullet, the operator holding the camera had a lucky escape. Evidence from the capture of over 200 photographic images taken that day revealed that the damage was better than had been thought. The Wing Commander would have been unaware of the intelligence gathered from the images. Along with his crew, they were grounded at Akyab and the opportunity had unexpectedly presented itself to take some rest and relaxation. The crew were able to go swimming at the sandy beach and enjoy the warm waters of the Bay of Bengal while they awaited collection. Their aircraft was not going to be airworthy for some period of time. The ground crew engineers at Akyab had located the damage; a bullet had pierced the number two engines crankcase. The Pratt & Whitney engine had a main crankcase, which consisted of three sections that in turn supported individual main bearings. In all probability, the damage caused by the enemy gunfire would have entailed significant work to address secondary damage inflicted upon the engine systems.

Rather strangely, from all of the flight crews at Digri, it was Johnny Haycock and his crew who were briefed to collect the lucky survivors from Akyab. The crew taxied their Liberator from its protected standing along the long perimeter runway, which led to one of the two main runways. These were connected at the far extremity forming the shape of an inverted letter 'V'. Taking off at 6 a.m. on 19 May, they flew to Akyab and collected their Wing Commander and his crew and return them safely back to base.

Flight Lieutenant John Eustace Haycock later received news of having been recommended for a Distinguished Flying Cross medal. The recommendation read:

Flight Lieutenant John Eustace Haycock DFC NZ422396 & 133869.
This officer has completed a highly successful tour of operations. This included many sorties against various objectives. Early in his tour during low-level attacks on a bridge [on 13 December 1944] his aircraft was attacked by an enemy fighter but by skilful manoeuvring and accurate fire he was able to destroy it. On another occasion [on 11 March 1945] when flying over Rangoon, his aircraft was seriously damaged by enemy action, with great skill and determination he regained control and successfully brought his damaged aircraft back to base, where he made a safe landing. Throughout his career Flying Officer Haycock has shown outstanding keenness, skill and great devotion to duty. In the incident over Rangoon mentioned above the flight engineer repaired the rudder control cables with parachute cords. On landing, 197 holes were counted in the fuselage. The aircraft was so badly damaged it did not fly again.

With everyone back safely at Digri, temperatures were starting to rise as the monsoon season commenced. The shower block water was hand pumped from deep wells and it was always refreshingly cold when it arrived; however, this was always just short relief from the stifling weather. Everybody without question experienced the uncomfortable heat even when simply sitting in the shade; fresh, dry short-sleeved shirts were likely to be wringing wet within less than half an hour of being worn. Not that this really mattered as the regular monsoon rains would always douse everyone on a daily basis. Regardless, the daily intelligence briefings for operations continued in a relentless fashion, despite the increasing odds of last minute cancellations due to weather conditions. For Thomas Reynolds and his crew, there was a welcome break with no further operations for them until the following month, however, David Jones with his crew had two further sorties to complete before the close of May 1945. Having lost their Liberator of choice, as KH352 remained at Akyab, on 22 May the Wing Commander took Liberator KH116 to attack another railway bridge, recorded in David Jones' flying logbook as Lang Suan on the Chumphon–Singapore line. This may well be a bridge name used by him and his crew members, but the squadron record books once again records Bridge TF104 as their target. This was the same bridge they had attempted to destroy on their ill-fated exploits five days previously and one which they had been exceptionally fortunate to have survived.

Another fifteen-hour-plus flight lay ahead, which David Jones navigated as pathfinder, with eleven aircraft from his squadron following in staggered times. KH116 took off at 6.20 a.m., while the final Liberator, flown by Flying Officer Mitchell, departed at 7.43 a.m. Some bad weather conditions were experienced *en route* to this target. Two aircraft from the Squadron strength were forced to return early as a result of it, while the remaining aircraft got through and attacked the target. Two of the attacking Liberators reported seeing a large collection of rail rolling stock in the sidings just north of Ban Kanon, which was then strafed with gunfire. Another pair of Liberators saw a locomotive and a selection of rolling stock south of Tako Bridge, which was also duly attacked at very low level. Typical train configurations seen on the tracks normally comprised of box wagons for troops, flat carriages, which carried motor transport or light armoured fighting vehicles, and short-base coaches carrying Japanese officers. Photographic interpretation of this type of rolling stock frequently revealed the identity of the Japanese troops. This was achieved simply by examining the hardware carried on the flat bed carriages. A further sighting south of Kra Buri by a pair of Liberators allowed for another attack on the active enemy railway infrastructure. These and additional sightings were later debriefed to the intelligence officer (Flight Lieutenant George Betterley) at Digri and the photographic evidence secured would later be examined once developed and printed.

Returning to the primary target, bridge TF104 received serious damage. The bombers had approached along the railway line with a closing speed of 160 miles per hour at around 100 feet. The bomb aimers took control to make the final crucial minor adjustments on the bomb sight mechanism, in effect flying the aircraft and the pilot awaited the bombs away call before he once again took the controls. The massive weight loss caused the aircraft to surge upwards. The short fuse of the bombs meant the crews could hear the explosions below and behind and feel the concussion of the blast. The pilots would wait in anticipation for their rear gunners who had glorious views to hopefully report that the bridge had been destroyed. The southern span of the bridge had in fact been successfully deposited into the water leaving the northern span remaining intact. However, this was sufficient to render the bridge incapable of carrying out its function. A satisfying result, but once again the target destination caused three Liberators problems in achieving a safe return. Those aircraft had left the target area, having climbed up to a safe height and, with the flight engineers managing the fuel calculations, they reported that they had insufficient to reach their home station. These Liberators were forced to divert and land at the sanctuary island of Akyab, a venue now frequently associated in saving aircrew lives. These fuel deficiencies could have easily been induced by weather diversions or simply flying into heavy winds, which consumed more fuel. Wing Commander Ercolani safely arrived at Digri and David Jones simply wrote in his logbook, 'War Operation Railway Bridge at Lang Suan'. It was to him no more than another operation, which would count towards the completion of his second tour of duty.

Bridge busting remained a priority and, just two days later, 159 Squadron dispatched six Liberators under the 'A' Flight Commander, Squadron Leader Freddie Stroud. Interestingly, this operation was to clearly illustrate the high proportion of Commonwealth crews serving in 159 Squadron—five of the Liberators were being flown by Canadian pilots. These aircraft were to return to the Singapore line where Railway Bridge TF102 was demolished at its southern section and other partial separations of the bridge construction had also been achieved. This was one of a great many operations that excluded the participation of both Wing Commander Ercolani and Flying Officer Haycock's crews. It must also be remembered that several other Liberator-equipped Squadrons were operating around the clock against the numerous railway targets; for instance, on 22 May, the same day of the 159 Squadron attack on the bridge at Lang Suan, 99 Squadron attacked railway bridges at Pran Buri with excellent results. The headquarters of Eastern Air Command, Southeast Asia, created reviews from aerial reconnaissance intelligence in order to estimate the rolling stock and locomotives being used on the entire Burma–Thailand rail structure. It would entail a six-day period of good-weather opportunities to secure in its entirety and this was done repetitively whenever possible. The evidence was gathered from 18 March to 24 March 1945, where sorties were broken down into the various routes. These were allocated two-letter references or routes. These two-letter codes are frequently seen when bridge identification has been used elsewhere. In particular, the Burma–Thailand Railway with the adopted 'Q' code:

| Route | Stops |
|---|---|
| TA: Bangkok to Chiengmai | Bangkok Terminus, Makkasan, Government Oil Refinery, Klong Toi, Don Muang, Chieng Rak, Ayutha, Phitsanulok, Ban Tum, Uttaradit, Kohga |
| TD: Korat to Udon Thani | Khon Kaen, Udon Thani |
| TF: Banpong to Chumphon | Chedsamien, Rajburi, Gubua, Bhojpuri, Kao Tamone, Wangbhong, Kui, Prachuap Khiri Kan, Hnohng Hin, Bang Saphan, Bang Saphan one, Bang Son, Na Ja Ang, Chumphon |

| TG: Kra Isthmus to Chumphon | Na Nien |
|---|---|
| TH: Chumphon to Padang Besar | Sawi, Lang Suan, Rohnbhibun |
| Q: Burma to Siam | Bangkok Noi, Bang Bamru, Taling Chan, Ban Khmer, Nakhon Pathom, Hnohn Pladuk (Nong Pladuk), Banpong, Dhapa, Mile 242, Bang Bhang, Kanchanaburi, Ban Kao, Ban Tha Kilen, Ban Lum Sum, Ban Wang Yai, Tha Daeknoa, Sra Si Muli, Mile 146, Mile145, Gaizat Yok, Kui Zang, Prang Kasi, Kaklang, Kui Yong, Dha Khanun, Yohnodi, Dhamayiew, Kui Chang, Ban Naunglu, Phadaw, Shitpyit, Mile 56, Anankwin, Mile 26 |
| TI: Tung Song to Ban Kantang | Ban Kantang |

The intelligence interpretation of the photographic coverage along all of the seven routes and sixty-six individual locations revealed the presence of twenty-three locomotives and 2,977 individual types of rolling stock. The Burma–Thailand Railway alone was found to have only five locomotives present, but 1,363 various types of rolling stock, the vast majority of which were being held in sidings or by pass links both present and still under construction. The Japanese became adept at keeping the Burma–Thailand Railway open, with rapid repair facilitated by prisoners of war who were given unenviable tasks to achieve in the most difficult of circumstances. With bridges in particular, one of the most obvious routes for continuing repairs was facilitated by the roads built by the labour force. Bypass constructions were on occasions built and these were reinforced with corduroy matting in an attempt to make them last longer in wet conditions.

Where bridges were destroyed that spanned over wide rivers, ferry services were swiftly put into place. The bridge known as bridge Q691 on the Burma–Thailand line was seen to have been repaired as a simple footbridge, the evidence of which came from photographic reconnaissance. Large barges would then transport materials to the site, and these were capable of carrying freight from additionally constructed jetties with individual access slip roads down to the river banks. The construction of rail lines to the water's edge followed and, once in place, rail ferries were capable of transferring loaded freight cars across the river. At Kanchanaburi, the Tamarkan prisoner of war camp and a nearby Japanese anti-aircraft battery were located adjacent to the bridges over the River Kwai. Both the substantial bridge and its temporary wooden bridge had been well-constructed. In the dry season, the Japanese innovation saw them build a causeway across the partially dried up river approximately 200 yards from the wooden bridge. This temporary structure had a short span across the river, but it did allow bullock carts to move freight while damage caused to both bridges by aerial bombing was being fixed.

It was around this time that the retreat of the Japanese forces was virtually split apart. A huge force of men and equipment were segregated between the swollen monsoon-struck rivers of the Sittang and Salween. The Japanese headquarters in Moulmein became a rallying location for masses of troops, and these were targeted by the Allied forces from the air. Significant effort was direct towards Moulmein as Ba Maw had fled there during the Japanese retreat and was at this time deemed to be within the Japanese headquarters complex. Moulmein had been the administrative capital of British Lower Burma, with the important port on the Gulf of Martaban near the mouth of the Salween River.

Moulmein was to be the subject of a major strike by four squadrons consisting of approximately forty-eight aircraft. The target was to be the munitions and supply centre for the Japanese army fighting along the Sittang River front. Additionally, the anti-aircraft defensive gun emplacements were to be attacked and disabled in the hope of protecting the main force. This task fell to 159 Squadron and, on 28 May, the crews were comprehensively briefed at their various stations for an attack the following day. The briefing officers advised and illustrated an area immediately adjacent to the primary target that was to be identified from the air and avoided at all costs. This was the prisoner of war camp, where several hundred men were held as a workforce to repair the railroads. At 2.24 a.m. on 29 May 1945, Wing Commander Ercolani took off in B-24 Liberator KH275 to bomb defensive gun emplacements at Moulmein. He was to act as master bomber, carrying a mixed bombload of red target indicators and high explosive ordinance. The route into the target was to be marked for the main force of aircraft. A further five crews followed him into the air, with the specific target of bombing four heavy anti-aircraft guns. Once they arrived at the target area, they found the defences to be fully operational and actively engaged in directing exploding flak towards them. The gun battery sites were straddled by several sticks of bombs, which resulted in fairly good results, but not direct impacts. Sufficient damage was done to silence the guns and they enabled target markers to be dropped onto the main target. Although Moulmein was still capable of putting up moderate anti-aircraft fire, none of the 159 Squadron aircraft sustained any serious damage. The supporting force of Liberators, having flown independently, arrived at 10,000 feet and followed their briefing instructions by commencing bombing runs upon the target indicators from about 7,000 feet. After dropping their bombloads, they turned off their course by 90 degrees on a left trajectory, a manoeuvre designed to avoid any mid-air incidents or collisions. All twelve Liberators from 99 Squadron successfully completed the task and turned away, leaving Moulmein burning. Likewise, the nine Liberators from 355 Squadron all reported good marking and only two of their aircraft failed to accurately plaster the target. Even so, their bombs still contributed to the entire operation. No. 356 Squadron supplied eight Liberators, who arrived on time over Moulmein and also reported success. One aircraft, having suffered an unserviceable bombsight and bearing in mind the presence of the prisoner of war camp, considered the matter too dangerous to bomb. They diverted to use their bombs against the trestle bridge on the Burma–Thailand Railway.

Admiral Mountbatten announced from his South East Asia Command headquarters on 5 May 1945 that, between 1 February 1944 and 30 April 1945, the Japanese Fifteenth,

Twenty-Eighth, and Thirty-Third Armies had been routed by the Allies. The Japanese casualties were estimated to have been 347,000. He added:

> You have given the enemy such a beating … and harried them so hard that the vaunted Japanese Army, about whose toughness and fanaticism we have heard so much, has in some cases pulled out rather than face your final assault.

The Strategic Air Force itself comprised of a high percentage of Commonwealth crews. The number of Canadians who ended up in Royal Air Force Far East Liberator units was impressive. Robert Farquharson's book, *For Your Tomorrow: Canadians and the Burma Campaign, 1941–1945*, advises that 159 Squadron alone had 237 members of the Royal Canadian Air Force within its ranks. In the final year of the war, half of the Liberator aircrew personnel, which was estimated to number 1,672, were Canadians spread over the twelve squadrons, and one 166 lost their lives in action or flying accidents.

On 1 June 1945, the infrastructure of the Allied Air Force's capability changed with the withdrawal of the United States Army Air Force from Air Command South East Asia. The Allied front against the Japanese had narrowed significantly, primarily due to the capture of Rangoon. The threat of Japanese supply lines into China was almost extinguished, regardless of the huge numbers of Japanese troops cut off, but still present in central Burma. The Royal Air Force and her Commonwealth Air Forces progressed south into the Malay Peninsula towards Singapore, while the United States Air Forces turned their attention towards China. The British and American Southeast Asian forces had created an aerial strength that had been fundamental in the success thus far in taking Burma. Meanwhile, the British airfield construction program was being heavily prioritised, examples being the Rangoon area airfields of Zayatkin and Mingaladon, both of which became all-weather airfields with 2,000-yard runways. For the heavy Liberator bombers, Pegu aerodrome was nominated as being ideal, but would require far more time than the anticipated completion date of August 1945 set for Zayatkin and Mingaladon. The long transit from India-based airfields was to become of greater significance as target ranges inevitably lengthened. The skill in balancing bombloads and fuel strategy measures remained vital for the B-24 Liberators.

The title 'Strategic Air Force', which had encompassed the British and American Squadrons, ceased to be officially used with effect from 1 June 1945, however, the Royal Air Force 231 Group would continue to be used independently upon strategic operations. That date also saw another change in targets for 159 Squadron. Fourteen Liberators were dispatched to the natural shipping anchorage at Satahib Bay. This was a significantly large bay, south of Bangkok, where assorted shipping from the Thailand Navy was likely to be found. It was a target that was a considerable distance from their airfield. From the strength of crews briefed for this operation, four Liberators would carry sea mines that would be dropped into the waters and, if shipping was present, these would discourage any immediate moves to escape. The remaining ten Liberators were led by Wing Commander Ercolani. He and his crew would act as master bombers in directing the attack upon their primary target, which was the prized *Anthong*-class submarine depot ship. The Thailand Naval anchorage at Satahib Bay had been targeted previously, but medium to high-level bombing against shipping targets had failed to produce any acceptable results. This operation was designed to be another operation undertaken at a medium height, but it was hoped that the adventurous low-level exploits developed by 159 Squadron pilots would be capitalised upon. The Wing Commander had five experienced Canadian pilots, supported by four from the Royal Air Force, who would engage with the shipping targets. Some of those experienced crews would come in at very low level, in a similar fashion to the effective bridge busting techniques.

The Liberators departed from Digri before 6 a.m. and they were not expected back until 8 p.m. David Jones would have required intensive concentration to navigate the Wing Commander's aircraft to what he hoped would be an easily recognisable target on the Thailand coastline. However, concentrating and calculating accurately for over fourteen hours was always going to be challenging and, as ever, a huge reliance was placed upon the Liberator aircraft to endure such long operational flights. David sat in a small area between the bomb aimer and the nose wheel compartment. He sat facing the pilot's feet, with a small navigation table fixed to the bulkhead. On both sides of him he had a small window where he had the opportunity to conduct visual sightings. The crew's regular rear gunner, Fred Smith, also faced long hours within his turret, but the expectation of being able to put his guns to good use against enemy shipping was highly motivational. Smithy was a very experienced air gunner, having completed one full tour of duty in the Far East between 1943 and 1944. He had been personally selected as the Wing Commander's rear gunner. Luckily for Thomas Reynolds, he was excused the ardours of being the flight engineer and managing fuel on such a long sortie as Jonny Haycock's crew were not flying that day. Acting Squadron Leader Robin Williams and his crew had been selected by Wing Commander Ercolani to participate in the low-level shipping attack. It would prove to be an extraordinary day for this pilot and would lead to him being recommended for a Distinguished Flying Cross.

The planned attack went exceptionally well for all of the participating crews, no doubt a reflection of the detailed briefing they had received and excellent navigation. The weather had created some problems on the way to the target, but once they had crossed the high hills into Thailand it was perfect and a good omen for the attack. The bay was sheltering several vessels including the instantly recognisable submarine depot ship. The initial medium-level bombing run was to prove successful, with one direct hit on a vessel. Highlighting the skill in bomb aiming achieved by the squadron's constant training and growing efficiency, the low-level Liberators followed in as planned, including the aircraft being flown by the Wing Commander. The large enemy vessel, which could be better described as a tanker, was hit and burned fiercely from end to end, the damage eventually causing it to keel over and sink completely. A smaller tanker was also subjected to a direct hit from the Liberator captained by the Canadian Flight Lieutenant Williams. That vessel immediately exploded and burst into flame, billowing thick black smoke and sinking just a few minutes later leaving debris and oil on the sea. Acting Squadron Leader Williams had sighted the submarine depot ship on his first bombing run, but saved his bombs as it was obvious to him that the ship was mortally damaged. He took another low-level bombing run on what may well have been the small tanker, but his bombload failed to release, causing his flight engineer an immediate problem to resolve. His Liberator once again took another approach at low level, ignoring the rather inaccurate light anti-aircraft flak that was being fired. Witnessing the tankers explosion, he sought out yet another target and attacked an enemy sloop; a direct hit was scored on the stern of that vessel, adding to the tally of destruction.

Wing Commander Ercolani had witnessed a most successful operation. Two significant vessels had been sunk and others, including small torpedo boats, had been badly damaged. He noted the impressive work of the Canadian bomb aimer Flying Officer Drew, who had been exceptionally accurate in his bombing of the primary objective, the depot ship. Also of note was the Canadian pilot Flight Lieutenant Roy Borthwick, who, while initially affording cover for aircraft attacking at low level, he not only drew the fire of the anti-aircraft defences, but pressed home his own attack and obtained a hit on the enemy depot ship, setting it on fire.

Leaving Satahib Bay, the Liberators made for home while additionally seeking out any targets of opportunity, always eager to inflict as much damage as possible upon the Japanese transport infrastructure. One of the returning Liberators had been able to allow their air gunners to strafe trains at Bhojpuri with great success, Pilot Officer Temple-Smith later reporting to the intelligence officer that various box cars had exploded, violently producing brilliant red flashes and heavy black smoke. All of the aircraft returned safely to Digri, with the exception of one that had been forced to land at Ramree on the way home with a failing engine. This had been a remarkable day for 159 Squadron.

June 1945 saw further bombing of the enemy troops, who were now frantically endeavouring to reorganise. Many Japanese soldiers were widely scattered and cut off in the area around Moulmein. The Japanese Headquarters at Moulmein and the villages along the road from Papun to Bilin were still accessible to the retreating enemy and were systematically attacked from the air. New fragmentation bombs were brought into use by the Liberator crews and these became responsible for inflicting significant casualties to the Japanese troops sheltering and massing in the jungle. On 10 June, Wing Commander Ercolani led twelve 159 Squadron Liberators to attack two precisely briefed areas around the village of Kamamaung. Intelligence had accumulated, indicating that an estimated 1,000 Japanese troops had congregated at that location. It was not uncommon for the many villages, areas, and other locations to appear in numerous documents spelt differently. David Jones, in his flying logbook, recorded the target as he pronounced it, which frequently creates confusion. Once again, he navigated to a very small target area within dense jungle. The route had been from Digri to Kyaukpyu then Gwa Bay and Elephant Point turning inland to Shwegun in order to locate the small target, which was very close to the Salween River. Flying in Liberator KH275, the bombload consisted of twelve 250-lb fragmentation bombs and nine equally large yellow target indicators. The intelligence was interpreted to indicate splitting the force between two locations. The Canadian Flight Lieutenant Williams was also carrying target indicators that were green. Both dedicated markers had another supporting Liberator to re-mark the respective areas if required. Among the crews that took off just before 7 a.m. were the crews of Flying Officer Haycock and Thomas Reynolds, who by now was rapidly approaching his end of tour, this being his thirtieth operation. Despite the bad weather with low cloud and rain, all of the Liberators accurately dropped their respective markers and bombloads. Thomas Reynolds noted in his logbook that they were at a height of 1,700 feet when their bombs were dropped. Due to weather conditions, nothing could be seen in relation to ground activity, but the intelligence reports were confidently advising that the Japanese troops, now numbering around 6,000, were attempting to cross the river at this target. The concentration of bombing was good and numerous fires were seen to have broken out by several of the crews. The air gunners strafed the jungle, additionally hoping to add to the bombing results. On the return to Digri, Pilot Officer Haycock sighted some railway rolling stock at Thaton, near Thailand's northern border with Burma. Thomas Reynolds witnessed the crews air gunners plaster the target effectively when the Liberator was banked around the railway, allowing all of the gunners the opportunity to shoot at the target. The Wing Commander, however, was experiencing another fraught situation with an engine fire on his Liberator as he made for base and he was once again forced to find sanctuary at Akyab. This island was like an aircraft carrier in the middle of the ocean and once again it was responsible for rescuing him. The Liberator landed safely, but the initial inspection by the ground crew revealed that the aircraft was in need of major repairs. Wing Commander Ercolani and his crew would remain at Akyab for a few days and miss out on what was to prove to be an important operation undertaken by 159 Squadron.

On 13 June, two Japanese tanker vessels being protected by two destroyers had been sighted and urgent measures were put into place to search for and attack these important vessels. They had been sighted in the Gulf of Thailand, formally the Gulf of Siam. The Gulf waters are in the main quite shallow along its coastal areas. Many rivers flow into its expanses, which are some 350 miles wide and 450 miles long. For Thomas Reynolds, navigating to the last sighting in the gulf would be simple once they had crossed the Asserim Hills. Thereafter, the finding of the convoy would engage a detailed square search pattern to be flown, which would need detailed plotting to accurately cover the water without leaving any areas uncovered. Climbing into Johnny Haycock's Liberator just before 6a.m., they departed with five other bombers. Fairly swiftly, Flight Lieutenant Borthwick developed engine trouble and was forced to drop his bombs over the Salbani bombing range and return to Digri. This was not a good omen as the remaining aircraft then hit monsoon weather in the Bay of Bengal and Warrant Officer Brown was forced to withdraw from the operation. He elected to put his bombload to good use by attacking the Moulmein Railway near to Kalumpa. His bomb aimer, Sergeant Holden, once again proved his ability, rewarding his crew with the sight of a large locomotive being completely lifted off the rails and broken apart with a torrent of steam. The remaining four B-24s had reached the Gulf and commenced searching for the tankers. Each aircraft carried six 500-lb bombs in their bomb bays. The respective flight engineers calculated the time available against the fuel and eventually a decision was made by Flight Lieutenant Williams to abort the search and bomb the secondary target at Satahib Bay before returning to the airfield at Digri. No doubt disappointed at not finding the shipping prize, they were again disappointed when they found Satahib Bay covered in fairly thick cloud, hampering efforts to bomb with any accuracy. Enemy shipping put up light flak and bombing runs were made, but no results were observed as a result of the frustratingly thick cloud. Fortunately, this long protracted and exasperating operation concluded with all of the Liberators returning safely. Thomas Reynolds recorded another fifteen hours and ten minutes operational flying in his logbook. These men must have been exhausted after such long sorties and will have hoped to receive at least a full day's rest to recover. The intelligence gathered upon the important enemy convoy suggested that they had steamed south, and immediately six 159 Squadron Liberators were dispatched to fly to Akyab. From that location, they would be able to refuel and strike further southwards in the hope of locating the convoy. The move to Akyab would provide the Liberators with an additional 300-mile range and it was hoped that would be sufficient for this cat and mouse search.

At 2 p.m. on 14 June 1945, Wing Commander Ercolani, who had only recently departed Akyab, returned there in Liberator EW173. Five aircraft followed him with great anticipation of attacking a target so far away from Digri. Once again, there was a huge Canadian presence as the Wing Commander was backed up by Flight Lieutenant Borthwick, Flight Lieutenant Foot, Flying Officer Kinnear, and Flight Lieutenant Hamilton (all Canadians), supported by Pilot Officer DeNett of the Royal Air Force. The Wing Commander landed at Akyab at 4.15 p.m., and his six Liberators were joined by another detachment of aircraft from 355 Squadron, who would support him on the operation to be mounted the following morning.

The crews were fed early and fully briefed, which included the unpredictable monsoon weather. The combined strength of Liberator bombers would be taking off at around 9 a.m., with the set route from Pagoda Point to High Island and across the short mainland to the area south-west of the Bay of Ko Samui. In daylight, with significant coastal areas providing easily recognisable features and good weather, this should have been a relatively simple sortie to navigate. However, at the southern tip of Burma, Pagoda Point, the aircraft hit the very worst of monsoon conditions. Such were the conditions experienced that some aircraft were forced to return to India and make for base at Digri. The remaining Liberators were no more than halfway to the target area, although as they continued the weather conditions fortunately began to improve. The Wing Commander's old 99 Squadron at Dhubalia had frequently supported him on many operations over Burma and Thailand, and this important operation to Ko Samui Island was no exception. Seven 99 Squadron Liberators attempted to join his strike force, but were forced to take-off with a gathering monsoon present over the airfield. Only three aircraft would eventually reach the target. The minds of the pilots and crews were focused upon the main target, a 10,000-ton oil tanker. Rarely would they ever be able to attack such an important shipping target. The oil it carried was of utmost importance to the Japanese forces. The last sighting confirmed by a Rangoon-based Sunderland Flying Boat plotted the tanker heading towards the islands that they were now fast approaching.

In Wing Commander Ercolani's Liberator, David Jones would join the second pilot Warrant Officer Devlin on the flight deck. A heavy responsibility suddenly fell upon their bomb aimer Sidney Wells, who would ultimately hold the key of success against this most prized Japanese target. The tanker was sighted being shadowed by a destroyer and other smaller, but well-armed vessels. Immediately, the tanker turned southwards and as expected the escorts took evasive action. The first Liberator to take a bombing run was flown by Pilot Officer Williamson of 355 Squadron. He came across low and scored a direct hit aft of the tanker, Wing Commander Ercolani led and directed the operation and made two bombing runs on the tanker. He later wrote:

> Sid Wells our bomb aimer really was on form and hit it twice on our two bomb runs, very pleased.

The tanker was on fire with thick black smoke rising to several thousand feet. Pilot Officer DeNett of 159 Squadron delivered his attack on the tanker when it was submerged about two-thirds underwater. However, the attack was far from having been unopposed; Flight Lieutenant Ludbey of 99 Squadron made two bombing runs, but suffered heavy anti-aircraft fire and he was forced to return home severely damaged. Flying Officer Wheeler also of 99 Squadron was repeatedly hit by fire from the escort ships. Unable to drop his bombs through a mechanical fault, he had to be satisfied with his air gunners raking the target. They reached Akyab, but the emergency landing saw their Liberator burst into flames causing the death of the flight engineer who had been crushed and lost to the intense flames—a terrible death. The third and final 99 Squadron Liberator, flown by Flying Officer Parkin, also suffered badly with its tail fin shot away by flak. Two crew members baled out, but remarkably the aircraft, with some fatal casualties on board, managed to reach Mingaladon where it crashed, killing the pilot. One of the parachutists who had escaped from the ill-fated B-24 also lost his life and the sole survivor was captured and taken prisoner.

Wing Commander Ercolani had redirected his remaining force to attack the evading destroyer, but no hits were scored. The surviving Liberators, however, left the target area with great satisfaction, having destroyed what was thought to have been one of the largest Japanese tankers in the Far East conflict. David Jones recorded in his flying logbook that the Liberators engines were finally switched off after an operation lasting eleven hours and forty-five minutes. His had been the first aircraft to take-off from their airstrip and the second to last in returning on a round-trip sortie of some 2,500 miles. No. 159 Squadron records provide evidence of four bombs scoring direct hits upon the tanker and all participating aircraft from their Squadron returning safely. This aerial operation saw the final oil supply tanker to Japan lost. Fuel oil, one of the valuable resources that Japan sought in her plan of expansion, was now denied to them. This was an important blow that the B-24 Liberator crews were quite rightly proud of.

The men who undertook these duties had families who knew little of what they were doing in Southeast Asia. Little comment has been made upon their lives. Men like Wing Commander Ercolani had many other duties. Organising the Squadron's operational strength was difficult, ensuring men and crews were rested as best possible during their operational tour of duty. Crews overlapped with other crews, forming daily bomber strengths, while others who had returned from long sorties into Thailand needed rest before they could fly again. This created a constant ebb and flow of differing crews, aircraft, and leadership in the air and the constant pressure on ground crew personnel who were crucial in maintaining the aircraft. On 19 June 1945, Wing Commander Ercolani turned his thoughts to his home and his wife as it was the date of his fourth wedding anniversary. He carried his countries recognition of bravery with gallantry medal ribbons, knowing very well that his survival in a ditching into the sea in November 1941 so very nearly took his life when he had been sucked down into the depths of water. His own mortality would have been frequently in his mind each time he wrote to the wives and parents of the men he commanded who never returned. In many instances, he was unable to comfort them with the knowledge of what had actually happened and the fear of them having fallen into the hands of the Japanese was far different from that of having become a prisoner of war in Europe. He was all too aware that many of his own operations were to destroy the Japanese railway infrastructure. Knowingly flying low to attack trains, bridges, and railway lines crowded with vast numbers of Allied prisoners of war created conflicting emotions. They flew so low that they frequently witnessed these enslaved men, encouraging them as they sped past those terrifying places to destroy the forces that were creating such hardship and death to the hundreds and thousands of prisoners and labourers.

Despite the progress made in Burma by the Allies, the now famous bridge on the River Kwai became a vital target to be destroyed. The first wooden bridge over the Khwae Yai had been finished in February 1943. The substantial concrete and steel bridge built nearby was completed in June 1943. Both of these bridges had been bombed by the United States Air Force B-24s on several occasions, with repairs immediately carried out by prisoner of war labour, and the wooden trestle bridge was inevitably fully operational in a very short period of time. This vitally important target was subjected to constant aerial inspection, which gave evidence of the Japanese providing good defensive anti-aircraft guns, both light and heavy, supported by machine guns to protect them. The Royal Air Force, in particular 159 Squadron, supported by 355 and 356 Squadrons, was required to fly B-24 Liberators on one decisive and final operation to destroy both bridges. Using their expertise and master bomber techniques on 24 June 1945, the railway bridges were to be put out of commission for the rest of the war.

The briefing plan that took place in the afternoon on 23 June was for 159 Squadron to attack the main bridge, 356 Squadron to attack the bypass bridge, and 355 Squadron to deal with the Japanese ground defences. A total of twenty-four aircraft were to engage on the attack against what they describe as bombing the Kanchanaburi Bridges or Bridge No. 654. All of the crews engaged in this operation were well aware of the large prisoner of war camps proximity to the primary targets and the bombing runs were calculated to avoid that area. Flying a large B-24 Liberator against such small targets at between 200 and 500 feet above the ground was exceptionally challenging to those crews. Johnny Haycock's crew had been selected as one of the crews to bomb the primary steel bridge. It had been ten days since they had been on operations, but Thomas Reynolds knew that, at such low level, light machine-gun fire had great capabilities to inflict serious damage to his Liberator. Fuel and oil lines in particular were highly vulnerable, all of which would fall to him to repair or regulate while in the air during what was to be his thirty-first operation against the enemy. His thoughts would also be upon surviving. Fate had a terrible hand to play on many occasions, especially as he was exceptionally close to completing a full tour of duty, which was no mean achievement. Some comfort came from the meteorological officer who predicted reasonable weather conditions, despite being at the height of the monsoon period.

At 6.36 a.m. on Wednesday 24 June 1945, Johnny Haycock opened up the throttles and the four powerful engines of his Liberator roared as the propellers cut into the air to haul the massive weight along the airstrip. The bomb bays that day held five large 1,000-lb general-purpose bombs, fitted with eleven-second delay fuses. The flight engineer Thomas Reynolds assisted in the management of the engines as they slowly gathered speed and the aircraft commenced to take to the air. A few hundred yards from the end of the airstrip, the crew felt the Liberator lifting slightly. The control column was pulled back by Johnny Haycock to place the elevators a few degrees above the tail plane. This movement caused the air stream to force down the rear of the aircraft and the pull of the engines lifted up the nose slightly. The Liberator began to gently rise and the wheels eventually cleared the ground with very little runway to spare. Once airborne, the wheels were retracted safely and locked into position. At this point, the rear gunner would leave the flight deck area to negotiate his way along the fuselage and eventually climb into his turret. The weight distribution of him and the other crew members had been vitally important to the take-off technique required in the heavily fuel-laden aircraft. This standard take-off procedure was followed by all eleven 159 Squadron Liberators that were engaged in this operation, commanded by the two Canadians, Flight Lieutenant Bothwick and Squadron Leader Watson. The various aircraft take-off times were as follows:

| Pilot | Aircraft | Take-off Time |
| --- | --- | --- |
| Flight Lieutenant Williams | Liberator 'M' KL660 | 6.19 a.m. |
| Flight Lieutenant Mitchell | Liberator 'H' KH893 | 6.20 a.m. |
| Warrant Officer Brown | Liberator 'Z' GV968 | 6.31 a.m. |
| Flying Officer Haycock | Liberator 'B' EW173 | 6.36 a.m. |
| Warrant Officer Green | Liberator 'Q' EW246 | 6.37 a.m. |
| Pilot Officer Lee | Liberator 'D' EV981 | 6.39 a.m. |
| Squadron Leader Watson | Liberator 'C' KL653 | 6.40 a.m. |
| Flying Officer Dowding | Liberator 'X' KL677 | 6.46 a.m. |
| Flight Lieutenant Foot | Liberator 'R' KL491 | 6.48 a.m. |
| Flight Lieutenant Bothwick | Liberator 'A' KH398 | 6.49 a.m. |
| Warrant Officer Newman | Liberator 'U' EV966 | 6.51 a.m. |

Aircraft 'M', 'Z', and 'H' were carrying a total of thirty-nine fragmentation bombs, which were to be dropped on the Japanese anti-aircraft positions. These cluster units of 100-lb bombs were exceptionally effective when deployed against enemy troops and it was hoped that they would destroy the anti-aircraft sites during the initial stages of the operation. These Liberators were briefed to patrol the area after the initial bomb run and deploy other fragmentation bombs on targets of opportunity.

All 159 Squadron aircraft were equipped with 8-inch vertical cameras, a precaution to facilitate complete photographic coverage in order to assess the effectiveness of the bombing. Six of the Liberators additionally carried a larger handheld oblique-mounted camera, which was designed to provide images from an angle that was beneficial for the interpretation of damage to the bridge structures. It was commonplace for the flight engineers to operate the large cameras from the position of the Liberators' beam gunners. They were instructed to take several exposures at one time to enable the position to be easily recognised, and additionally record the exposures on the navigation log. Those measures ensured that any important enemy facility would be correctly identified and plotted with exact geographical positions. The flight engineer in Liberator EV981, Colin Clinton, was responsible for taking several photographs of the operation conducted against the bridges on 24 June 1945.

The surviving operational records for the attack upon the bridges over the River Kwai indicate that the two bridges were identified as Bridge 654 and Bridge 654A. Additionally, the records show that the crews were also tasked with dropping Nickel propaganda leaflets. Nearly 140,000 leaflets were distributed from the Liberator crews of 355 and 356 Squadron. Those particular leaflets were identified as leaflets SJ122,

SJN43, and SJG26. All material issued by the British Psychological Warfare Division for the Far East had leaflet coding that bore an identification serial for easy reference and security. These reference numbers and letters are to be found at the bottom left-hand corner of the single-side leaflets, and at the reverse bottom left-hand corner of the double-sided leaflets.

SJ122 were standard Japanese leaflets with text and images.
SJN43 were pictorial Japanese news sheets, frequently of a cartoon nature.
SJG26 were Japanese news text sheets.

The route to be navigated to the target was via Sagar Light, Pagoda Point, and Heinze Basin. The weather conditions were found to be good, with some cloud base over the actual target area. The morale among the 159 Squadron crews was exceptionally high; no doubt the result of recent achievements against the shipping targets and the general Allied progression against the Japanese forces. Wing Commander Ercolani was not engaged with this important operation against the famous bridge. That day he had flown to Alipore, 65 miles from Digri for conference duties. He had, however, conducted the briefing for his crews and personally emphasised that his men should take exceptional care in respect of the labour camps that were in close proximity to the bridges.

The 159 Squadron Liberators reached the target area safely, arriving overhead at approximately 1 p.m. The anti-aircraft defences had been suppressed by the immediate attacks upon their emplacements and the 159 Squadron Liberators commenced their bombing runs. The master bomber Squadron Leader Watson made the first run, checking the approach and dropping a single bomb. He then witnessed Johnny Haycock and Flight Lieutenant Bothwick both hit the main bridge accurately. All of the pilots succeeded in making five passes along the river, each time dropping a single 1,000-lb bomb. The bombs disappeared into the muddy water next to the bridge before exploding eleven seconds later. One of the first set of bombs destroyed a span of the steel-and-concrete railway bridge, immediately making the operation a success. An additional two bridge spans had been dislodged and tipped into the river, undoubtedly knocking other spans out of alignment before the master bomber switched the remainder of aircraft to attack the wooden bypass bridge. As a result of the consistently impressive bombing successes, this bridge had also been badly damaged before the arrival of the 356 Squadron Liberators who were tasked with its destruction. The eight 356 Squadron Liberators contributed to the damage by dropping their bombs, repeatedly straddling the construction, and the bridge was left completely broken in two positions. The Canadian nose gunner Flight Sergeant Dalton, who had recently joined 356 Squadron and was flying in Flight Lieutenant Whidden's Liberator, took the opportunity to fire his guns in anger at the Japanese on what was his first low-level bombing operation. The additional seven 356 Squadron Liberators were captained by the Canadians Flying Officer Veitch, Flight Lieutenant Payne, Flight Lieutenant Dick, Squadron Leader Evans, Flying Officer Bradley, Flying

Officer Myers, and Flying Officer Hunt, who had bombed and badly damaged the northern approach route to the bypass bridge. Seven of the eight 355 Squadron Liberators tasked with supressing the anti-aircraft defences had been just as effective in their efforts. One Liberator had failed to reach the target as a result of weather conditions and diverted to attack bridge H161 at Lampang. Another Canadian contingent within 355 Squadron, Flight Lieutenant Fuller and Flying Officer Collins, had attacked both heavy and light gun emplacements with accuracy, silencing the gunfire. A Canadian pilot from the same squadron, Flying Officer Wardell, had initially drawn the heavy anti-aircraft flak by flying at an ideal height for the Japanese gunners. He then came down low to accurately drop his bombs and destroyed one of the heavy gun emplacements, allowing his gunners to target the remaining defensive emplacements. The crews from 355 Squadron additionally reported two small fires having broken out as they turned away from the target area.

As the force of Liberators departed the target area, they also left behind strafed locomotive and rolling stock and many thousands of propaganda leaflets gently floating down to earth. The attack had been a resounding accomplishment of flying skills in all respects. The 159 Squadron Liberator KL491, flown by Flight Lieutenant Foot, had been exceptionally lucky during their bombing runs. One of their empty fuel tanks, which would have retained its lethal mix of gasoline fumes in the fuselage, had been struck by a piece of flak. These additional tanks were positioned in the forward bomb bay area and, if struck like this, inevitably exploded into a fire ball. For reasons unknown, this did not happen. The crew had most unexpectedly survived and experienced a hazardous return, ensuring everybody eliminated the risk of any sparks. The 159 Squadron aircraft all returned safely landing within a time period of one hour and thirty-one minutes.

| Pilot | Time Landed |
| --- | --- |
| Squadron Leader Watson | 7.05 p.m. |
| Flight Lieutenant Bothwick | 7.43 p.m. |
| Flying Officer Dowding | 7.47 p.m. |
| Flying Officer Haycock | 7.56 p.m. |
| Warrant Officer Green | 8.03 p.m. |
| Flight Lieutenant Williams | 8.06 p.m. |
| Pilot Officer Lee | 8.10 p.m. |
| Flight Lieutenant Mitchell | 8.15 p.m. |
| Flight Lieutenant Foot | 8.21 p.m. |
| Warrant Officer Brown | 8.31 p.m. |
| Warrant Officer Newman | 8.36 p.m. |

Thomas Reynolds switched off the engines in Liberator EW173 after a flight of thirteen hours and twenty-five minutes. The ground crews would once again thoroughly check the Liberator for damage, service and repair anything in need, and turn the aircraft around as soon as possible, ready for the armourers to load the nominated bombload for yet another operation. The crews, having been debriefed, later made up their records. Thomas Reynolds made his entry in red ink, endorsing his flying logbook as having successfully completed yet another operation of 'low-level bridge busting'. He, along with all the other men who participated in the final destruction of this important bridge, had no idea of the importance that particular raid would have in the reflective history of the Second World War. Sergeant Frank Holden, the Pickle Barrel bomb aimer within the Liberator piloted by Warrant Officer Brown, recorded his log with the entry: 'War Operations attacking anti-aircraft sites while main force attack railway bridges at low level both bridges destroyed, heavy anti-aircraft fire'. He later pasted a news cutting into his logbook, the article read:

Kandy, June 25. Heavy bombers of Air Command in a low level attack yesterday destroyed three spans of the main bridge at Kanchanaburi, on the Burma–Siam Railway, 80 miles west of Bangkok, and made a large break in the centre of a bypass bridge, says todays S.E. Asia Command communique. Anti-aircraft sites nearby were bombed and engines and rolling stock strafed. The approach to a bridge seventy miles south of Moulmein, on the railway to Ye, was damaged.

The bridge on the River Kwai had been finally destroyed and it was unable to contribute any further to the Japanese forces, least of all assist in the supply of reinforcements to the Japanese troops steadfastly fighting along the Sittang River front. It was at the Sittang River three years earlier where the British Army had suffered a heavy defeat, but the tide had turned and now thousands of Japanese troops were cut off and any immediate retreat was thwarted by that influential river.

On 27 June 1945, the Air Officer Commanding 231 Group sent a message of congratulations upon the accuracy of bombing connected to the destruction of gun sites and bridges recently carried out by 159 Squadron. The war in Burma was nearly won and thoughts turned to the recapture of Malaya, but, before that, 159 Squadron would be called upon to fly some further operations including supporting the Allied Army who were still engaging significant Japanese stronghold forces on the ground.

On 30 June, the Army once again called on 159 Squadron to conduct a pathfinder accurate-bombing operation against Japanese troop concentrations in the area of the Boyagyi Rubber Estate, situated just to the east of the Sittang River. Johnny Haycock, fresh from the exhilaration of having been responsible for such accuracy against the bridge on the River Kwai, would once again engage with the enemy. On this occasion, seven other crews from his station would accompany him. Squadron Leader Stroud was the master bomber who, alongside his bombload, would drop the yellow target markers. These would attract the primary bombloads from the following B-24s, all of which carried twelve 500-lb bombs. The bombing force was also tasked with dropping over 400,000 propaganda leaflets, the majority of which were Japanese text messages of surrender titled 'Guard this paper, you will need it'. The intelligence officer briefing indicated that the Japanese troops were congregating at the target area and it was thought that military stores were also present. The weather conditions were not predicted to be good, with a heavy cloud base expected. Thomas Reynolds, in Johnny Haycock's crew, would once again be responsible for the handheld camera and would no doubt assist in dispatching the propaganda leaflets.

David Jones, the Wing Commander's navigator, found himself fitting in his last operational sortie against the Japanese. It was to be his sixty-third and he would thence be regarded as having completed his second full tour of duty, a remarkable achievement that was rarely attained. This final operation was to navigate for Flight Lieutenant Ellis in Liberator KL683, one of the new Mk VIII aircraft recently supplied to the Squadron. The new mark of Liberator brought with it a radical rearrangement of some crew positions. David Jones, as navigator, moved from his usual position deep within the nose section of the aircraft up onto the pilot's flight deck. Squadron Leader Stroud, also in a new Mk VIII Liberator, took off at 6.11 a.m. on 30 June to lead the force. Within the next twenty-eight minutes, all seven Liberators were in the air and making for the target. The route was to be via Sagar Light, Pagoda Point, to the significantly large Heinze Basin, and then directly onto the target area. The western coastline of Burma became instantly recognisable to experienced crews, providing weather conditions were favourable, and this route would not have been particularly challenging for David Jones. His Liberator had been the second to last in taking off. After an uneventful trip, having arrived over the target area, nothing could be detected in the way of enemy activity. The target was identified from the photographic reconnaissance images and the pathfinder markers were dropped. A level bombing run was made through the heavy rain, which was falling across the entire target area. The bombing was accurate and aircraft reported seeing a large sheet of blue flame run through it, indicating what was presumed to have been a vapour explosion. A fire was started and several Liberators reduced height to strafe the numerous buildings seen within the woods. All seven Liberators returned safely and David Jones navigated his aircraft home to arrive at exactly 5 p.m., the final aircraft to land. He simply entered 'War Op Boyagi' in his flying logbook, and calculated that his final operation had been achieved within 1,201 hours and fifty minutes of flying, which he subsequently recorded in his logbook.

Flight Lieutenant David Jones was now regarded as tour expired and his name would no longer feature on any bombing orders within 159 Squadron. Wing Commander Ercolani endorsed his flying logbook record as being correct and measures were put in place for him to be repatriated to England. In the meantime, he continued to fly with the Wing Commander on general duties, which would include squadron preparations to move to the Coco Islands. New orders were in place advising that the Squadron would eventually operate from those islands supporting the planned invasion of Malaya.

The length of an operational tour on the Burma front was one year or 200 operational hours, whichever was completed first. In the case of pilots, they then rested from operations for six months, normally being posted to ferrying duties, after which they were required to fly a further tour. Similar duties engaged other aircrew. In 1945, what was known as the duty scheme advised that at the end of three years, if married, or four years, if single, these men would be repatriated. Therefore, if married, those men were required to complete two tours with two rest periods prior to repatriation. If they were not married, they were required to undertake three tours, plus two rest periods. It would appear that at a high level within the Air Force, an interpretation existed that the monsoon period reduced flying significantly, whereas in fact these men in the Far East were flying whenever possible in those terribly dangerous conditions. During the period of the 1943 monsoon (July to October), the Royal Air Force flew nearly 8,000 sorties. Forty-two aircraft were lost and nearly all of those casualties resulted from the treacherous climate and the merciless flying conditions, not enemy action.

Thomas Reynolds remained operational in 159 Squadron, both his and Johnny Haycock's tours of duty were rapidly nearing completion. Well aware that they both needed a few more operations and that the Squadron's anticipated duties were engaged in retaking Malaya, their thoughts would have turned to home. However, before those events, 159 Squadron was still receiving orders relative to the final actions over Burma. The Japanese railway line from Banpong to Singapore had been completely removed from service by the consistently repeated bombing of vulnerable points. The loss of that supply route resulted in the Japanese seeking to deploy small shipping coasters northwards in the Gulf of Thailand, into Bangkok, and onwards to the Japanese troops situated east of the Sittang River. To thwart this, 231 Group Command required 159 Squadron to plant sea mines at the specific locations of the Mae Khloung River, Prachuap Khiri Kan, and Chumphon. On 4 July 1945, four Mk VI Liberators and two of the newer Mk VIII Liberators were to fly on this operation. The crews were briefed and the targets were allocated to the pilots:

Flying Officer Haycock: Mae Khloung River
Flight Lieutenant Marcou and Flying Officer Myles: Prachuap Khiri Kan
Flight Lieutenant Mitchell, Warrant Officer Green, and Warrant Officer Newman:
    Chumphon

Taking off from Digri, Johnny Haycock lifted off the runway at 5.40 a.m. on 4 July. Thomas Reynolds had completed ten operational sorties in their Liberator, EV173, which carried the identity letter 'B'—the crew no doubt held total confidence in that particular aircraft. All six Liberators formed up and flew to Pagoda Point, where they split towards their respective target areas. Johnny Haycock would fly alone to Heinze Bay and thence to the south-west tip of the Mae Khloung River estuary. They dropped all four mines precisely, as required, and safely returned at 6.30 p.m. The entire operation was unopposed for all of the crews, and a total of twenty-four sea mines had been planted. Flight Lieutenant Mitchell, in Liberator KL683, endured the longest period of flying time. His crew returned home having been in the air for fifteen hours and forty minutes.

The Kanchanaburi prisoner of war camp and a nearby Japanese anti-aircraft battery were located near to the bridges on the River Mae Klong (River Kwai). The substantial bridge and its temporary wooden bridge both became targets of priority for the B-24 Liberators to destroy. This image was taken from a significant height by an unknown pilot during an Allied photo-reconnaissance sortie. Kanchanaburi was approximately 1,000 statute miles from the Allied Liberator airfield at Digri, India.

An aerial reconnaissance image of both bridges on the River Kwai, evidence of previous American high-level bombing operations having been undertaken can be clearly seen. There were several near misses, with strings of bombs having landed in close proximity to the permanent bridge. The wooden bridge appears to have had some temporary supporting structure, no doubt to facilitate repairs or maintenance. The Japanese had four heavy anti-aircraft gun sites protecting the bridges.

The Royal Air Force operation finally destroyed the River Kwai bridge on 24 June 1945. The concrete bridge supports bear multiple and varied scar damage inflicted by shrapnel and bomb casings from explosions in the water beneath and adjacent to the target area. The second span from the right can be seen to have been dislodged from its mounting; thereafter, the destroyed steel spans can be seen making the bridge incapable of any use whatsoever.

No. 159 Squadron B-24 Liberator 'T' crash-landed at Digri after sustaining Japanese anti-aircraft flak damage. It would appear that both engines on the dropped wing were not operating at the point of landing as both propellers are not to be seen with the classic bent tips forced backwards by contacting the runway. This rare image was taken by Frank Holden, but insufficient detail exists to establish the full facts of this particular incident.

General purpose bombs ready to be loaded into the bomb bays of the 159 Squadron Liberator. Fuses were installed in the bombs at the time they were loaded on the aircraft. The bomb shackle that carried the bomb had three points, the end two held the bomb by releasable hooks and the third held the arming wire. The arming wire was a long wire that was inserted into the fuse. The arming wire was retained and simply pulled out of the fuse as the bomb dropped. A small propeller, called the arming vane, rotated to arm the fuse—the bomb was fully armed while in the air. Among many other targets, these bombs were inevitably always used to attack the numerous bridges built on the Burma–Thailand Railway.

Top logbook, with pasted-in news clippings:

**MINES LAID IN ENEMY WATERS**
KANDY, June 22.—Air Command fighters on offensive reconnaissance over the Sittang river damaged a large number of rivercraft, says today's SE Asia Command communiqué. Liberators laid mines in enemy waters.

| Date | Hour | Aircraft Type and No. | | Duty | | Remarks (including results of bombing, exercises, etc.) | Flying Times Day | Night |
|---|---|---|---|---|---|---|---|---|
| | | | | | | Time carried forward :— | 176.50 | 176.00 |
| 24.6.45 | 8.30 | EV.968 | W/O Brown | AIR BOMBER | | WAR OPERATIONS SIAM. MINELAYING IN BANGKOK RIVER. ATTACKED BY H.A.A AND L.A.A | 7.00 | 7.00 |
| 24.6.45 | 16.30 | EV.968 | W/O Brown | AIR BOMBER | | WAR OPERATIONS — SIAM ATTACKING ANTI-AIRCRAFT SITES WHILE MAIN FORCE ATTACK RAILWAY BRIDGES AT LOW LEVEL Pos 14° 01′ N 99° 32′ E KANCHANABURI BOTH BRIDGES DESTROYED. HEAVY ANTI-AIRCRAFT FIRE. | 12.00 | 3.00 |
| 27.6.45 | 09.00 | Kt. | W/O Brown | AIR BOMBER | | MEDIUM LEVEL BOMBING. 8 BOMBS | 1.35 | |
| 30.6.45 | 15.30 | Kt. 124 | W/O Brown | AIR BOMBER | | BASE TO JESSORE | 55 | |

**BURMA-SIAM RAILWAY BRIDGES DAMAGED**
KANDY, June 25.—Heavy bombers of Air Command in a low-level attack yesterday destroyed three spans of the main bridge at Kanchanaburi, on the Burma-Siam railway, 80 miles west of Bangkok, and made a large break in the centre of a by-pass bridge, says today's S.E. Asia Command communiqué. Anti-aircraft sites near by were bombed and engines and rolling-stock strafed. The approach to a bridge 70 miles south of Moulmein, on the railway to Yé, was damaged.

Sergeant Frank Holden's flying logbook entries for June 1945. Warrant Officer Brown flew his Liberator EV968 on the famous raid against the bridges over the River Kwai. Frank Holden was responsible for the accurate bombing of anti-aircraft emplacements protecting the bridges and Len Moore, in the front turret, shot up the emplacements on the approach for their bombing runs. The pasted-in news clippings show the importance of this particular operation, which took fourteen hours to complete. (*Frank Holden via Nicky Swann*)

| Date | Hour | Aircraft Type and No. | Pilot | Duty | Remarks (including results of bombing, gunnery, exercises, etc.) | Flying Times Day | Night |
|---|---|---|---|---|---|---|---|
| | | | | | Time carried forward :— | 501.25 | 129.55 |
| 6.6.45 | 12.00 | LIBERATOR "B" | F/O HAYCOCK | CO-PILOT | BASE - ALIPORE - BASE | 1.05 | |
| 7.6.45 | 09.00 | "D" | F/O HAYCOCK | ENG. | PRACTICE BOMBING | 2.00 | |
| 8.6.45 | 07.00 | "B" | F/O HAYCOCK | ENG. | OPS- BILIN - TROOP CONCENTRATIONS - HT. 2,000 FT - BOMB LOAD - 5,000 LBS | 10.15 | |
| 10.6.45 | 07.00 | "B" | F/O HAYCOCK | ENG. | OPS - KAMAMAUNG - TROOP CONCENTRATION HT. 1,700 FT - BOMB LOAD | 11.00 | |
| 13.6.45 | 05.45 | "B" | F/O HAYCOCK | ENG. | OPS- SHIPPING STRIKE- GULF OF SIAM - 1 CRUISER - 2 DESTROYERS AND MERCHANT VESSELS. | 15.10 | |
| 24.6.45 | 06.30 | "B" | F/O HAYCOCK | ENG. | OPS- KANCHANABURI- LOW LEVEL BRIDGE BUSTING - HT 500 FT- B.L. 5000 LBS DIRECT HIT- HEAVY A.A. | 13.25 | |
| 30.6.45 | 06.20 | "B" | F/O HAYCOCK | ENG. | OPS- BOXAGAYI - ARMY CO-OP- JAP TROOP CONCENTRATION - HT 1500 FT- B.L. 6000 LBS | 10.05 | |

Thomas Reynolds's flying logbook entries recording, among others, the legendary operation to finally destroy the bridge over the River Kwai. He records having attacked at just 500 feet above this well-defended target. Of note is the prior entry, showing the shipping strike that engaged them in the air for over fifteen hours. Liberator crews in the Far East undertook exceptionally gruelling and demanding operations.

*Above and below*: A sequence of images taken from a low-level Liberator attack upon two Japanese road bridges between Pegu and Martaban, Burma. The consistent bombing of the railway enforced additional road-building bypass routes, which were in turn targeted by Liberators of the Strategic Air Force, Eastern Air Command. These images, taken at exceptionally low level, show the bombs falling in the air and exploding on both the primary and secondary bridge. The wooden trestle construction is seen to have collapsed and debris is strewn about in the explosion, debris is then seen floating in the river. (*Thomas Reynolds*)

*Above*: The two white-painted bars on a black background on the rudder identify this Liberator to be from 215 Squadron. An example of the American Emerson nose gunner turret can be clearly seen, the undercarriage is locked down as this B-24 approaches the runway at Digri, India.

*Below*: The unusual main gear landing wheel assembly can be seen on this 99 Squadron Liberator at Dhubalia, India. The assembly, when retracted, folds towards the body of the aircraft and upwards to rest in the wing. Warrant Officer Biccard from the Royal Australian Air Force is checking his revolver in preparation for the operation to bomb Mandalay on 13 January 1945. Returning from that raid, the undercarriage would not lower; fortunately, they had sufficient fuel to circle the airfield while the crew undertook the protracted process of winding down the undercarriage by hand. The nose wheel, however, defied all efforts to lower. The pilot Biccard placed all the crew at the rear of the Liberator in order to counter balance the Liberator in the landing. The aircraft came down safely with no injuries to the crew and minimal damage to the lower nose section, which eventually made contact with the runway. Seven days following this incident, Biccard and his entire crew were killed in an aerial collision with another Liberator during the preparations to bomb Ramree. (*Australian War Memorial*)

*Above*: Warrant Officer Biccard's ball gunner, Flight Sergeant Greeves, Royal Australian Air Force, completing checks to his claustrophobically small turret before embarking on the raid to Mandalay, 13 January 1945. Once airborne, the gunner had to slide into the turret feet first, past the Sperry gun sight, and sit in a curved position within the ball. His feet were apart so they would go into the stirrup arrangements on each side of the window built into the bottom of the sphere. Insufficient room was available for the gunner to wear his parachute and it was a complicated procedure to extract him in any emergency. Flight Sergeant Greeves had been within his ball turret when his aircraft collided with Liberator KG974. The entire crew was buried in a collective grave in the Maynamati War Cemetery. (*Australian War Memorial*)

*Below*: No. 159 Squadron bombing section intelligence room where bomb aimers and other crew were able to study target recognition. Japanese shipping features on the far wall, while the important railway targets can be seen to the left. Rail track plans and photographs were updated regularly, while general awareness of anti-aircraft guns is demonstrated in posters. A rare example photographed by Sergeant Holden. (*Frank Holden via Nicky Swann*)

*Above left*: Air Ministry photograph, dated April 1945, of Liberator bombers attacking bridges on the Burma railway. This photograph illustrates the accuracy with which these heavy bombers carry out their assignments. At a height of 500 feet, bombs burst on and near the railway bridge built near Kalawthut, south of Moulmein on the Moulmein–Bangkok Railway. Significant embankment works can be seen, as well as Japanese trenches and defensive gun emplacements around this target.

*Above right*: The terminus of the railway to Mandalay on the lower Chindwin was situated at the Burmese township of Yeu, 22 miles north-west of Schwebo. The River Mu flows into the Irrawaddy at this location. This Air Ministry photograph, taken in January 1945, reveals the damage done by Liberator bombers that had destroyed the relatively substantial bridge across the river.

*Below*: No. 159 Squadron bomb aimers, with Sergeant Holden behind the desk (third from the right). On the wall are posters displaying bomb aiming diagrams detailing the Liberators Mk XIV bomb Sight and autogyro. Bomb aimers were able to control the aircraft selecting adjustments in flight. Directional stabilisers held the sight on its target during these adjustments. Sergeant Holden was a very skilful bomb aimer, having been awarded the prize of hitting the Pickle Barrel during bombing competitions by Wing Commander Ercolani. (*Frank Holden via Nicky Swann*)

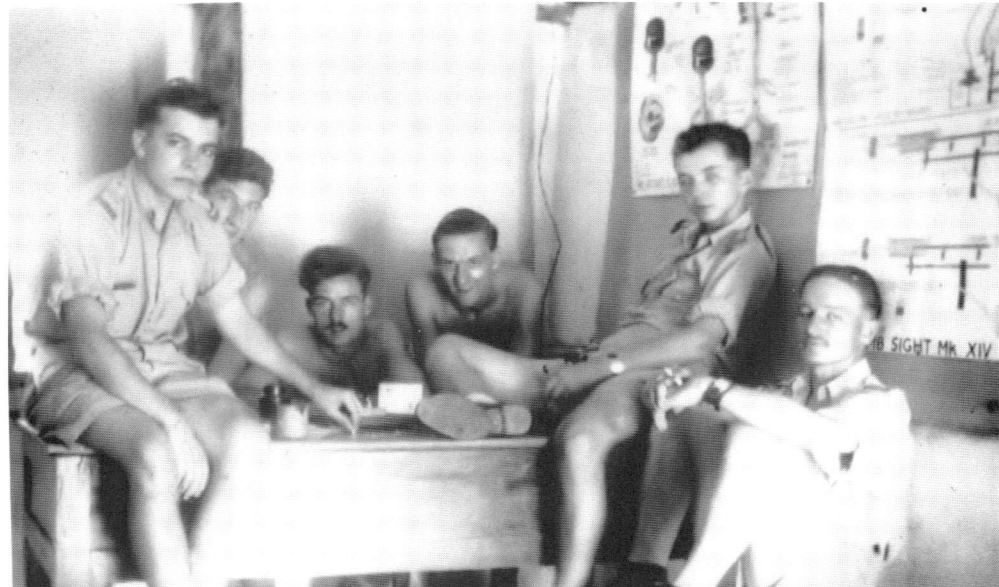

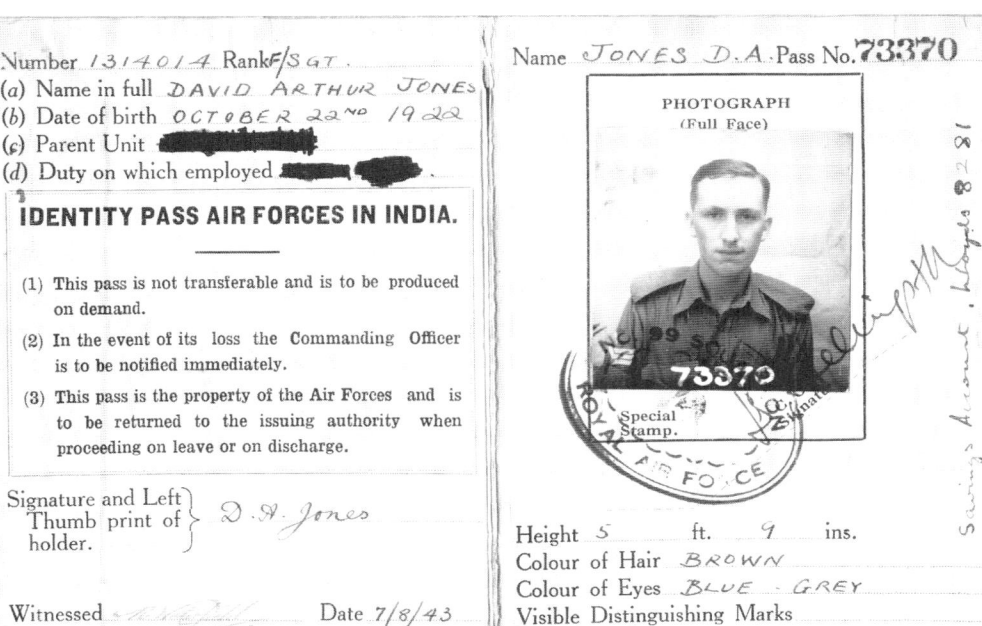

Number *1314014* Rank *F/Sgt.*

(a) Name in full *DAVID ARTHUR JONES*

(b) Date of birth *OCTOBER 22ND 1922*

(c) Parent Unit ██████████

(d) Duty on which employed ██████ .

## IDENTITY PASS AIR FORCES IN INDIA.

(1) This pass is not transferable and is to be produced on demand.

(2) In the event of its loss the Commanding Officer is to be notified immediately.

(3) This pass is the property of the Air Forces and is to be returned to the issuing authority when proceeding on leave or on discharge.

Signature and Left Thumb print of holder. } *D. A. Jones*

Witnessed *[signature]* Date *7/8/43*

MGIPC—82—720(RAF)MFP(PD)—(3386/E/C-201)—13 8-42—60,000.

Name *JONES D.A.* Pass No. **73370**

PHOTOGRAPH
(Full Face)

Special Stamp.

Height *5* ft. *9* ins.

Colour of Hair *BROWN*

Colour of Eyes *BLUE - GREY*

Visible Distinguishing Marks

AIR FORCE (I.) FORM 557-A.

Sergeant David Jones's Air Forces in India identity pass stamped 99 Squadron and dated 7 August 1943. He was promoted to Flight Sergeant in November 1943, Pilot Officer in May 1944, and finally to Flying Officer in February 1945. (*David Jones*)

Photograph capturing the results of a successful bombing run on the Burma–Thailand Railway. The lower bridge and high embankment illustrate the enormous work undertaken to build this railway section, which was cut through the Burma jungle. Two bridges are present, the foremost being a large construction that crosses a relatively small waterway within a gully or pass. Photo interpretation would establish the dimensions accurately from the shadow detail, however, this image tends to indicate that the lower bridge is devoid of railway track.

*Above left*: Bombing the main railway line of the Burma–Thailand Railway, 8 March 1945. The tracks ran through the dense jungle, with a large side cutting constructed to facilitate train movement or simply built to navigate past devastation caused by previous attacks. In keeping with the vast majority of bombing operations, the crew dropped thousands of propaganda leaflets at designated points on their flight plans. This 159 Squadron photograph was taken from the Liberator flown by Flight Lieutenant Gee. (*Air Ministry*)

*Above right*: No. 159 Squadron 'nose art' painted upon an unidentified Liberator at Digri. It is known that Canadian members of the Squadron were very adept at creating these impressive artworks. This one was entitled *Rita*. Instantly recognisable as Rita Hayworth, this image appears to be an excellent representation taken from the 1941 iconic *Life* magazine photo, in which she posed in a negligee with a black lace bodice. (*Frank Holden via Nicky Swann*)

*Below*: Liberator 'Q' *Queenie* photographed at Digri with the tarpaulins stretched across the cockpit and front turret. Fixing points are provided for these covers, which were used to block the sun beating into the aircraft. The impressively large artwork also illustrates that this aircraft had completed thirty-one operations from India. The bomb bay doors are clearly seen in this image, as are the access ladders positioned leading into the nose wheel compartment. This was one of the main crew entry points for the Liberator. (*Frank Holden via Nicky Swann*)

*Above left*: Flying Officer Haycock and his crew engaged in the operation to bomb the Japanese supply dump and railway facility at Amarapura, near Mandalay, on 26 January 1945. The bombing was highly successful, this image illustrating the Liberators leaving the area. In the distance, the important bridge that spanned the Irrawaddy River has been demolished and plumes of smoke continue to rise upwards from the target area. (*Air Ministry*)

*Above right*: More than eighty B-24 Liberators took part in a mission to bomb comprehensive railway sidings at Na Nien, south of Chumphon, Thailand. The target was attacked at very low altitude and the crews reported seeing prisoners of war waving at them during their bombing runs. The sidings were destroyed, trains set on fire, and a large oil fire belched black smoke. This image, taken from the waist position using a handheld camera, illustrates the aircraft leaving the target. (*Air Ministry*)

*Below*: Thomas Reynolds's flying logbook recorded a remarkable daylight sortie on 13 December 1944. This was his third long trek into Thailand, but it was to specifically attack the railway line and the first precise bridge busting target at a location called Hninpale. The sortie commenced at 7.40 a.m. and they would not return until after 5 p.m. Johnny Haycock reached an altitude of approximately 2,500 feet in Liberator EW255, when a Japanese Oscar fighter attacked their Liberator. One of the waist gunners' positions was manned by Thomas Reynolds, who managed to shoot down the attacking fighter, writing these events in his logbook.

| | | | | | | Flying Times | |
|---|---|---|---|---|---|---|---|
| | Hour | Aircraft Type and No. | Pilot | Duty | Remarks (including results of bombing, gunnery, exercises, etc.) | Day | Night |
| | | | | | Time carried forward :— | 196·55 | 82·15 |
| 44 | 10.05 | LIBERATOR "R" | P/O HAYCOCK | W/OP | OPS. — PRANG KZIA — LOCOMOTIVE BOMBING AND STRAFING. — B. LOAD 3000 LBS. | 8·30 | 4·30 |
| 44 | 07.40 | "M" | P/O HAYCOCK | W/OP | OPS. — HNINPALE RLY. BRIDGE — ONE ENEMY A/C — OSCAR — DESTROYED. — HEIGHT 100FT. BOMB LOAD 6000 LBS. | 9·25 | |
| 44 | 07.50 | "M" | P/O HAYCOCK | W/OP | GLAXO OPERATION BASE — BOMBAY. | 10·40 | 3·20 |
| 44 | 05.58 | "M" | P/O HAYCOCK | W/OP | OPS. — TAUNGUP — SUPPLY DUMPS HEIGHT 6,500 FT. BOMB LOAD 8,000LBS | 6·30 | 0·30 |
| 44 | 13.00 | "T" | F/O HAYCOCK | W/OP | H.L.B + L.L.B. SIM. ATTACK L.L.B. RAILWAY BRIDGE | 2·20 | |
| 44 | 10.30 | "V" | F/O HAYCOCK | W/OP | AIR TEST | 2·05 | |
| 44 | 09.00 | "T" | F/O HAYCOCK | W/OP | L.L.B. SIM. ATTACK RLY. BRIDGE | 2·20 | |

*Above*: An aerial reconnaissance image of two unidentified Japanese bridges both destroyed by bombing. The wooden road bridge was built as a result of the more substantial metal and concrete built having been demolished. The steel and wooden span has been moved a considerable distance from its concrete-pillar foundation, while another rests on the far river bank. The river bed is severely cratered, with numerous explosions showing the concerted efforts to destroy both bridges. (*David Jones*)

*Below*: An aerial photograph dated 15 March 1945. The 159 Squadron Liberators wing tip is visible as the aircraft flown by Flight Lieutenant Busbridge banks around a high ridge to observe an apparent Japanese defensive position. The target that day had been bridge 147 on the Burma–Thailand Railway. The terrain below was thick jungle and deep gullies, a formidable environment to survive within for any crew who should be forced to escape from any ill-fated Liberator. (*Air Ministry*)

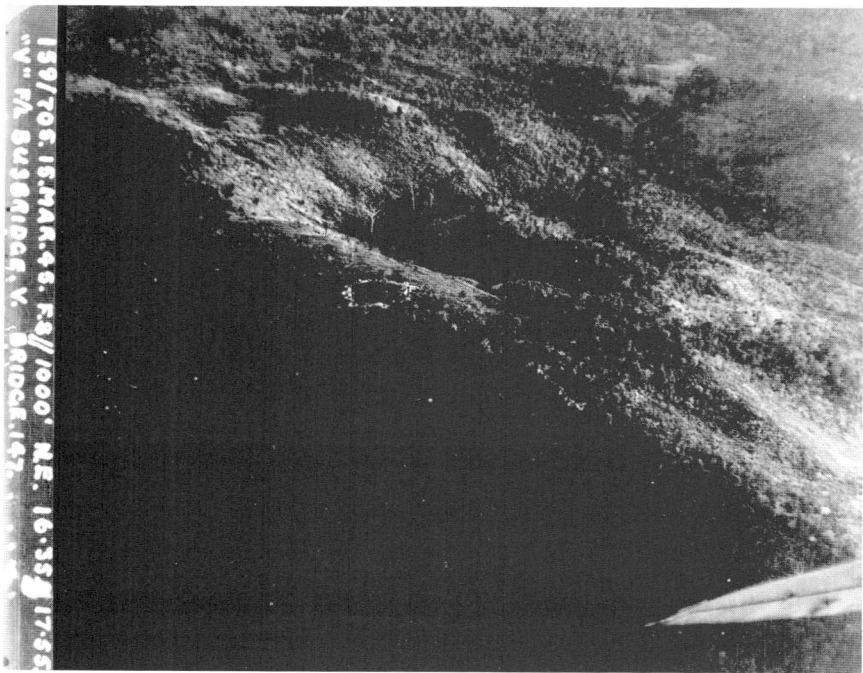

*Above*: The Japanese railway infrastructure frequently provided targets of opportunity for Allied aircraft to attack. Liberator bombers often sighted rail movements during their transit flights to and from targets. Flying the heavy bomber low and offensively, the crews attacked any target at every opportunity. This attack on a locomotive carrying open bed trucks and enclosed carriages is sited on a section of railway facilitated with passing tracks. This image represents a classic example of the terror imposed by the aerial firepower that was used to destroy railway transportation within Burma.

*Below*: Squadron Leader Gauntlett's aerial image of cutting MS41 on the Burma–Thailand Railway, the new main cutting crosses the road while a damaged track runs below. Both track and rail sleepers appear to have been purloined from the lower rail line. On 15 February 1945, this target was completely obliterated by a force of sixteen 159 Squadron Liberators. (*Air Ministry*)

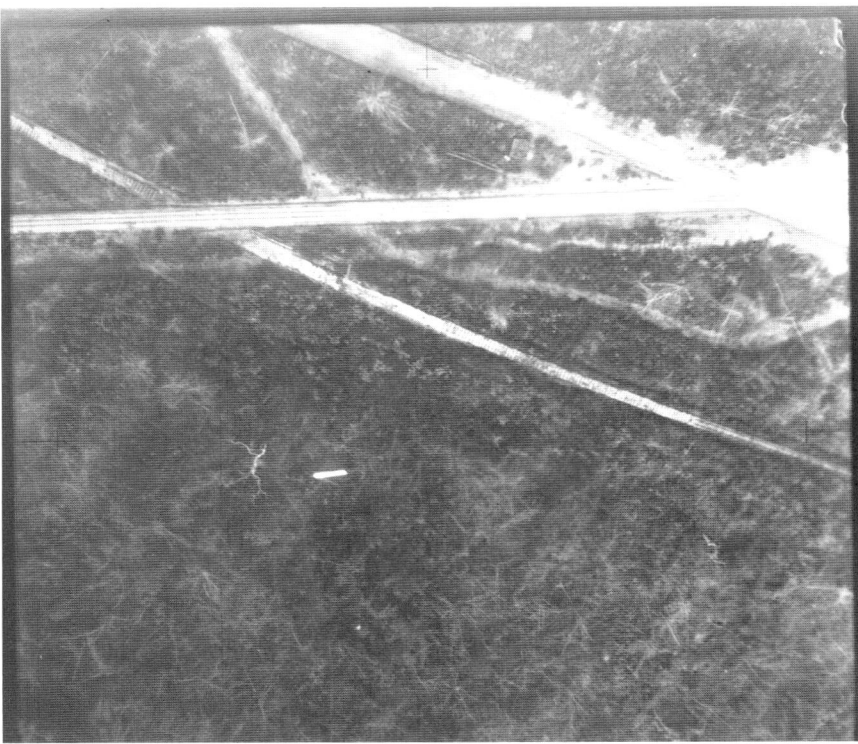

Air Ministry photograph from a low-flying B-24 Liberator illustrating a typical enemy held waterway that was targeted to receive precisely dropped aerial sea mines. No. 159 Squadron in particular became renowned for its capabilities in these hazardous duties and confirmed reports rewarded their achievements in successfully destroying Japanese shipping.

Sergeant Frank Holden and his crew frequently operated in Liberator 'V' KH366. This image illustrates the unusual undercarriage mechanism that folded into the wing void and allowed a view of the waist gunners' position in the fuselage. The crew are identified as Len (WO Len Moore, front gunner) Roy, Jock, Les, and Stan. (*Frank Holden via Nicky Swann*)

Squadron Leader Robin Williams standing centre with his crew, who had attacked the bridge on the River Kwai, 24 June 1945. This 159 Squadron crew stand in front of their B-24J Liberator, which has an Emerson nose turret fitted. Of note is the large bulged side window, which was a greatly appreciated modification for the navigators who gained much improved visibility and natural light.

The bombing of the bridge at Kanchanaburi, 24 June 1945.
(*Colin Clinton Flight Engineer 159 Squadron*)

Another image of the bombing of the bridge at Kanchanaburi, 24 June 1945. (*Colin Clinton Flight Engineer 159 Squadron*)

No. 356 Squadron B-24 Liberator being made ready for a deep penetration raid against the Japanese railway infrastructure in Burma.

During the previous year, the Royal Air Force, together with the Americans, had laid a total of 1,149 mines in the Far East. In 1945, the more sophisticated Mk VII mine was used in preference to other mines, and each of the Liberators engaged in the aforementioned operation were carrying these mines—all of which were set to operate over a sixteen-week period. Additionally, they carried the American M13/5 mines, which were set to operate over a thirty-six-day period. The vast majority of mines deployed in the Far East were operated by magnetic detonation and it is estimated that the Royal Air Force alone dropped 4,374 mines during their operations in the Far East.

Allied intelligence indicated that the Japanese were gathering supplies and constructing fortifications for a defensive stand at Nakhon Nayok, north-east of Bangkok. During June, it became known that the Japanese had moved officer-rank prisoners of war from the large Kanchanaburi camp, which supplied labour for the bridge on the River Kwai, to Nakhon Nayok. This was in itself not unusual as the Japanese sought to move significant numbers of Allied prisoners of war during their retreat from Burma. At one time, conjecture existed that the movement of Allied prisoners was likely to indicate the use of these men as a physical defensive measure towards their mainland. The journey for these men was arduous as the train journeys were broken up between smashed bridges. At the Naromchase Bridge, which crossed a moderately sized river, three central spans had been destroyed by the Royal Air Force. These had been replaced by a very flimsy bamboo construction. The prisoners from the train were forced to cross this swaying construction on foot and await a further transportation link towards Bangkok. All of these transits were fraught with danger from aerial attack, in particular the free-ranging British Beaufighters, who eagerly swooped on all forms of enemy transportation.

On 10 July 1945, 159 Squadron briefed ten B-24 Liberator crews to fly from Digri to Bangkok in order to destroy the railway workshops and warehouses adjacent to the main railway terminus. Two aircraft were to drop sea mines in the Bangkok River, and Johnny Haycock was to fly as the deputy pathfinder. Among their bombload were four yellow target indicators, which were to be dropped upon Squadron Leader Stroud's direction. All ten aircraft departed shortly before 6 a.m. on what was likely to be a long operation of up to fifteen hours. Bangkok continued to be a heavily defended location, with radar predicting heavy anti-aircraft guns. Poor weather conditions forced one of the minelaying Liberators to return to Digri, however, the other aircraft managed to clear the heavy weather and, on reaching Bangkok, the conditions improved greatly. Heavy anti-aircraft fire was of some concern to all of the bombers. Two Liberators sustained damage, although none of the crew were injured. Thomas Reynolds, in Johnny Haycock's aircraft, was well aware that they were over the target for longer periods of time than the bombing force. He kept a constant lookout for any signs of broken fuel or oil lines, items that could easily be severed by small fragments of flak. The Canadian pilot Flight Lieutenant Marcou, flying in the Mk VIII Liberator KL662, had the misfortune to have his number four engine struck by flak while over

Bangkok. It was a long haul back to India on just three engines, with the additional worry that the new Stromberg carburettors fitted on the new Liberator were likely to consume much more fuel than the old type of Ceco carburettor. No. 355 Squadron also supplied eight Liberators on this operation, six of the aircraft added to the bombing of the yellow target-marking pathfinders, while two diverted, most probably due to weather conditions, and used their bombloads upon the secondary target of the bridge at Rajburi, a target previously visited by 159 Squadron. Flight Lieutenant Marcou eventually returned to base with his flight engineer nursing the remaining three engines, the crew thankful that the Japanese Air Force no longer offered any threat to limping Liberators. It was quite possible that Marcou's Liberator had suffered other undetected damage as it crashed down upon the runway when it landed at 7.55 p.m. Three members of the crew suffered superficial injuries, an incident that marked the first significant operational accident of 1945. That particular B-24 was completely written-off and became a source of parts for the maintenance units.

The four men focused upon in this account are Wing Commander Ercolani, Flying Officer Haycock, Flying Officer Jones, and Warrant Officer Reynolds, who all completed their operational flying tours with 159 Squadron in July 1945. Their flying logbooks would see no further bridge busting or general bombing sorties entered. They would, however, remain on strength in the Squadron and engage on various other duties, some of which were of a general flying nature. The announcement that the Burma Star Medal had been inaugurated and that they would be entitled to the medal provided great satisfaction to them. However, for the men serving in India and Ceylon, the burden of overseas service and commitment was not to be recognised. They were in receipt of notification that they would not be entitled to the Burma Star—they would only be entitled to the award of the Defence Medal. (An explanation to the basic award of medals is explained in Appendix VII.)

Between May and September 1945, the realigned tours of duty for men having completed their operational flying duties in the Far East saw over 2,000 airmen and over 500 officers released from command. During that same period, over 2,000 officers and 12,000 airmen were repatriated, many originating from Canada and Australia. The men repatriated to the United Kingdom returned home to a country that was embarking on a general election of government and those men still serving in the Far East were to receive postal votes. Over 30,000 completed postal votes were eventually returned from Air Command South East Asia.

In Germany, at what became known as the Potsdam Conference conducted on 17 July to 2 August 1945, the results of the general election would become known; therefore, the opposition leader Clement Attlee accompanied Winston Churchill to that conference. The terms of Japan's surrender were agreed between the President of the United States of America, the Soviet leader Joseph Stalin, and Winston Churchill. However, Attlee became the British prime minister on 26 July and Churchill returned to England midway through the conference after what must have been a huge disappointment at his defeat in the British general election. The newly appointed

Labour Prime Minister Clement Attlee saw the conference through on behalf of Britain. Among many matters discussed, the decision was made to hold war trials and the Council of Foreign Ministers were tasked with drawing up peace treaties. The conference agreed on the terms of surrender for Japan, to be managed by a council of foreign ministers in charge of peace settlements. The Japanese government were called on to proclaim unconditional surrender and President Truman received word of the successful atomic bomb test soon after he had arrived at Potsdam, he confided in Churchill, but mentioned 'a new weapon' only casually to Stalin.

Despite all this, the war against the Japanese continued in the ferocity that was associated with the Far East conflict and no sign existed that the Japanese were entertaining any kind of surrender. The Allied Air Forces, in anticipation of victory, had already begun to drop propaganda leaflets on Japanese forces and one type in particular was dropped on their soldiers who were trapped in the Pegu Yomas of Southern Burma. These leaflets not only called upon the enemy to surrender after telling them of the hopeless position of their homeland, but, on the reverse side, offered them a safe conduct through the Allied lines with the added assurance that they would be given food, medical attention, and honourable treatment. The Japanese Twenty-Eighth Army was ordered to break out of the Pegu Yomas and the Japanese Thirty-Third Army was ordered to make a diversionary attack across the Sittang River, which they did on 3 July. However, they had attacked too early—the Twenty-Eighth Army was not planned to move until 17 July. When they did, they were ambushed by concentrations of British artillery that had been placed along the predicted route. Hundreds of Japanese drowned trying to cross the swollen Sittang on improvised bamboo floats and rafts. Burmese guerrillas and bandits killed huge numbers of stragglers east of the river. The breakout cost the Japanese nearly 10,000 men, half the strength of their Twenty-Eighth Army.

The Liberator Squadrons were tasked with yet more significant bridge busting operations and 159 and 355 Squadrons in particular were detailed to bomb bridges on the Banpong–Singapore Railway on 27 July 1945. Squadron Leader Stroud would lead 159 Squadron's eight new Mk VIII Liberators, which were armed with the lighter 500-lb general-purpose bombs. The armourers had received orders to load the Liberators with these lighter bombs as decisions had been made that they were sufficient to destroy the bridges TF44 and TF28 on that particular railway. Unopposed, the aircraft carried out a classic low-level attack on the bridges and at 500 feet, the bombs were released with accustomed accuracy, but they lacked the demolition power to cause sufficient damage. The bridges remained operable and could only be classified as superficially damaged. The six 355 Squadron Liberators, however, attacked their target bridge and damaged the buttress supports and destroyed the eastern bridge spans. Additionally, buildings on the eastern end of the bridge were destroyed and the crew's air gunners were provided the opportunity to shoot up the Bhojpuri marshalling yards with no opposition. It had been a most gratifying sortie for 355 Squadron, but for 159 Squadron there was a great disappointed with the new Mk VIII B-24, which had not brought with it greater efficiency. Two days later, those thoughts were compounded by the ground crews having to deal with the failure of four aircraft not being able to gather sufficient power from the engines to lift off with a standard bombload. This proved to be a problem associated with the carburettors. Any crew faced with the thoughts of a take-off procedure being aborted late, while hauling a full bombload down the runway, was highly likely to be seriously worried and no doubt brought forth serious concern over their safety. The three 159 Squadron crews that did manage to get aloft carried five dependable 1,000-lb bombs and flew to attack the railways in Bangkok. In company with 355 Squadron, they found the anti-aircraft defences were just as effective as ever over that target. One overshot bomb was acknowledged to have struck the hospital, where an anti-aircraft gun emplacement had been established by the Japanese gunners. The five Liberators from 355 Squadron all struck at the eastern end of the joint target, Bangkok's number one marshalling yard. They dropped their bombs accurately, destroying not only rail tracks, but also a large locomotive. No. 355 Squadron's aircraft successfully returned to their station at Salbani in India. Unbeknown to them, this had been the penultimate operation for 355 Squadron in the Second World War.

The Supreme Commander Allied Forces South East Asia Command, Lord Louis Mountbatten was leading the planning of the recapture of Malaya, Singapore, and the territories generically termed East Indies. The plan was ambitious and engaged glider assaults, with the Army advancing overland from the north. The operation was codenamed 'Zipper' and the heavy bombers were required to support the Army advance by destroying strategic targets as they had done during the push through Burma. Approximately 1,000 miles from Singapore lay the Cocos and Keeling Islands. These islands were administered as a British Colony of Singapore. The largest island, known as Browns West Island, had an airstrip constructed of pierced steel sheeting. The runway was long enough for B-24 bombers to safely take-off and land upon, and it would become a key location in which Operation Zipper support would operate from. No. 231 Group and 159 Squadron were to be based on the island, which became simply known as 'The Cocos'. The Commanding Officer of the island was Major-General J. T. Durrant, an officer of the South African Air Force. In 1944, he had been seconded to the Royal Air Force and, in 1945, he was posted to the Far East as Officer Commanding 231 Heavy Bomber Group, with the rank of Major-General.

On 3 August 1945, Major-General Durrant was in Dum Dum, India, and sought passage to the Cocos Islands. Wing Commander Ercolani received instructions to fly his Liberator KL660 to Dum Dum and transfer the Major-General to the airfield at Kankesanthurai. This was situated on the northern tip of Ceylon, now known as Sri Lanka, and thence onto the remote islands in the Indian Ocean. On 5 August, David Jones navigated a route from Ceylon, southwards over endless miles of sea, to the rather oddly shaped Cocos Islands to land on what appeared to be bare beach; the landing ground had been hewn from the palm tree-covered idyllic island. From the air, the breaking waters on the coral reef were a beautiful sight, but landing on the pierced steel matting would inevitably be rather noisy and very sandy when compared to other conventional landing grounds. They touched down safely after ten hours and twenty minutes of flying. The island had only recently received the Liberator-equipped Squadrons 356, 99, and the Dutch 321, all of whom eagerly awaited the impending operations to retake, including the significantly historical British territory of Singapore. Wing Commander Ercolani must have immediately felt very much at home on the remote Island as both 99 and 356 Squadron had only recently departed from Digri. Remarkably, those men were now operating from an island no more than 1,000 miles distant from Perth, Australia. Two days previously, three 99 Squadron crews had participated in the first operation from the Cocos, engaging in ship hunting, receiving the accolade of having participated in the Squadron's first operation in the South West Pacific theatre. On 7 August, four Liberators of 99 Squadron engaged on an attack against the Japanese airfield at Bencoolen (also described as Bengkulu) in Sumatra.

Despite being operationally tour-expired, David Jones would have experienced the trepidation of seeing several of his friends embarking on operational flying to Malay and further afield into mainland Japanese territories. Neither he nor the Wing Commander would be taking part in those operations. At 6.14 a.m. on 7 August 1945, Wing Commander Ercolani took off from the island and David Jones set the course to return to Ratmalana in Ceylon. That sortie would then be followed by a short trip to Kankesanthurai and thence to Digri, entailing some twenty hours of flying.

At around the same time in India, on the morning of 7 August 1945, ten 159 Squadron crews were receiving a final briefing and instructions to undertake a bridge busting operation. The Mk VIII Liberators were required to strike attacks on two bridges on the main Singapore railway line, bridges TF30 and TF69. The Canadian pilots Flying Officer Williams, Flight Lieutenant Marcou, and Squadron Leader Stroud, accompanied by Flying Officers Clarke and Dowding, were allocated the target TF30. Flight Lieutenant Mitchell, Flying Officer Myles, and Flight Lieutenants Atkins, Ellis, and Owens were allocated bridge TF69. Unusually, each B-24 had been armed with a range of bombs—one 250-lb bomb, two 500-lb bombs, and two 1,000-lb bombs. If the weather was bad over the target, the Liberators were permitted to seek out any target associated to the railway. The attacking Liberators reached the bridges at around midday and, having anticipated that the cloud base would be acceptably high, both bridges were found to be in good visibility with no enemy opposition encountered. At bridge TF69, rolling stock was seen to be in close proximity and the attack saw some first-class bombing. The bridge was completely destroyed and rolling stock was left having been set afire by the air gunners strafing. At bridge TF30, the bombing caused serious damage, with foundations disrupted and the bridge thrown out of alignment. The bombing also targeted the railroad lines and its bypass facility with impressive results. This was the outcome of efficiently trained air crews, who had developed techniques specifically designed to destroy the plethora of railway bridges utilised by the Japanese military forces in its occupied territories. The photographic images taken by each crew would be developed and printed to be pinned up on the intelligence briefing boards for all the station personnel to see. Unbeknown to all, the final bridge busting operation undertaken for Wing Commander Ercolani's squadron had taken place.

The first atomic bomb was dropped on the centre of Hiroshima at 8.15 a.m. the preceding day. The bomb had an explosive yield of around 13 kilotons. At the moment of detonation, the weapon created a fireball that generated temperatures to some 4,000 degrees Celsius. President Harry S. Truman announced the news, stating that the device was more than 2,000 times more powerful than the largest bomb ever used in the war. He also announced that the Potsdam Declaration issued ten days prior, which called for the unconditional surrender of Japan, had been the last chance for the country to avoid utter destruction.

News of the bomb was published in *The Daily Telegraph* newspaper, 7 August 1945:

The Allies have made the greatest discovery in history, the way to use atomic energy. The first atomic bomb has been dropped on Japan. It had over 2,000 times the blast power of the largest bomb ever used before, which was the British 'Grand Slam', weighing about 11 tons; and more power than 20,000 tons of TNT. Yet the explosive charge is officially described as 'exceedingly small'. A spokesman at the Ministry of Aircraft Production said last night that the bomb was one-tenth the size of a 'block buster', yet its effect would be 'like that of a severe earthquake'.

The first atomic bomb, a single one, was dropped on Hiroshima, a town of 12 square miles, on the Japanese main island of Honshu. Tokyo radio said that the raid was at 8.20 a.m. yesterday, Japanese time, and that the extent of the damage was being investigated.

The official announcement yesterday of the existence of the bomb was made sixteen hours after its first use. Late last night no report had been made on the damage done because it had been impossible to see the result through impenetrable clouds of dust and smoke.

Statements were yesterday issued by Mr Churchill from Downing Street, by Mr Truman from the White House, by Mr Stimson the United States Secretary of War, giving an account of the research which led to the development of the new weapon; of the terrible fate awaiting Japan if she does not immediately yield; of the future use of atomic energy as a source of power and an instrument for keeping the world's peace.

In the Downing Street statement, Churchill was quoted as saying:

By God's mercy, British and American science outpaced all German efforts. The possession of these powers by Germans at any time might have altered the result of the war and profound anxiety was felt by those who were informed.

Mr Stimson said the bomb would prove a tremendous aid in shortening the war against Japan. It had an explosive power that 'staggered the imagination'.

President Truman described the results as the greatest achievement of organised science in history. The Allies had spent the sum of $500,000,000 on the 'greatest scientific gamble in history', and had won. If the Japanese did not now accept the Allies terms, he said, they might expect a rain of ruin from the air the like of which had never been seen on this earth.

The method of production would be kept secret, while processes were being worked out to protect the world from the danger of sudden destruction. Congress would be asked to investigate how atomic power might be used to maintain the future peace. British, American, and Canadian scientists collaborated in developing this tremendous new source of power. Mr Stimson also disclosed that Dr Niels Bohr, the Danish Nobel Prize winner, had been whisked from the grasp of the Nazis and had helped in the bomb's development. By agreement between Churchill and Roosevelt, research was carried out in the United States and in Canada, safe from enemy attacks.

The British Prime Minister Clement Attlee, who was still fresh from having overturned and replaced Winston Churchill, read out a statement prepared by his predecessor to the House of Commons. It echoed his previous statement that the atomic project had such great potential that the government felt it was right to pursue the research and to pool information with atomic scientists in the United States:

By God's mercy, Britain and American science outpaced all German efforts. These were on a considerable scale, but far behind. The possession of these powers by the Germans at any time might have altered the result of the war.

Churchill's statement said considerable efforts had been made to disrupt German progress, including attacks on plants that were making constituent parts of the bomb. He ended:

We must indeed pray that these awful agencies will be made to conduce peace among the nations and that instead of wreaking measureless havoc upon the entire globe they become a perennial fountain of world prosperity.

Three days later, on the morning of 9 August, the Allied forces were still engaged in fighting a resolute and tenacious Japanese Army. Moreover, no recognition of the call to surrender had been received from Japan. Consequently, a second United States B-29 bomber took off from the airbase at Tinian Island in the Pacific Ocean; this aircraft carried a second nuclear bomb. The bomb was of a differing design and utilised plutonium as opposed to the uranium deployed in the previous bomb. The device was designed to detonate at an altitude of approximately 1,800 feet and had an estimated yield of 21 kilotons. With instructions to drop the bomb only on a confirmed visual sighting at the primary target of Kokura Japan, the adverse weather prevented the operation from having a successful outcome. The crew therefore headed for its secondary target, Nagasaki, where at 11.02 a.m. the world's second offensively deployed atomic bomb was dropped and detonated as desired.

Two days later, David Jones wrote the following letter to his parents:

Dear Mum and Dad,

Once again I am behind with my letter writing. This time it is due to having been away on a job for two weeks.

I have been feeling fine myself during the last two weeks. No doubt the change has helped a lot. There has been no reoccurrence of those pains. The doctor said it was bladder trouble, but it couldn't have been serious.

None of the tobacco has reached me yet, but I did get five hundred Senior Service cigarettes a while back. I believe I thanked you for those in my last letter. Did I tell you that there are two parcels on the way to you containing among other things honey and butter. Two navigation books i.e. *Hughes' Tables* and Brown's *Air Navigation* have arrived, also those traverse tables, but not the last one.

Until a week ago, my overseas tour was definitely still a full four years. Now that the Japanese have sued for peace I don't know for certain what will be decided on, but I guess it will still be four years. Even if the Japanese in Japan pack in it is not certain that those in Java and Sumatra, etc., will, and in that case our war is still on. And if they do, there will still be plenty of work to be done here, as in Europe, so do not expect me home yet. The feeling here is of suppressed hope and a lot of uncertainty as to the future.

Just now it is raining cats and dogs outside as we are in the middle of one of our famous thunder storms. Water is dripping from the roof near my bed in large quantities. I have just finished one letter to you and as I do not want to get wet on the way to dinner I am starting on another to pass away the time.

I was writing about the Japanese request for surrender terms. We first heard about it over the radio last evening. It makes the third big headline in three days. First the atomic bomb, the thought of which frightens me, second the Russian declaration of war, which is most gratifying, and then this which I view with mingled hope, suspicion, and concern, because I may soon be out of a job. The general feeling was of course a very jubilant one. Most people as is common on happy occasions in the mess began to imbibe large quantities of liquor. This process continued late into last night and disgusting drunken scenes were numerous…. I don't feel like making merry about it. My inclination is to sigh with relief and relax, but I don't think there is justification for that just yet.

The Allies may turn down the offer and destroy the Japs completely with this atomic bomb. That thing by the way makes me feel that our effort is ridiculously small. On the other hand the Japs in this area, being fairly strong, may continue to resist and we would then have to continue with our puny efforts. But I am hoping things will not turn out that way…

The two atomic bombs, combined with the Soviet declaration of war against Japan on 8 August 1945, left the Japanese no choice. Japan finally accepted the previously requested unconditional surrendered to the Allies on 14 August 1945.

At noon on 15 August 1945, Emperor Hirohito of Japan accepted the Potsdam Declaration of an unconditional surrender. The Japanese Federal Communications Commission had recorded the Emperor's words, which was broadcasted to his people and later published in the *Nippon Times*. The formal radio address announcing the Emperor's words was effectively the surrender of Japan. It was the first time that ordinary Japanese people had ever heard their Emperor's voice. He used precise and intricate formal language, which would have been unfamiliar to most of his subjects. Not only did this speech signify the end of the Second World War, it meant the end of the Emperor's status as a deity or god to the Japanese people.

The Emperor's words translated into English:

To our good and loyal subjects. After pondering deeply on the general trend of the world and the actual conditions pertaining to our Empire today, we have decided to effect a settlement of the present situation by resorting to an extraordinary measure. We have ordered our government to inform the government of the United States, Britain, China, and the Soviet Union that our Empire accepts the provisions of their joint declaration [the Potsdam Declaration]. To strive for the common prosperity and happiness of all nations, as well as for the security and well-being of our subjects, is the solemn obligation which has been handed down by our imperial ancestors and which lies close to our heart. Indeed, we declared war on America and Britain out of our sincere desire to ensure Japan's self-preservation and the stabilisation of East Asia, it being far from our thought either to infringe upon the sovereignty of other nations or to embark upon territorial aggrandisement. But now the war has lasted for nearly four years. Although the best has been done by everyone, the gallant fighting of the military and naval forces, the diligence and assiduity of our servants of the state, and the devoted service of our hundred million people the war situation has developed not necessarily to Japan's advantage, while the general trends of the world have all turned against her interests.

The enemy, moreover, has begun to employ a new most cruel bomb, the power which to do damage is indeed incalculable, taking toll of many innocent lives. Should we continue to fight, it would only result in the ultimate collapse and obliteration of the Japanese nation ... but would lead also to the total extinction of human civilisation. Such being the case, how are we to save millions of our subjects, or ourselves, to atone before the hallowed spirits of our imperial ancestors? This is the reason we have ordered the acceptance of the provisions of the joint declaration of the Powers.

We cannot but express the deepest sense of regret to our allied nations of East Asia, who have consistently cooperated with the Empire toward the emancipation of East Asia. The thought of those officers and men who have fallen on the field of battle, of those who have died at their posts of duty, or those who have met with untimely death, and of their bereaved families, pains our heart night and day. The welfare of the wounded and war victims and of those who have lost their homes and livelihood are objects of our profound solicitude. The hardships and sufferings to which our nation is to be subjected hereafter will certainly be great.

We are keenly aware of the inmost feelings of all our subjects. However, it is according to the dictates of time and fate that we come by enduring the unendurable and suffering what is insufferable. Having been able to save and maintain the structure of the Imperial State, we are always with you, our good and loyal subjects, relying upon your sincerity and integrity. Beware most strictly least any outburst of emotion, which may engender needless complications, or any fraternal contention and strife, which may create confusion, lead you astray and cause you to lose confidence of the world. Let the entire nation continue as one family from generation to generation, ever firm in its faith in the imperishability of its divine land, and mindful of its heavy burden of responsibilities and the long road before it. Devote your united strength to construction for the future. Cultivate ways of rectitude, further nobility of spirit, and work with resolution, so that you may enhance the innate glory of the Imperial State and keep pace with the progress of the world.

At 4.05 p.m. on 15 August 1945, Prime Minister Attlee made the following announcement in the House of Commons:

Mr Speaker, at midnight last night the terms of the Japanese surrender were announced to the world. The House will, I trust, bear with me while I repeat them, for I feel that it is fit and proper that they should be for ever on record in the annals of this ancient and honourable House. They are as follows.

With reference to the announcement of 10 August, regarding the acceptance of the provisions of the Potsdam Declaration and the reply of the Governments of the United States, Great Britain, the Soviet Union, and China, sent by Secretary of State Byrnes on the date of 11 August, the Japanese Government has the honour to communicate to the Governments of the four Powers as follows.

(1) His Majesty the Emperor has issued an Imperial rescript regarding Japan's acceptance of the provisions of the Potsdam Declaration.

(2) His Majesty the Emperor is prepared to authorise and assure the signature by his Government and the Imperial General Headquarters, of the necessary terms for carrying out the provisions of the Potsdam Declaration.

(3) His Majesty is also prepared to issue his command to all military, naval, and air authorities of Japan and all the forces under their control, wherever located, to cease active operations, to surrender arms, and to issue such other orders as may be required by the Supreme Commander of the Allied Forces for the execution of the above-mentioned terms. [Signed] Togo.

Thus the long and grievous Second World War was at an end, and it was thought that peace on earth had been restored. On 16 August 1945, the Allied Combined Chiefs of Staff confirmed the appointment of General Douglas MacArthur as the Supreme Commander of the Allied Powers in Japan. This also covered the areas controlled by South East Asia Command, which were previously bounded by the eastern border and coastline of Thailand, Malaya, and Sumatra. This was also extended to include the entire Dutch East Indies, French Indochina, Hong Kong, and the area of the South China Sea—in effect all the territories previously controlled by the Japanese Southern Area Army.

The Allied Air Forces spread the news of the enemy's surrender by dropping leaflets on principal towns, villages, and known prisoner of war camps. By 31 August 1945, many millions of leaflets had been distributed and some ninety prisoner of war camps had been targeted with air deliveries of food and medical supplies. One of the immediate actions had been the distribution of over 1 million Atabrine tablets a week; this was the bold yellow prophylactic tablet that fought against malaria. The immediate medical plan for evacuated prisoners of war used advanced base hospitals in Rangoon. The following weeks into September saw significant efforts to evacuate the prisoner of war camps and, by the middle of September 1945, 9,000 men had been transported by air from Bangkok into Rangoon. A total accommodation of 10,000 beds had been achieved in the Rangoon hospitals. These units were expected to facilitate 16,000 prisoners of war who were to be evacuated from Burma, Thailand, and French Indochina by air into Rangoon. The majority of emaciated men were flown from Bangkok, which had been developed into a medical transit staging post. The hospitals in Rangoon quickly became effective in processing the sick prisoners of war, the vast majority of whom were expected to recover within a three-month period, after which they would be suitably fit enough for repatriation to their home country. Many of those were from the survivors who had built the Burma–Thailand Railway.

# 9

# 159 Squadron: Japanese War Crimes

The Allied liberation of Rangoon brought immediate relief to the many hundreds of prisoners of war that had been confined within the squalid walls of its jail. Rangoon jail was a most repulsive place. Prisoners were kept in barracks or wings of the jail, segregated by nationality and rank. The blocks were long buildings all converging onto a central courtyard, like spokes of a large wheel. The blocks housed prisoners of war from America, Australia, India, and China, as well as from the other British Commonwealth countries. The numbers of Royal Air Force prisoners within the Japanese prison camps were, by comparison to the European camps, exceptionally low, however, these men were despised and loathed by the Japanese. Any aviator taken to Rangoon was exclusively dealt with by the Japanese, held in block five solitary confinement before again being collectively segregated within what was known as block eight.

The unexpected and sudden abandonment of the jail by the Japanese was an event that preceded the actual Allied liberation of Rangoon. Four days prior, the Japanese had marched approximately 400 fit and able prisoners away with the intention to reach Pegu and then onwards into Thailand. These men were themselves unexpectedly abandoned by the Japanese when they arrived in Pegu. The men still held within the jail at Rangoon painted a message on the roof of one of the cell blocks. The large white lettering displayed 'Extract Digit', a phrase that the Royal Air Force pilots overflying the area would instantly understand. Moreover, it was one that could only have been placed by an Allied captive. A photograph showing the newly added message was taken by an overflying Beaufighter from 211 Squadron. The pilot returned from his sortie and, shortly after the photograph had been interpreted, orders were passed to instigate aid supplies to be dropped into the jail as soon as possible. Three Liberators, one aircraft each from 99, 356, and 159 Squadrons, flew to Rangoon prison in the afternoon of 3 May and dropped Red Cross parcels and Army rations into the jail. The Army rations, known as K-packs, consisted of cigarettes, chocolate, biscuits, and chewing gum and were dropped right into the compound. The first-aid packages with fresh clean bandages were items not seen in the jail for several years, and these were immediately put to good use on the many prisoners who were suffering with open wounds. The 159 Squadron supply dropping Liberator EV981 was flown by Pilot Officer Lee. Known to all as 'Red', he and his crew observed the prisoners hurrying to the supplies, not realising that amongst them were several fellow 159 Squadron men. Among them were all six survivors from the crew of Liberator BZ926, which had been shot down by Japanese night fighters over Rangoon on 29 February 1944.

Rangoon jail was finally liberated by the British Indian Division later that same day. The 159 Squadron rear gunner Jack King, from the crew of BZ926, experienced the joy of liberation. Although he received immediate care, like several other men who were seriously sick, he died twenty-eight days later from Beriberi. His symptoms had been induced by the Vitamin B-1 deficiency caused by the grossly inadequate food provided by the Japanese. Jack King had witnessed the death of his fellow crew mate Johnnie Westermark, who had died in similar circumstances on 10 December 1944; however, from that crew, four men survived. Pilot Officer Lentz, Warrant Officer Lomas, Sergeant Harris, and Sergeant Davis all survived, along with several other flight crew members from 159 Squadron. The unfortunate ball gunner from 215 Squadron, Flight Sergeant Reekes, who parachuted out of his Liberator after misconstruing the thumbs-up signal, was also among the survivors.

The graves of prisoners buried in close proximity to Rangoon jail were exhumed by the Allies and the Imperial War Graves Commission in late 1945—the recovered remains were later interned in the Rangoon War Cemetery. The body of rear gunner Jack King was never conclusively identified, as was often the case with exhumed remains. He now has a grave marker on Plot 9 B6 in Rangoon War Cemetery, which is inscribed with 'buried near this spot'. Also within Rangoon War Cemetery are a number of men who suffered beheadings by the Japanese. Flight Sergeant Stanley James Woodbridge served as a member of the Royal Air Force Volunteer Reserve within B-24 Liberators of 159 Squadron. Woodbridge had been attached to the 159 Squadron special duties 'C' Flight, undertaking Japanese radar detection duties within an especially equipped Liberator. Under great secrecy, two B-24 aircraft had first engaged in this work in early 1944. The capability to locate radar used by the enemy in various capacities was of significant importance and Flight Sergeant Woodbridge was among very few men who knew some of the intricacies of the special electronic detection capabilities undertaken within those very technically equipped Liberators. He was not, however, the special operator within the crew who was directly responsible for the electronic equipment. That role was undertaken by Flying Officer Lowery.

At 3.30 p.m. on 30 January 1945, Liberator BZ938 took off from the airfield at Digri with nine men on board. The special operation objective was to try and locate Japanese radar stations in Rangoon, Mandalay, and Bangkok. In addition to Lowery, the crew comprised of two officers—Squadron Leader Bradley, the pilot, and the navigator Flying Officer Jeffrey. There was also a trio of NCOs, a wireless operator, and air gunners, Warrant Officer Williams and Flight Sergeants Woodage and Woodbridge; Flight Sergeant Adams was the air gunner, Flight Sergeant Snelling the flight engineer, and Flight Sergeant Bellingan acted as the second pilot. The Liberator failed to return from that operation and the circumstances of their fate only became known when Squadron Leader Bradley and Flying Officer Jeffery were found to be among the liberated prisoners of war from within Rangoon Prison. Their horrific ordeal unfolded as they recounted that their aircraft had crashed in Burma as a result of engine failures and Flight Sergeant Woodbridge had been captured by Japanese forces along with four other members of his crew. Unlike European flight crews, who inevitably wore identifiable brevets on their battledress jackets, the Far East crews, due to the harsh environment, were not so distinguishable. The tropical jackets and general uniform worn by these men were subjected to intense dampness, with constant washing and drying in the sun. Conventional crew brevets, which were woven silk or similar material, simply fell apart, unable to withstand those conditions. The Japanese selected Flight Sergeant Woodbridge, whom they identified as the aircraft's wireless operator, as being in a position to give them information about secret wireless equipment, codes, and wavelengths, so they subjected him to a period of the most brutal torture. Three of the prisoners, Bellingan, Snelling, and Woodage, were made to dig their own grave trench and then stand in line. The Japanese officer, Lieutenant Matsui, invited his soldiers to abuse the prisoners with violence. The airmen were then brought to the immediate edge of the trench, blindfolded, and forced to squat. Matsui ordered two of the airmen to be beheaded by sword and then ordered a corporal under his command to undertake the beheading of the third airman—all the bodies were additionally subjected to bayoneting. Flight Sergeant Woodbridge was forced to witness the beheading of his three fellow crew mates. His final interrogation was then undertaken at the place of execution so that Woodbridge would have been in absolutely no doubt that he would meet the same fate as his crew if he refused to talk. When all efforts to make him speak proved futile, the exceptionally brave young airman was decapitated by a Japanese officer's sword. The sword had been yielded by another Japanese officer, Lieutenant Okami. Having died valiantly and steadfastly defiant in the most gruesome of circumstances, his body was unceremoniously pushed into the grave situated in woodland at Myaungmya on 7 February 1945. They were later removed to the Commonwealth War Graves Rangoon Cemetery, where they jointly rest in the Collective Grave 3F, plots 6–9. A total of 1,417 Allied casualties are now cared for alongside them.

Flight Sergeant Stanley James Woodbridge was aged twenty-three when he was executed. He was the husband of Florence Woodbridge and the son of James and May Woodbridge. The fate of the remaining crew members of Liberator BZ938 was as follows:

Squadron Leader J. W. Bradley (84656), pilot, and Flying Officer A. G. Jeffrey (147114), navigator/bomb aimer: both taken prisoner and later rescued from Rangoon Prison in May 1945.

Flying Officer W. J. J. Lowery (156576), special operator, Warrant Officer A. R. Williams (421484), wireless operator/air gunner, Royal Australian Air Force, and Flight Sergeant J. Adams (1493958), navigator, are commemorated on the Singapore War Memorial for those with no known graves.

The South East Asia Command, Supreme Allied Commander, Admiral Lord Louis Mountbatten had been placed in charge of the minor war crimes trials of Japanese nationals. Investigators collected statements from former prisoners of war, most of which related to war crimes against the prisoners themselves. Many thousands of statements were collated on what became known as the military 'Q Form'. Those surviving documents can be viewed at the National Archives, Ref. WO311/59. The trials lasted from May 1946 to November 1948. Japanese names are normally presented first with their family name and followed by their given name and are represented accordingly in the majority of files.

On 15 January 1947, the case against those suspected of the abovementioned war crime, Lieutenant Colonel Murayama Seichi, Lieutenants Kanno Yasutaka and Okami Hiroshi, and Corporals Joko Hisachi, Katayama Shiro, and Tsukamoto Fukuichi was opened. The defendants were represented by a Japanese lawyer, Ito Toshio, with Captain John Gurney-Champion representing the War Crimes Courts as the British Advisory Officer to the Japanese legal teams to advise on British military law. The War Crimes Court prosecution was headed by Major Airey, who advised the court that the deceased Bellingan, Woodage, and Snelling had been beheaded about 8 a.m. on 7 February 1945, while Woodbridge was beheaded at approximately 1 p.m. An interpreter at the trial had himself been present when the Japanese were interrogating the prisoners in Myaungmya. Evidence existed that the defendants had tortured the men by beating them with bamboo canes, fists, and swords in their sheaths. Additionally, the evidence confirmed that the deceased Bellingan, Woodage, and Snelling had been forced to dig their own graves before being executed and that Woodbridge steadfastly refused to divulge any information and, after further extreme torture, was duly beheaded by Lieutenant Okami.

The Japanese defendants argued they were not there at the time of the execution and endeavoured to produce alibis. James Woodbridge, the father of Stanley, unexpectedly became engaged in examining the alibi evidence and successfully obtained witnesses to verify that the Japanese defendants were there at the time of the war crime offences being committed. On 21 March 1947, a sentence of death was passed on the defendants Murayama, Kanno, Okami, and Katayama, although the sentence against Murayama was subsequently reduced to ten years' imprisonment. Kanno, Okami, and Katayama were duly hanged at Rangoon on 27 June 1947. The two Japanese soldiers involved in the execution, Joko Hisachi and Tsukamoto Fukuichi, received two years' imprisonment and one year's imprisonment respectively. The post-war enquiry had also established that the Japanese Officer Lieutenant Matsui had been killed in action during the Japanese retreat from Burma. The National Archives in Kew hold the

Judge Advocate General's War Crimes Case Files for these trials within documents WO235/1009, and these can be publically examined.

In 1948, Stanley James Woodbridge was posthumously awarded the George Cross in recognition of his courage and devotion to duty. The citation for the award was announced in *The London Gazette* 28 September 1948:

> The King has been graciously pleased to approve the award of the GEORGE CROSS to 1393806 Flight Sergeant Stanley James Woodbridge (deceased), Royal Air Force Volunteer Reserve, 159 Squadron.
>
> Flight Sergeant Woodbridge was a wireless operator in the crew of a Liberator aircraft which crashed in the jungle in Burma whilst engaged in an operation against the Japanese on 31 January 1945. Together with five other members of the crew, he was captured by the Japanese. All six were subjected to torture at the hands of their captors in an endeavour to obtain information which would have been of use to the Japanese Intelligence Service. Eventually, the four non-commissioned officers were separated and conveyed by motor transport to a forest, where they were put to death by beheading. Three officers and three non-commissioned officers of the Imperial Japanese Army were subsequently brought to trial by a Military Court charged with the torture and murder of the four airmen, they were all found guilty. Three of them were hanged and three were sentenced to terms of rigorous imprisonment. At the trial, it was revealed that the Japanese concentrated their efforts on Flight Sergeant Woodbridge, the wireless operator, in an endeavour to obtain technical information regarding wireless equipment, secret codes, wavelengths, etc.
>
> A Japanese technical officer was detailed to carry out the interrogation, and the services of two interpreters were engaged, but, in spite of repeated torture which included kicking, beating with belts and with a sword, Flight Sergeant Woodbridge steadfastly refused to reveal any information whatsoever. The final interrogation took place at the site of the execution; when it was obvious to the unfortunate prisoner that he was to be put to death, he maintained his courageous attitude to the end, merely remarking that if the Japanese were going to kill him they should do it quickly. After all efforts to make him speak, including further torture, were found to be fruitless, this gallant non-commissioned officer was beheaded on 7 February 1945. Flight Sergeant Woodbridge behaved throughout with supreme courage. His fortitude, loyalty to his country and his complete disregard for his own safety, even unto death, constitute one of the highest examples of valour in the annals of the Royal Air Force.

A government report issued in June 1946 (HMSO CMND 6832) had stated that there were 5,102 Royal Air Force men captured by the Japanese in the Second World War. In addition, there were men from the Royal Canadian Air Force, the Royal New Zealand Air Force, and the Royal Australian Air Force serving within numerous squadrons and units. A great many died either by execution, murder, or due to the accumulative brutality inflicted on them by their captors. The same document evidences that 1,714 Royal Air Force men captured in the Far East were subsequently 'killed or died in captivity'. The majority of these casualties died of disease and malnutrition. Of the 619 who died at sea, some 362 died as a result of ships being sunk by Allied action.

Among the immediate post-war investigations were the efforts to trace the Japanese soldiers responsible for the heartless deaths of the nurses on the Island of Banka. They were suspected to have been committed by men from within 'O' Battalion of the 229th Regiment. Sister Vivian Bullwinkel was among those who gave evidence at the initial Tokyo war crimes trials in December 1946. *The Australian Women's Weekly* expressed in print the general mood of the Australian public at that time:

> If ever, anywhere in the world, a plea for mercy or leniency for the Japanese race is heard, there will rise before Australian eyes the accusing picture of twenty-two gallant women walking, with heads held high, into the sea as the Japanese machine-guns opened their murderous fire.

The Australian investigators were unable to bring any identifiable Japanese to trial for the murder of the nurses. One lieutenant from the 229th Regiment had, as a result of investigations, been located in Manchuria. This man was suspected of being the Japanese officer who issued the orders to execute the nurses and had been seen in person by the nurse Vivian Bullwinkel. However, the suspect took his own life by slashing an artery in his neck and bled to death in Sugamo prison before he could be tried (*Hidden Horrors: Japanese War Crimes in World War II*, 1966).

The International Military Tribunal for the Far East comprised of three classes of trials 'A', 'B', and 'C'. In brief, Class 'A' were those accused of crimes against peace, the planning, preparing, initiating, or waging a declared or undeclared war of aggression, or a war in violation of international law and treaties. Class 'B' were those suspects charged with conventional war crimes, people engaging in violations of the laws and customs of war, including the maltreatment of civilians and prisoners of war. Class 'C' were all those accused of crimes against humanity. Those who had carried out torture, murder, extermination, enslavement, deportation, and other inhumane acts before or during the war, or persecution on political, religious, or racial grounds ordered by superiors.

Crimes against humanity, Class 'C', were tried by the governments of Australia, Great Britain, China, France, Holland, the Philippines, and the United States. Brigadier Davis, the Deputy Judge Advocate General, oversaw the British legal proceedings that were held at various locations throughout the Pacific region. The Americans conducted most of their Class 'B' and 'C' trials in Yokohama, and the accused were shuttled back and forth from trials in Tokyo and Yokohama to Sugamo prison, which was located in north-west Tokyo. Immediately after the war, it was converted to be the primary prison for holding Japanese war crime prisoner. All Japanese Class 'A' war criminals were to be tried by the International Military Tribunal for the Far East in Tokyo.

The Allied prosecution team consisted of justices from eleven nations: Australia, Canada, China, France, Great Britain, India, the Netherlands, New Zealand, the Philippines, the Soviet Union, and the United States.

Military trials were also undertaken in Manila, Shanghai, and Guam. The British military conducted a great many war crimes trials in the Far East, in which hundreds of Japanese war criminals were tried and punished. Between June 1946 and July 1947, a total of 111 Japanese and Korean soldiers were convicted for crimes on the Burma–Thailand Railway. Death sentences were pronounced upon thirty-two of these men.

Colonel Wild, the British officer who had carried the white flag of surrender at Singapore, had first-hand experience of the brutality of the Japanese against prisoners. He had himself suffered as a prisoner of war and had been forced to do labour, building the Burma–Thailand Railway. Following his release, he became the chief war crimes detective in the Far East. Wild had lived in Japan before the war and he spoke fluent Japanese; his official title was the War Crimes Liaison Officer, with responsibilities over Malay and Singapore. He later provided evidence in several courts, but tragically he lost his life on 26 September 1946 in a flying accident commuting between the trial centre in Tokyo and Singapore. Ironically, he had been required to give evidence against Japanese and Korean guards charged with war crimes during the construction of the Burma railway when he died. That particular joint British and Australian case engaging the commander of the guards, Lieutenant Colonel Banno Hirateru, naturally faulted, but progressed with other substantive evidence to a satisfactory conclusion.

# Eastern Air Command Personnel Structure

Royal Air Force and United States Army Air Force Combined Operational Command.

Air Chief Marshal Sir Richard Peirse November 1943–November 1944.

Air Marshal Sir Guy Garrod December 1944–February 1945.

Air Marshal Sir Keith Park February 1945.

Eastern Air Command.

Royal Air Force and United States Army Air Force, Eastern Air Command structure of personnel from December 1943–June 1945.

Lieutenant General G. E. Stratemeyer, Air Commander, 15 December 1943–31 May 1945 USAAF.

Air Marshal Sir W. A. Coryton, Assistant Air Commander. 4 December 1944–31 May 1945 RAF.

Air Vice-Marshal T. M. Williams, Assistant Air Command RAF.

Air Vice-Marshal A. Gray, Assistant Air Commander RAF.

Major-General C. B. Stone, Chief of Air Staff USAAF.

Brigadier General A. R. Luedecke, Deputy Chief of Air Staff USAAF.

Air Vice-Marshal C. E. Gibbs, Deputy Assistant Air Commander RAF.

Air Vice-Marshal The Earl of Bandon, Air Officer Commanding, 224 Group RAF.

Air Marshal Sir John Baldwin, Air Commander, Third Tactical Air Force RAF.

Air Vice-Marshal S. F. Vincent, Air Officer Commanding, 221 Group RAF.

Air Commodore F. J. Mellersh, Air Commander, Strategic Air Force RAF.

Brigadier General F. W. Evans, Commanding General, Combat Cargo Task Force USAAF.

Brigadier General W. D. Old, Air Commander, Troop Carrier Command USAAF.

Major-General H. C. Davidson, Air Commander, Strategic Air Force USAAF.

Brigadier General J. F. Egan, Commanding General, Northern Air Sector Force USAAF.

Group Captain S. G. Wise, Air Commander, Photographic Reconnaissance Force RAF.

Colonel M. W. Kaye, Air Commander, Photographic Reconnaissance Force USAAF.

Group Captain R. Boyd, Commanding Officer, Defence of Calcutta Wing RAF.

The Eastern Air Command Public Relations Section published the following statement in May 1945:

Teamwork of British and American air power, fused by the organisation of Eastern Air Command, blasted the Japanese from India and the Burma skies.

# APPENDIX II

# Map of Burma

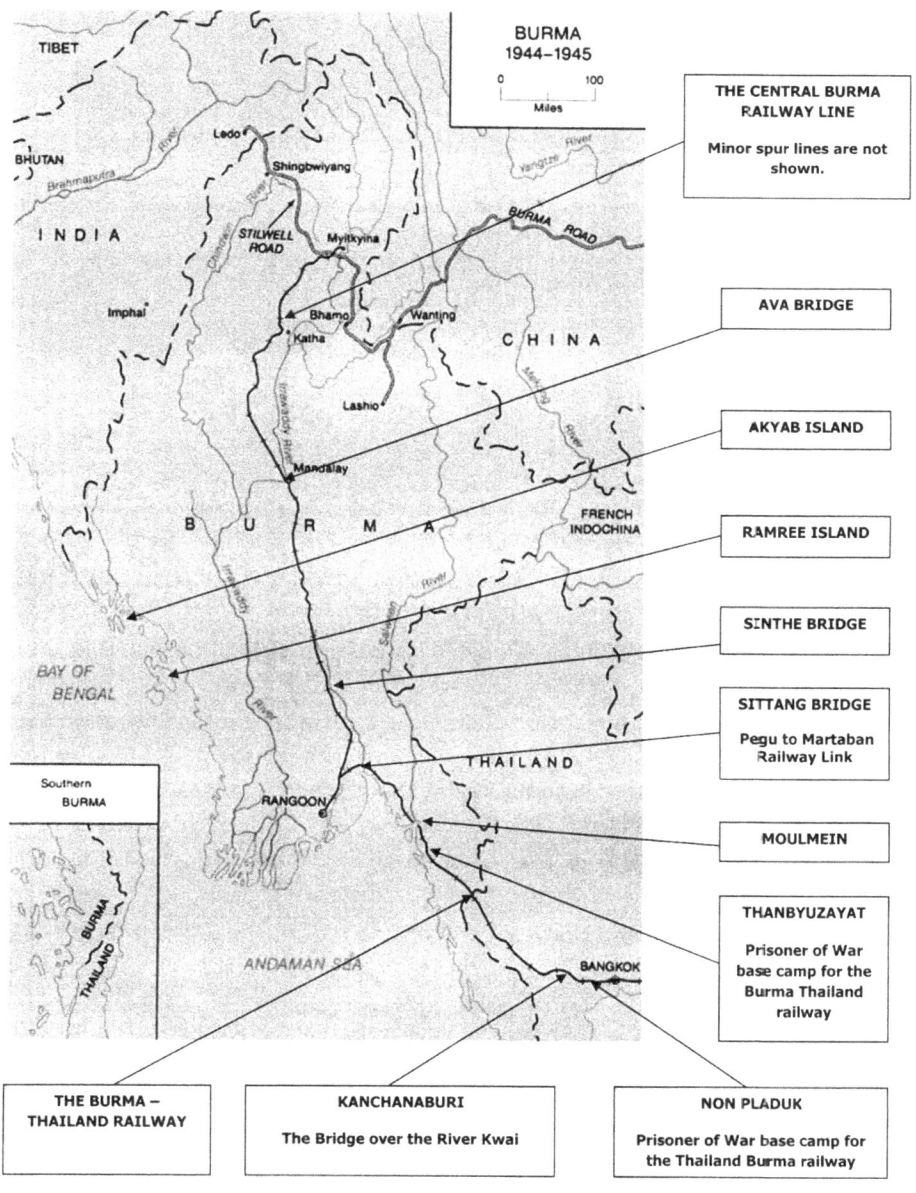

# Detailed Interpretation Report: Burma–Thailand Railway

SECRET

AIR H.Q., INDIA C.P.I.S. DETAILED INTERPRETATION REPORT NO. 0.28.

BURMA–SIAM [Thailand] RAILWAY.

1. GENERAL STATEMENT

On 25 October 1943, the new Burma–Siam Railway was photographed from Thanbyuzayat for a distance of 86¼ miles. This cover was continuous, but in two places detail was obscured by cloud.
TRACK IS LAID AND THE LINE IS BEING USED THROUGHOUT THE LENGTH COVERED BY THESE PHOTOGRAPHS.

It is, of course, not possible to say whether the line is open right through to Bangkok, but the fact that a number of new camps are under construction round about Mile 80 rather suggests that railway construction work is still in progress further down the line. Furthermore, new goods jetties and sidings, recently constructed at Moulmein, Martaban and Sittang, have been noticeably inactive and not consistent with the volume of traffic which would be using this line, were it in use throughout its length.

Full details of bridges, sidings, camps, etc. are given in the Appendix to this report and a set of maps showing the alignment of the railway is attached.

2. ACTIVITY

Railway activity and movement were not great on the line covered; a total of 11 locomotives and 143 wagons were present, which does not represent much traffic on 86 miles of track. Only two trains were actually in motion; one, consisting of

7 wagons and a probable coach, was moving north at Mile 39, whilst the other, consisting of 10 wagons, was moving south at Mile 56.

A train of 12 wagons, double engine-headed facing north, was stationary at Mile 32 and a train of 22 wagons, double engine-headed facing south, was stationary at Mile 50.

Four locomotives were in the sidings at Mile 28; the layout of this siding suggests that it is being developed as a locomotive depot.

This lack of traffic movement is reflected in the inactivity of the ferries at Moulmein–Martaban and Sittang, which should be active if traffic was passing north from Siam. Details of recent activity at these places is as follows:

## MOULMEIN–MARTABAN FERRY

There has as yet been little or no traffic passing over the new goods jetties at Moulmein and Martaban. At Moulmein, the sidings serving the new jetty have always been very lightly loaded, while on only two occasions have any craft been seen at the jetty. The new sidings and jetty at Martaban were covered five times during October 1943, but only one wagon was ever seen in the sidings and no craft have yet been seen at the jetty, the ends of which are still being extended. Nor do the number and size of craft at the older jetties indicate any large traffic from south to north, only a few small craft having been seen at Martaban.

Rails are still being ferried from the north siding [Martaban] to the old goods jetty [Moulmein] as shown by changes in the dumps of rails on each successive cover. The craft employed are two rafts, each consisting of a pair of 60 ft lighters decked over amidships.

There are a considerable number of lighters or cargo boats at Moulmein and, as motor vessels no longer visit the port, these craft are free to carry the increased goods traffic foreshadowed by the construction of the new ferry sidings and jetties. As regards passengers, recent cover has shown three creek steamers at Moulmein, but of these only one has been active. Another has been lying idle at the B. R. Passenger Jetty at the north end of the waterfront, while a third is beached by the Moti Rahaman and United Saw Mills, probably undergoing repairs. At least two launches are probably also being repaired at the latter site, while the fact that the railway flat is lying at the rice mill immediately to the west, suggests that minor repairs or alterations may also be in progress on her.

The Moulmein–Mataban ferry crossing is about 5 miles long. ND/672—3009 to 3012, 4013 to 4016

## SITTANG FERRY

Since the new bridge over the Sittang has been washed away, the Japanese have been augmenting the ferry facilities already existing immediately north of the old bridge by extending the sidings and by constructing additional jetties on the left bank. On the last cover there were about 11 craft in the immediate vicinity of the terminals, the largest being a launch of about 55ft. in length. There are no facilities for ferrying rolling stock, so that all goods must be transhipped. The ferry crossing is about 500 yards long. ND/624—5080, 5081

## 3. SIDINGS

Passing loops have been constructed at intervals throughout the line, in addition to which sidings have been constructed as follows: Miles 18½, 26, 28 [this is a probable locomotive depot], 37½, 44, 50, 68 and 81½.

## 4. RAILS AND SLEEPER DEPOTS

There has been a big reduction in the quantity of rails and sleepers in the depot at Thanbyuzayat, which now appears to be little used. Now depots have been built in two places; at Mile 38 there is a rail dump which has 9 stacks of rails, whilst at Mile 50 is an extensive depot, served by a specially constructed loop line. This depot has very considerable stacks of sleepers and 9 large stacks of rail lengths, and at the time of photography 20 wagons were present on the serving lines.

## 5. CAMPS

Hutted camps have been built approximately every 2 to 3 miles throughout the length of the line photographed. In all cases they are located immediately adjoining the line, and are used both for personnel and stores. Many camps at the Burma end of the line have already been or are in the course of being demolished; these are at Miles 0 [Thanbyuzayat], 5, 8, 11, 12, 14, 15, 21, 24, 27, 32, 37. In addition, a small camp at Mile 84 also appears to have been removed.

Camps, which appear normal and active, are located at Miles 18, 30, 35, 39, 40, 42, 44, 45, 48, 50, 54, 55, 56, 58, 60, 64, 66, 73, and 80. Camps, which are partly built and still under construction are located at Miles 71, 76, and 81.

The camp at Mile 30 has a large cross painted on the ground, and is presumably a hospital. The previous hospital buildings have been removed from Thanbyuzayat. At many of these camps, stacks of stores are seen on the ground. The main stores depot appears to be at Mile 81, where 18 motor vehicles are seen amongst the huts and large stacks of timber and stores are present.

## 6. TARGETS

There are several points on the railway, which offer suitable targets and where damage would cause serious operating difficulties and delay. They are as follows:

1. Mile 26. The line runs immediately at the foot of a steep cliff and at point 632019 (Map 95 E/14), the line could be blocked by damage to the cliff face.

2. Mile 28. Extensive sidings and locomotive depot at 659002 (Map 95 I/2).

3. Mile 44½. Viaduct, 28 arches, length 380', over Mezali Chaung at 848797 (Map 95 I/2).

4. Mile 50½. Sidings with extensive sleeper and rail depot at 223243 (Map 95 I/3).

5. Mile 81½. Very extensive sidings, hutted camps and stores depot at Ban Naung Lu, 525837.

7. BRIDGES

All railway bridges over 40' in length have been pinpointed in the appendix. There are numerous bridges of 20' and under throughout the line, which have not been indicated.

Bridge construction is of two types; (a) girder bridges with normal spans of up to 100' in length, and (2) bridges of viaduct type. These are not true viaducts, but consist of numerous concrete piers, often of great depth, and built very close together. The largest bridges are at:

Mile 44 where a viaduct of 23 arches, total length 380', crosses the Mezali Chaung.
Mile 52 where at 210' bridge crosses the Zami River.
Miles 70 and 71 where there are 3 viaducts of 230'.
Mile 73 where a bridge 300' in length crosses the Saung Galia River.
Mile 82 where a bridge whose length including the approach spans is 1,100' crosses the Ran Ti River.
Mile 83, bridge 240'.

ROADS

The new road has been completed and runs alongside the railway throughout the distance covered by photographs. It appears serviceable throughout and at several points motor vehicles were seen in movement. Numerous road bridges have been constructed over streams and rivers.

MIS/APIS Distribution MWD/JC/ARP      4 Nov. '43

# Appendix to Interpretation Report

[Author's note: the original maps and photographs were not attainable.]
A.P.I S. SECRETAIR H.Q., INDIA APPENDIX TO DETAILED INTERPRETATION
REPORT NO. 0.28 4 Nov. '43

| Miles | Map 95 E/9 Coordinates | | Photo |
|---|---|---|---|
| 0 | 337357 | THANBYUZAYAT  There has been a big reduction in the quantities of rails and sleepers previously stored here. This is probably due to the fact that many have been destroyed by our bombing attacks, whilst a new main stores depot has been constructed at Mile 81. Since 3 August 1943, all the buildings have been removed from the hutted camp and hospital situated immediately to the southwest of the sidings. The station sidings held ten wagons, whilst the stores sidings were empty. The line runs parallel to and east of the existing Moulmein–Ye line for a distance of 1½ miles. | 3014 |
| 1½ | 349328 | Line bifurcates, Moulmein–Ye line continuing south, whilst the new Siam line continues in a south-east direction. | 3018 |
| | 353322 | Bridge, 40', over stream. | |
| | 354319 | Bridge, 100', over Karonpaik Chaung. | 3052 |
| | 357315 | Bridge, 80', over stream. | |
| | 362310 | Bridge, 40', over stream. | |
| 4 | Map.95 E/13 | Two short cuttings. | 3054 |

| | | | |
|---|---|---|---|
| | 379289 | Bridge, 30', over Weyet Chaung. | |
| | 380287 | Bridge, 80'—no apparent stream. | |
| 5 | 385283 | Passing loop about 370 yards long. Five wagons present Camp: Situated to north of line, consists of the following huts: 225' × 25' (1); 190' × 25' (1); 100' × 25' (1). About 12 huts of various sizes have been demolished. Track activity is not very marked and suggests site is being abandoned. | 3055 |
| | 393279 | Bridge, 180', over Mayan Chaung. | 3057 |
| 6 | | Bridge, 80', followed closely by bridges of 80', 20', 40', 20', and 60'. | |
| | 406269 | Bridge, 60', over Taunggya Chaung, both approaches being on short embankments. Short cutting, followed closely by three bridges, each of 60'. | 3059 |
| | 418250 | Bridge, 2 spans each of 100', over stream. | 3060 |
| 8 | 423243 | Bridge, 2 spans each of 100', over stream. | |
| | 427238 | Bridge, 80', over Salnwin Chaung. Camp: Situated south of line, consists of one hunt, 60' × 35'. Probably 8 huts have been removed; cloud shadow makes detailed interpretation impossible. Four small bridges. | |
| | 434229 | Bridge, 100', over stream. | 3062 |
| | 436226 | Bridge, 40', over stream. | |
| | 442218 | Bridge, 60', over stream. | |
| | 443217 | Bridge, 40', over stream. | 3063 |
| | 447213 | Bridge, 40', over stream. | |
| | 448209 | Bridge, 40', over stream. | |
| 10½ | 449207 | Bridge, 80', over Kalonkala Chaung. | |
| 11 | 453201 | Camp: Situated east of line. Consists of the following huts: 150' × 40' (3), 65' × 30' (1), 50' × 30' (1). Several huts have been removed and others are in course of demolition. The camp appeared active at the time of photography, but it is probably only occupied by the demolition gang. | 3064 |
| | 458196 | Passing loop, 270 yards long. | 3066 |
| | 464193 | Bridge, 40', over stream, both approaches being on short embankments. | |
| | 467189 | Bridge, 30', over stream. | |
| | 468186 | Bridge, 80', over stream; approach from north on short embankment, whilst southern approach is on embankment 250 yards long. Line runs down valley with hills to east. | 4068 |

AIR H.Q. INDIA APPENDIX TO DETAILED INTERPRETATION REPORT NO. 0.28

| Miles | Map 95 E/13 Coordinates | | Photo |
|---|---|---|---|
| 12½ | 468182 | Camp: Situated west of line. Consists of one hut, 65′ × 25′, with 4 huts in course of demolition and 3 huts already demolished. | |
| | 473179 | Bridge, 30′, over stream. | |
| | 474177 | Bridge, 40′, over stream. | |
| | 477173 | Bridge, 40′, over stream. | |
| | 479170 | Bridge, 40′, over stream. | |
| 14 | 485161 | Bridge, 40′, over stream. | |
| | 486160 | Bridge, 40′, over stream. | |
| | 487158 | Camp: Situated east of line. About ten huts, approximately 250′ × 30′, have been removed from this site, which is now completely abandoned. Four small bridges over streams in next 700 yards. | 4071 |
| | 493153 | Bridge, 40′, over stream. | |
| | 495150 | Bridge, 40′, over stream. | |
| | 499145 | Bridge, 60′, over stream. | |
| | 500144 | Bridge, 60′, over stream, followed by several small bridges and culverts. | |
| 15½ | 501143 | Camp: Situated on both sides of the line. Approximately fifteen huts have already been removed from this camp; the remaining huts are as follows: 190′ × 20′ (1), 100′ × 20′ (3), 160′ × 20′ (1), 110′ × 25′ (1), 65′ × 25′ (2) and 40′ × 25′ (2). This site has the appearance of being in course of complete removal. | 4072 |
| | 504137 | Viaduct, eight arches, overall length 140′, over stream Cutting. | 4074 |
| | 506135 | Viaduct, five arches, overall length 100′, over stream | |
| | 509132 | Viaduct, fourteen arches, overall length 250′, over stream. | 4075 |
| | 511130 | Bridge, 40′, over stream. | |
| | 512128 | Bridge, 60′, over stream. | |
| | 516126 | Bridge, 40′, over stream. | |
| | 517125 | Bridge, 60′, over stream. | |
| 17½ | 525126 | Bridge, 100′, over stream. Embankment 700 yards long. | 3076. |
| | 535123 | Bridge, 100′, over Tiphattan Chaung. | |
| 18 | 537123 | Bridge, 40′, over stream. | |

| 18½ | 544118 | SIDINGS: Through line plus two double-ended roads, about 370 yards in length. Possible small goods shed with side loading ramp. Sidings hold 10 wagons. Camp: Situated immediately to west of sidings. Consists of 16 huts as follows: 230' × 30' (8), 95' × 30' (3), 70' × 30' (1), 100' × 30' (3), and 100' × 60' (1). There are several small sheds and, from the marked track activity, the site appears to be occupied. No demolitions have so far been made. | |
| --- | --- | --- | --- |
| | 549114 | Bridge, 60', over stream. | |
| | 550113 | Bridge, 100', over Thittaku Chaung. | |
| 19 | 564101 | RETPHAW VILLAGE. Bridge, 80', over stream. | 3079 |
| | 570096 | Bridge, 40', over Tilay Chaw Chaung. | |
| | 577089 | Bridge, 60', over Tilay Chaw Chaung. | |
| 21 | 578088 | Passing loop, 250 yards. Long. | |
| | | Camp: Situated to east of passing loop. Consists of the following huts: 225' × 25' (1), 100' × 25' (2), 50' × 25' (1), and 35' × 25' (1). Five huts have already been removed and 3 more are in course of being demolished. | |
| | 582085 | Bridge, 40', over stream. | |

A.P.I S.      SECRET

AIR H.Q. INDIA APPENDIX TO DETAILED INTERPRETATION REPORT NO. 0.28

| Miles | Map 95 E/14 Coordinates | | Photo |
| --- | --- | --- | --- |
| | 589078 | Bridge, 40', over stream. | 3081 |
| | 597070 | Bridge, 80', over Paya Chaung. | |
| | | TANYIN VILLAGE. | |
| | 616044 | Camp: Situated to west of line. Consists of the following huts: 50' × 12' (2), 55' × 12' (1), 65' × 12' (3), and 100' × 30'. Three huts have already been removed whilst four are in course of demolition. There are a few small sheds in addition. | 3086 |
| | 618036 | Passing loop, 300 yards long. | 4088 |
| 26 | 631019 | Line runs immediately beneath the west face of a steep hill rang height about 1,200 feet, for approximately 1 mile. This is a very vulnerable point for blocking the line through bombing. | |

| | 633017 | SIDINGS: Line bifurcates and a branch line runs in an east and north direction for a distance of 1,500 yards, where it dead-ends. Immediately following the junction, there is a passing loop, 200 yards long, on the branch line; this line continues to the foot of the cliff, and at 644015, is a bridge, 100', over a stream. This line dead-ends at 644017. This branch line serves a stores dump and several stacks of materials are seen along its length. Fourteen wagons are present on the branch line. The main line continues in a south-east direction. | 4090 |
| --- | --- | --- | --- |
| | 637013 | Bridge, 40', over Beke Chaung. | |
| 27 | | ANAYKWIN VILLAGE. | 4091 |
| | 651005 | Bridge, 40', over stream. | |
| | 654005 | Bridge, 180', over Myettaw Chaung; this bridge has probably a 100' span, with short approach spans. A locomotive is moving in a southerly direction just north of the bridge.<br>Camp: Situated north of the bridge and on both sides of the line. Consists of five huts, 240' × 25', and a few small sheds. Six large sheds have already been removed and others are in course of demolition. | |
| 28 | 659002 | SIDINGS: Through line with passing loop, 300 yards long; to the east is a wide loop line with a branch line running from its northern end in an easterly direction. This branch line is 550 yards long and terminates in three short, dead-ended spurs. One locomotive and two wagons are seen on this branch line. To the west of the through line, there is also a wide running loop, with a reversing triangle running off it. This triangle has a short dead-ended spur at its N. extremity; at the end of this spur a possible engine shed is being built. At the west end of the triangle, a line runs in a westerly direction for a distance of 500 yards and terminates with two short, dead-ended spurs. The lay-out of these sidings suggests that the area is being developed as a locomotive depot with dispersal spurs; four locomotives are present, whilst eight wagons are seen in the area. | 4092 |

| | 663530 | Bridge, 60', over stream. | |
|---|---|---|---|
| | 675523 | Bridge, 60', over stream. | |
| 30 | | THANBAYA VILLAGE. | |
| | 694977 | Bridge, 40', over stream. | |
| | 699975 | Camp; Situated on both sides of the line. Consists of nine huts, 240' × 24', and 4 huts, 90' × 24'. A large cross has been painted on the ground in the centre of the camp, suggesting that this camp is used for medical purposes. No demolitions have taken place. | 3097 |
| | 724954 | Bridge, 120', over Khon Khan Chaung. | 3099 |
| | | Camp: Situated to west of line, immediately north of bridge (724954) Consists of the following huts: 150' × 40' (1), 105' × 30' (1), 65' × 40' (1), and 50' × 25' (1). One hut has been removed; this camp appears to be occupied. | |

A.P.I S.        SECRET

AIR H.Q. INDIA APPENDIX TO DETAILED INTERPRETATION REPORT NO. 0.28

| Miles | Map 95 E/14 Coordinates | | Photo |
|---|---|---|---|
| 32½ | | KHONKHAN VILLAGE. | |
| 35½ | | TAUNGZUN VILLAGE. | 3104 |
| | 764924 | Camp: Situated to east of line. Consists of the following huts: 125' × 25' (2), 70' × 25' (1), 100' × 25' (1), and 65' × 30' (2). There are also a number of smaller huts; this camp appears occupied. | |
| | 765923 | Bridge, 40', over tributary of Winyaw River. | |
| 37 | 776903 | Bridge, nine spans, concrete piers, total length 140', over Winyaw River. Camp: Situated to west of bridge (776903). Consists of five huts, 240' × 24'. This camp is in course of removal and some huts are seen to be partly demolished. | 4107 |
| | 777902 | Bridge, 80', over stream. | |
| 37½ | | SHITPYIT VILLAGE. | |

| | 786897 | SIDINGS: Consist of probably three double-ended roads, 450 yards in length, with a wide running loop to the west. To the south of the sidings and east of the through line, is the first leg of a reversing triangle, whilst, from the northern end of the sidings, a branch line runs in an easterly direction for about 370 yards. This line is uncompleted and its layout suggests that it will ultimately join up with the reversing triangle. At the northern end of the sidings, a loop line, 200 yards long, runs round a rail dump; there are nine separate stacks of rails at this depot. Five wagons are seen in the sidings. Immediately to the west of the sidings is a small camp of six huts, 60' × 25', which appear occupied. | |
| 39 | | LONSI VILLAGE | 4110 |
| | 802875 | Bridge, 80', over Tha Byu Chaung. | |
| | | Camp: Situated immediately north of the bridge (802875) and on west of line. Consists of the following huts: 80' × 20' (4), 90' × 25' (3), and 125' × 30' (1). This camp is situated in the village of LONSI and appears to be occupied. | |
| | 806872 | Bridge, 80', over Tha Byu Chaung. | |
| | 807871 | Bridge, 80', over Tha Byu Chaung. A train of eight vehicles, including a probable coach, is moving north at this point. | |
| | 811867 | Bridge, 80', over Tha Byu Chaung. | |
| 40 | | Camp: Situated immediately to west of the bridge (811867). Consists of the following huts: 250' × 45' (2), 240' × 45' (2), 80' × 30' (1), and some small sheds. | |
| | 817859 | Bridge, 40', over stream. Line now runs in the river valley and there are numerous bridges and cuttings. | 4112 |
| 41 ½ | 816843 | Bridge, eight spans, total length 120', over stream. | 4113 |
| | 817838 | Bridge, 60', over stream. Cutting 500 yards long. | |
| 42 ¼ | 824828 | Bridge, ten spans, total length 150' over stream. | 4114 |
| | | Camp: Situated to the north of this bridge (824828) and west of line. Consists of eight huts, 240' × 35', and three huts, 90' × 25'. (The next 1,200 yards of this line are cloud covered.) | |

| | 833817 | Bridge, 60', over Htihpomaw Chaung. | 4116 |
|---|---|---|---|
| | 838816 | Bridge, 40', over stream. | |
| | 836814 | Bridge, 60', over Htihpomaw Chaung. | |
| | | Bridge, 40', over Htihpomaw Chaung. | |
| 44 ¼ | 845804 | Sidings; Possibly three double-ended roads, 320 yards long, which holds four wagons. | 4117 |
| | | Camp: Situated immediately to the west of the sidings (845804). Consists of the following huts: 175' × 35' (1), 90' × 25' (1), and 50' × 25' (4). Trees hide track activity, so occupation is not certain. | |

A.P.I S.          SECRET

AIR H.Q. INDIA APPENDIX TO DETAILED INTERPRETATION REPORT NO. 0.28

| Miles | Map.95 E/14 Coordinates | | Photo |
|---|---|---|---|
| | 847803 | Bridge, five spans, with concrete piers, total length 80'. | |
| 44¾ | 848797 | Viaduct, 23 equal arches, concrete piers, total length 380', over Mezali Chaung. | 4118 |
| | 849793 | Bridge, 60', over stream. | 4119 |
| | 853791 | Bridge, 40', over stream | |
| | | Cutting 340 yards long. | |
| 45½ | 855787 | Camp: Situated east of line. Consists of the following huts: 275' × 40' (1), 250' × 35' (3), 100' × 35' (4), 115' × 35' (2), 175' × 40' (10), 60' × 25' (1), and 'L' shaped 175' × 100' × 35' (1). No demolitions have taken place and the camp appears occupied. | |
| | 856787 | Viaduct, nine arches, concrete piers, total length 160', over stream. | |
| | 858785 | Viaduct, six arches, concrete piers, total length 130', over stream. | 4121 |
| | 860783 | Viaduct, five arches, concrete piers, total length 70', over stream. | |
| 46 | 862782 | Viaduct, six arches, concrete piers, total length 90', over stream. | |
| | Map 95 I/3 1733303 | Viaduct, two arches, concrete piers, total length 80', over stream. No approach on embankment. | 4122 |
| | 178299 | Viaduct, possibly eight arches, concrete piers, total length 110', over stream. Cutting 550 yards long. | |

| | | | |
|---|---|---|---|
| 47½ | 186291 | Viaduct, possibly seven arches, concrete piers, total length 100', over stream. | 3123 |
| | 199271 | Viaduct, possibly ten arches, concrete piers, total length 130', over stream.<br>Camp: Situated immediately south of viaduct (199274) and west of line. Consists of the following huts: 250' × 50' (4), 300' × 45' (1), 225' × 40' (1), 165' × 40' (1), and 65' × 30' (2). This camp has every appearance of occupation. | 3125 |
| | 209264 | Viaduct, five arches, concrete piers, total length 80'. | |
| 50½ | 219253 | Bridge, possibly ten spans, total length 150', over Apalon Chaung. | 3128 |
| | 223243 | SIDINGS: Consist of four double-ended roads 400 yards long they held forty-five wagons including a length of 22', engine-headed south. To the west of the sidings is an extensive rail and sleeper depot, with a loop line running through it. Many stacks of sleepers and nine stacks of rail-lengths are seen; twenty wagons are on the lines serving the depot. To the north and west of the sidings is a reversing triangle, which appears to be still under construction.<br>Camp: Situated immediately to the S.W. of the Sidings; consists of the following huts: 235' × 35' (4), 100' × 35' (1), 125' × 35' (1), 45' × 25' (2), and 75' × 30' (1); there are a number of smaller huts and sheds (probably stores) and this camp appears occupied. | 3129 |
| 51¼ | | PHADAN VILLAGE | |
| | 223239 | Bridge, five spans, total length 70', over stream. | |
| 52½ | 239228 | Bridge over Zami River, Probably three spans of 40' each, with shorter approach spans total length approximately 210' (not clearly seen). | |
| | Map 95 I/7 & I/8 253207 | Bridge, four spans, total length 60', over stream. | 3133 |
| | 262204 | Camp: On the east side of the line, consists of the following huts: 235' × 35' (3), 225' × 35' (2), 155' × 35' (1), and 100' × 30' (4). On the W. side of the line are 3 huts, 250' × 35', one hut, 250' × 35' under construction, and two small sheds. Both camps appear active and occupied. | |
| | 262203 | Short cutting, 350 long, steep sides. | |

A.P.I S.        SECRET

AIR H.Q. INDIA APPENDIX TO DETAILED INTERPRETATION REPORT NO. 0.28

| Miles | Map 95 I/7 & I/8 Coordinates | | Photo |
|---|---|---|---|
| 54½ | 263202 | Viaduct, possibly twelve arches, concrete piers, total length 200', over stream. | 3134 |
| | | In the next 3 miles, the railway runs through country with many watercourses in consequence of which there are numerous bridges up to 80' in length. Steep hills border both sides of the track. | 3135 |
| | 280206 | Camp: Situated both sides of the line, consists of huts as follows: 110' × 25' (1), 90' × 25' (1), 80' × 25' (1), 60' × 20' (1), 50' × 20' (1), and 80' × 20' (2). This site has appearance of living-quarters and was occupied. | |
| 56½ | 291197 | Train of 10 vehicles moving S. | 3137 |
| | 294189 | SIDING: (not clearly seen) probably passing loop with short, dead-ended spur. Camp: Situated immediately south of siding (294189); consists of 5 huts, 250' × 40', two huts, 200' × 40', and two huts, 65' × 40', and some smaller sheds and stores. These huts are well hidden in the trees. | 3139 |
| 58½ | 308166 | Probably three or four bridges over Megathat Chaung, but cloud make interpretation impossible. | 4141 |
| | 310163 | Bridge, 80', over Megathat Chaung. | |
| | 313160 | Camp: Consists of one hut, 150' × 30', 1 hut 110' × 30' and two huts 80' × 25', plus some small sheds and huts. This camp appears occupied. | |
| | 320148 | Possible passing loop | 4143 |
| | 325140 | Camp: Consists of four huts, 175' × 30', 1 hut 210' × 30', and 3 huts 125' × 30', plus three small sheds. This camp is hidden in the trees and appears occupied. | |
| 64 | 373092 | Passing loop, 350 yards long. | |
| | | Camp: Situated immediately to west of passing loop. Consists of six huts 250' × 35' and one hut 110' × 30'. There are also a large number of small huts and probably stores and the camp appears active. | 4151 |
| | 375089 | Bridge, 40', over stream. | |

| 66½ | 406062 | Camp: This camp is partly hidden under trees and looks active. Several stacks of stores are seen. Consists of huts as follows: 250′ × 40′ (4). 250′ × 30′ (1), 100′ × 25′ (3), also one hut, 200′ × 35′ under construction. | 3153 |
|---|---|---|---|
| 68½ | 425037 | SIDINGS: Passing loop 350 yards long. At the south of the loop are two short loop lines, serving a stores dump, and a reversing triangle, which is still under construction. Only a few small stacks of stores are seen. | 3157 |
| | 441012 | BURMA–SIAM FRONTIER | |
| | Map 95 I/SW | | |
| 70¼ | 440007 | From this point to point 443997, a distance of under 1 mile, are the following seven viaducts; total length 230′ (sixteen arches), 40′, 80′, 40′, 230′ (sixteen arches), 230′ (fourteen arches), and 120′. | 3161 |
| 71½ | 453987 | Camp: Situated both sides of the line. A fairly large group of huts, approximately 20′, most under construction. In the next 2 miles are 11 bridges up to 80′, over streams. | 3164 |
| 73½ | 473964 | Bridge, total length 300′ over Menam Saung Callia. five main spans of 30′ with short approach spans. Camp: Situated immediately north and south of the bridge (473964). Consists of huts as follows: 150′ × 35′ (1), 100′ × 35′ (2), 90′ × 30′ (1), 80′ × 30′ (1), 225′ × 35′ (1 under construction), and 60′ × 20′ (1). This camp appears active. | 3166 |

A.P.I S.        SECRET

AIR H.Q. INDIA APPENDIX TO DETAILED INTERPRETATION REPORT NO. 0.28

| Miles | Map 95 I/SW Coordinates | | Photo |
|---|---|---|---|
| 76¾ | 496907 | Camp: Situated both sides of the line. Consists of huts as follows: 350′ × 40′ (2) and 285′ × 40′ (2). There are 30/35 stacks of timber, one row of stores, 220′ × 30′, and one row of stores, 175′× 30′. Three spaces have been cleared for further huts or stores. This camp is occupied and active. | 3172 |

| 80¼ | 506848 | Camp: Situated both sides of the line. Consists of three huts. 75′ × 30′ and 1 hut 100′ × 35′. Occupation is uncertain. | 4177 |
| | | BAN NAUNG LU VILLAGE | |
| 81½ | 525836 | SIDINGS: [not clearly seen]. There are possibly six double-ended roads, about 380 yards long, with a wide running loop to the south of the Sidings. To the north of the sidings, a dead-ended spur. 600 yards long runs in an easterly direction. A reversing triangle runs off this spur, its northern apex running into a further dead-ended spur. 1,000 yards in length, this runs parallel to the main siding. A transhipment shed, 120′ × 25′, is situated in the sidings which held about 20 wagons. 300 yards east of the sidings, a branch line runs south for about 350 yards, and serves the hutted camp. Camp: Situated immediately south of the sidings. This camp consists of the largest number of huts and stores yet seen on this line; the following huts are seen:- 125′ × 25′ (1), 75′ × 30′ (1), 300 ′ 40′ (1), 100′ × 25′ (1), 250′ × 40′ (2), 85′ × 35′ (2), 230′ × 30′ (1), 110′ × 30′ (2), 230′ × 40′ (1), 60′ × 30′ (4), 110′ × 30′ (2), 75′ × 30′ (6), and 100′ × 30′ (3), plus a large number of sheds and smaller buildings; other huts are under construction. A large number of stacks of timber and stores are present and about eighteen motor transport vehicles are in the camp, which appears very active. | 3178 |
| 82½ | 537837 | Bridge over Menam Ran Ti River. This bridge has ten spans with concrete piers actually over the river; total length 150′; there is a long approach on the western bank, apparently of very short spans, giving an overall length of 1,100′. | |
| 83 | 550839 | Viaduct, total length 300′. Number of arches not seen. | |
| | 556837 | Bridge, 240′ [not clearly seen owing to cloud]. | 3179 |
| | | The next 1200 yards are cloud covered. | |
| 84½ | 567825 | Camp: A small camp that appears to be in course of complete demolition. | 3181 |
| 86½ | 580794 | Photographic cover ends. The line continues. | 3183 |

# Chronological Sequence of Allied Aerial Attacks upon the Bridges on the River Kwai

The chronological sequence of Allied aerial attacks undertaken upon the bridges built by the Japanese on the River Kwai, collectively known as the Tha Makham bridges or simply the bridge on the River Kwai.

29 November 1944:
The first air raid on the bridges was by United States Army Air Force's 9th and 493rd Squadrons. This raid caused some damage to the steel bridge. Regrettably, a bomb fell into the nearby prisoner of war camp and a large number of men were killed or wounded.

13 December 1944:
The second raid by the United States 7th Bomber Group caused little damage to either bridge.

23 January 1945:
One 7th Bomber Group B-24 reached the target and no damage was inflicted. Bad weather and mechanical problems had reduced this attack to a single aircraft.

5 February 1945:
Four squadrons of B-24s from the United States 7th Bomber Group carried out the largest raid on the bridges. This attack badly damaged the track leading to the bridges, but left the bridges intact. This damage was quickly repaired and the railway resumed full operation.

9 February 1945:
A United States 7th Bomber Group B-24 attack finally demolished two spans of the wooden bridge, but again left the steel bridge undamaged.

13 February 1945:

The 493rd Squadron, United States 7th Bomber Group, first AZON (guided bomb) attack. Finally success was achieved, with two spans of the steel bridge demolished and more damage done to the timber bridge. However, within six weeks, reconnaissance photographs revealed that the wooden bridge was back in use and the main bridge was being repaired.

3 April 1945:

B-24s from two squadrons of the United States 7th Bomber Group attacked. Again a section of the wooden bridge was damaged.

24 June 1945:

The final bombing operation on the Tha Makham bridges. The only one exclusively targeted by Royal Air Force's B-24 Liberators. Twenty-six aircraft from 159, 355, and 356 Squadrons attacked the repaired and fully functional bridges. This ultimately successful raid destroyed three spans of the steel bridge and breached the wooden bridge in two places.

# Listing of Commonwealth and British Air Crew who Participated in Finally Destroying the Bridges on the River Kwai, 24 June 1945

The British and Commonwealth Air Crew Personnel who participated in the operation to destroy the bridge on the River Kwai 24 June 1945.

The 'Battle Order' and Operational Records for 159 Squadron and 355 Squadron in June 1945 are either no longer in existence or partially missing. This formal gap in the accuracy of research has led to the inability to collate the definitive list of personnel from the twenty-six B-24 Liberator aircraft that took part in the operation. The serial numbers of four Liberators and the fuselage letter codes of three Liberators are unknown. Nine Liberator crew lists are incomplete—six from 159 Squadron and three from 355 Squadron.

159 SQUADRON:

KL491 'R':
Captain: Flight Lieutenant E. J. Foot.
Crew: Plt Off. J. D. Robson, Plt Off. D. Carmichael, Plt Off. P. Sianchuck, Sgt E. Walde, FS E. W. Presley, Sgt E. J. Kearns, Sgt H. C. E. Taylor, and Sgt Wright.

EW246 'Q':
Captain: WO G. Green.
Crew: Sgt E. H. Keen, Plt Off. E. Rowe, Plt Off. A. H. Fryer, Sgt E. M. Lord, FS H. Parrish, Sgt D. McLean, Sgt D. Roberts, and Sgt Withers.

EV968 'Z':
Captain: WO P. A. Brown.
Crew: Sgt R. Drabble, Plt Off. D. Kaye, Sgt F. Holden, Sgt D. G. Godfrey, Sgt H. Parr, Sgt R. Kitchen, Sgt W. Moons, and Sgt F. Kirkpatrick.

KL653 'C':
Captain: Sqn Ldr T. W. Watson.
Crew: Plt Off. Tetlock, FS E. C. Smuin, Plt Off. N. L. Chornopysky, Sgt H. Smaile, Sgt
   Wadkin, FS Hill, Sgt Helm, and Sgt Phillips.

KH398 'A':
Captain: Flt Lt R. M. Borthwick.
Crew: Plt Off. C. F. Nesbitt, Plt Off. E. R. Kennedy, Plt Off. W. Drew, Sgt R. Meredith,
   FS E. Johnson, Sgt W. M. Ross, Sgt J. Knauts, and Sgt J. S. Blyth.

EW173 'B':
Captain: Fg Off. J. Haycock.
Crew: WO T. F. Reynolds (the only crew member known).

EV981 'D':
Captain: Plt Off. R. Lee.
Known Crew: R. Sayer, J. Waugh, C. Clinton.
Probable Additional Crew: J. Beavis, D. Mills, L. A. Payne.
(Service ranks and remaining crew members are unknown.)

KL660 'M':
Captain: Flt Lt R. W. Williams.
Crew: Unknown.

EV966 'U':
Captain: WO W. Newman.
Crew: Unknown.

KG893 'H':
Captain: Flt Lt T. Mitchell.
Crew: Unknown.

KL677 'X':
Captain: Fg Off. S. Dowding.
Crew: Unknown.

355 SQUADRON:

KG844 'X':
Captain: Flt Lt W. H. Fuller.
Crew: Plt Off. E. F. Aitkens, FS I. E. Jones, Plt Off. J. E. Smart, Plt Off. A. E. Smith, Sgt J.
   A. Westing, Sgt E. V. Dennison, Plt Off. R. A. Woodrow, and Plt Off. J. Schwartzman.

EW176 'R':
Captain: Fg Off. N. V. Todd.
Crew: FS J. Ferguson, FS A. E. Poole, FS R. Hawkins, Plt Off. G. D. Hunter, Fg Off. J. D. Sawyer, FS E. W. Titball, Sgt R. E. Vincent, and FS R. McLeish.

KH280 'L':
Captain: Fg Off. R. Wardell.
Crew: FS J. D. Willis, FS D. T. Brain, Plt Off. A. F. Masters, Plt Off. N. A. Goveia, Plt Off. H. R. Hodgson, Plt Off. R. J. C. Dixon, Sgt F. E. M. Walker, and Sgt C. A. Noble.

EW221 'B':
Captain: Fg Off. S. P. Collins.
Crew: Fg Off. J. W. Hammond, Fg Off. H. Jarvis, Fg Off. C. R. Krueger, Fg Off. J. W. K. Slack, Sgt G. R. Grey, Sgt W. Barber, Sgt H. C. Somerville, and Sgt N. A. Grain.

Fuselage letter codes unknown.
Captain: Unknown.
Crew: Sgt M. V. Winton (the only crew member known).

Fuselage letter codes unknown.
Captain: Unknown.
Crew: Unknown.

Fuselage letter codes unknown.
Captain: Unknown.
Crew: Unknown.

356 SQUADRON.

EW285 'V':
Captain: Flt Lt R. W. Dick.
Crew: Fg Off. C. G. Evans, Fg Off. J. S. Young, Fg Off. R. L. Payne, Sgt C. T. Stroud, Sgt W. B. Mills, FS G. W. Rose, and FS R. R. Savage.

KH357 'S':
Captain: Flt Lt F. W. Payne.
Crew: Fg Off. J. N. Goodwin, Fg Off. A. E. Fussell, Fg Off. G. Pearson, Sgt W. G. Prytherch, FS L. M. Silver, Sgt P. Taylor, and Sgt D. Carey.

KL556 'T':
Captain: Sqn Ldr L. F. Evans.

Crew: WO C. G. Kilsby, Fg Off. J. H. Bruce, Fg Off. R. Hurford, FS J. R. Sayer, FS D. C. Cartwright, FS D. W. Matear, and FS J. P. Fraser.

EV982 'A':
Captain: Fg Off. P. I. Bradley.
Crew: Fg Off. L. J. Otley, Plt Off. C. G. Walker, Sgt C. Kendall, Sgt R. Millward, Plt Off. D. Jackson, Sgt J. P. Hughson, and Sgt B. J. Wilson.

EW125 'D':
Captain: Flt Lt H. E. Whidden.
Crew: Plt Off. F. L. Sturdy, Fg Off. G. A. Forrest, Fg Off. R. T. Sullivan, Fg Off. C. L. Charbonneau, FS J. Mills, FS H. D. Hurren, and FS M. J. T. Fay.

KH270 'B':
Captain: Fg Off. E. N. Myers.
Crew: FS A. H. Willingham, Fg Off. T. W. Moseley, Plt Off. C. Cox, FS H. M. Todd, Plt Off. C. W. Howe, Sgt C. Clark, and Sgt F. Ashby.

EV911 'G':
Captain: Fg Off. D. F. Hunt.
Crew: Plt Off. D. C. Marshal, Plt Off. R. Fleming, Fg Off. A. J. Reid, Fg Off. W. R. Walters, FS L. Childs, Sgt G. A. Handford, and FS D.C. Tucker.

KH218 'K':
Captain: Fg Off. W. H. Veitch.
Crew: Plt Off. W. J. Borody, Fg Off. A. McDonald, Fg Off. R. Morrice, Sgt F. J. Kelly, FS E. Askey, Plt Off. J. D. McBeth, and Plt Off. J. M. McRae.

At the same time that these airmen were so desperately trying to destroy this most legendary bridge, almost directly beneath them was a British prisoner of war, John Michael Esdaile. He had enlisted in the British Army in December 1940 and gained an emergency officer's commission in 1941. He had been part of the defence force for Singapore, within the Indian Armoured Corps attached to the Royal Indian Army Service Corps. Despite fighting against the odds in light armoured and ineffective wheeled vehicles, he and many of his men acquiesced in compliance with the surrender to the Japanese on the 15 February 1942. Lieutenant John Michael Esdaile was aged twenty-two when he fell into the hands of the enemy. Imprisoned in Changi Jail and then other encampments, he eventually arrived at Kanchanaburi as part of the prisoner of war workforce, building the Burma–Thailand Railway.

At the time of the Royal Air Force's B-24 Liberator attacks at Kanchanaburi, Lieutenant Esdaile was almost underneath the bridge, naked in the water having been on an ablution. The spectacle of low-flying Liberators bombing the bridges, accompanied with the intense noise and drama of the unfolding events, was observed by few at such close quarters. Fierce Japanese defensive gunfire, consisting of both heavy and light anti-aircraft guns, supplemented by light machine guns, created a combined firepower that proved ineffective in warding off the attacking Liberators.

Lieutenant Esdaile had experienced what was in all probability a unique occurrence, while marvelling at the bravery and accuracy of the crews who were flying overhead. He had witnessed the only Royal Air Force mounted attack on this target, seeing the final destruction of what has now become an iconic bridge associated to the Second World War.

Unlike thousands of his fellow prisoners of war, Lieutenant Esdaile survived the privations at the hands of his Japanese captors. He later sought to contact the men who had engaged in the valiant attack, and immediately upon his liberation he sent a letter to 159 Squadron. In late 1946, following his repatriation and recuperation, he sailed from England to Canada eventually becoming a Canadian citizen. Twelve years later he returned to England where he had the opportunity to show his young family their ancestral roots. He never forgot the bravery he witnessed that day in June 1945. In 1995, Major-General Ian Grant, a veteran of the Burma campaign, proudly reiterated John Esdaile's words during a symposium on the Royal Air Force, Far East War:

> To those gallant fellows who did what they did to the Kanchanaburi bridge. As one who was down below and alongside the bridge, I am full of admiration. I was naked at the time of your attack, having just been on an ablution effort to the river. I do not remember when I have ever sweated more. My thanks go to the accuracy of your bombs and then to President Truman for having the guts to drop the big bomb. Without the two of you, I would not be here today.

# Gallantry Awards to a Number of 159 Squadron Recipients, 1944–1945

Gallantry awards to selected 159 Squadron airmen 1944–1945. This is not a comprehensive list of all recipients in this time frame.

Gallantry awards were published in the British Government newspaper of record, *The London Gazette*, on the dates indicated. The identity of the recipient, the date of the award, and a brief overview of the citation are explained within these collated excerpts.

Many awards to both officer and non-commissioned men do not contain the actual recommendation submitted, merely a generalised statement of service worthy of recognition. This in no way diminishes the achievement of being awarded such recognition of gallantry and service. Administrative procedures for the submission of recommendations advised officers to provide as much detail as possible, including sorties flown by those recommended and degree of injuries (where sustained). They were reminded that recommendations for posthumous awards could not be submitted except when a Victoria Cross or a Mention in Despatches was involved. However, recommendations for awards progressed, even if the person involved had in the meantime been killed, but only on condition that the initial recommendation had been submitted while the person was still alive. It is occasionally seen in such awards 'Since Deceased' against the official announcement procedures.

The Distinguished Flying Cross and Distinguished Flying Medal awards could be recommended in two respects—immediate and non-immediate, the latter also being known as a periodic. Immediate awards were for conspicuous deeds or individual acts. Periodic awards were more commonly made on completion of a first or second tour or recognition for a long term of competence. Awards were rationed and allocated on the basis of a mathematical formula—the number of hours flown by a squadron and how many awards were available. The award process began with a recommendation made by the squadron commander. The recommendation then passed through several hands increasing in seniority—station commander, base commander, and group commander. In practice, the original recommendation would be supported by those going up the line in seniority, but occasionally changes were made. For example, an award being upgraded or downgraded was a practice that tended to be associated with 'immediate' as opposed to 'periodic' awards. Once the recommendation had been approved by the Air Officer Commander-in-Chief, the confirmation of the award was published in *The London Gazette*.

The status between ranks was reflected in the quality of the cases in which these respective medals were sent to the recipients. The Distinguished Flying Cross was encased in a fitted velvet-lined box, with the box lid embossed with the letters DFC. The equivalent award to non-commissioned officers, the Distinguished Flying Medal, was dispatched in a cardboard box with no particular fittings other than tissue wrapping.

22 August 1944:

CLEGG, Sqn Ldr Charles Gordon (70797)—Distinguished Service Order, 159 Squadron.

> Squadron Leader Clegg is an outstanding operational pilot who has been employed on operations without a break since May 1941…. Since joining this Squadron as Flight Commander, he has completed his duties in a most able and skilful manner. He has completed a number of successful night bomber sorties over Burma and has twice flown his aircraft and crew safely to base on three engines after sustaining damage in combats with enemy fighters.

WALLACE, Fg Off. Eric Dale (404122)—Distinguished Flying Cross, 159 Squadron.

> Awarded for sorties over Europe, Middle East and Far East.

KIRKNESS, FS William Arthur (1114254)—Distinguished Flying Medal, 159 Squadron.

> As first wireless operator of an aircraft detailed to attack Rangoon on the night of 1 April 1944, Flight Sergeant Kirkness showed extreme coolness and courage when the aircraft was badly damaged by night fighter attacks. The rear gunner was killed in the first attack and it is almost certain that the attacking fighter was shot down by accurate return of fire from the Beam Gun manned by Flight Sergeant Kirkness. It was largely due to his very skilful use of his radio equipment, under extremely poor conditions that the aircraft was brought back safely to friendly territory and the aerodrome prepared for the landing. Throughout his operational tour he has at all times shown a fine spirit and carried out his duties with coolness and efficiency.

GAUNTLETT, Flt Lt John Reginald (106221)—Distinguished Flying Cross, 159 Squadron.

Flight Lieutenant Gauntlett has completed a tour of operational duty during which he has attacked a variety of targets in Burma. He has at all times displayed a fine fighting spirit, great skill and devotion to duty. In April 1944 he was captain of an aircraft detailed for an attack against Rangoon. When his aircraft was attacked and badly damaged by enemy night fighters and the rear gunner killed, it was largely due to Flight Lieutenant Gauntlett's superb airmanship that the damaged aircraft reached home safely. As Deputy Flight Commander his skill and keenness have done much to maintain a high standard of operational efficiency in his squadron

GOWING, Fg Off. Geoffrey Alexander (402099)—Distinguished Flying Cross, 159 Squadron.

Awarded for sorties over the Western Desert, Burma and India.

17 November 1944:

BRADLEY, Flt Lt James Wilson (84656)—Distinguished Flying Cross, 159 Squadron.

Flight Lieutenant Bradley has flown on many occasions through appalling monsoon weather to achieve his objectives. His aircraft has often been intercepted by enemy fighters and engaged by searchlights and anti-aircraft fire. In May 1944, one engine of this officer's aircraft failed. With great skill he successfully flew back to base, a distance of 600 miles, where he accomplished a night landing in adverse weather. Both in the air and on the ground, Flight Lieutenant Bradley has inspired the personnel under his command with the greatest keenness to achieve results.

PRITCHARD, Fg Off. James Anthony (142030)—Distinguished Flying Cross, 159 Squadron.

This officer has served in both the Mediterranean and Far East theatres of war. He has displayed exceptional keenness in his work. On several occasions Flying Officer Pritchard has continued steadfastly with his allotted tasks despite enemy opposition in the form of anti-aircraft fire, searchlights and night fighters. His skill, determination and devotion to duty are worthy of the highest praise.

8 December 1944:

BLACKBURN DSO DFC, Wg Cdr James (70067)—Bar to Distinguished Service Order, 159 Squadron.

This officer has an outstanding record. He has completed five tours of operational duty. He has commanded this squadron for the past few months and during the period has participated in a number of bombing attacks and several minelaying missions. During these operations, despite very bad weather, not once has he failed to attack his allotted target, both in the air and on the ground.

2 January 1945:

MURPHY, Plt Off. Maurice Blaney (415217)—Distinguished Flying Cross, 159 Squadron.

Awarded for many sorties of a long and arduous nature in Monsoon weather.

ALCORN, Flt Lt Kenneth Pearce (415599)—Distinguished Flying Cross, 159 Squadron.

Awarded for courage displayed in long and hazardous flight over sea.

SANDILANDS, Fg Off. Jack Dalton (405937)—Distinguished Flying Cross, 159 Squadron.

Awarded for the completion of a wide variety of missions, day and night sorties.

QUINN, Flt Lt William Stewart (421048)—Distinguished Flying Cross, 159 squadron.

Awarded for fine fighting spirit on many sorties as Captain of his aircraft.

26 February 1945:

KINNEAR, Flt Lt Samuel (J10566)—Distinguished Flying Cross, 159 Squadron.

This officer has completed a successful tour of operations. At the commencement of it he participated in one of the longest missions of the war to mine Penang Harbour, a flight lasting over twenty hours. He also made many low level attacks against the Bangkok-Singapore railway, all of them with great success. He has flown throughout the monsoon period, forcing his way through most adverse weather and never failing to reach his objective. Flight Lieutenant Kinnear has always shown courage, a high degree of skill, and great devotion to duty.

23 March 1945:

HEYNERT, Flt Lt Felicite Pierre Andre (149322)—Distinguished Flying Cross, 159 Squadron.

As captain of a Liberator aircraft this officer has completed many operational missions of a varied nature, including bombing and minelaying by night and by day. In March 1944, he was detailed to attack Rangoon. Opposition from anti-aircraft fire was intense over the target and difficulty in identifying the target was experienced. Five runs had to be made before the exact objective was located and, on the fifth, the aircraft was illuminated by search lights and attacked by two night fighters. Despite this, Flight Lieutenant Heynert continued the run until the bombs had been released and a photograph obtained. Several further attacks were made by the fighters. Flight Lieutenant Heynert, displaying great skill, eventually evaded the attackers and returned to base safely. This officer has proved himself an exceptionally able pilot who has, at all times, displayed the utmost gallantry and devotion to duty.

Dutch DFC Awarded on the 22 September 1945: Royal Decree No. 75.

In recognition of his courage, perseverance, capability, and devotion to duty, whilst attached to a unit of the Royal Air Force taking part for a considerable time in operations against the enemy.

23 March 1945:

CAMPBELL, Plt Off. Arnold Ernest (J90742)—Distinguished Flying Cross 159 Squadron.

This officer has completed a tour of operational duty. He is a first class navigator and bomb aimer who has never let either adverse weather or enemy opposition deter him from completing his allotted tasks. At all times Pilot Officer Campbell has displayed outstanding courage, determination and devotion to duty.

3 April 1945:

COLES, FS Victor Arthur (1382302)—Distinguished Flying Medal, 159 Squadron Special Flight.

This NCO has at all times set a magnificent example. It is unfortunate that details of the results obtained by his efforts in his duties as Special Operator are of a secret nature and cannot be revealed. It is sufficient to say that they have been of vital importance to the Royal Air Force. Due to the loss by enemy action of certain key personnel, he has carried out work normally allocated to two operators with a cheerfulness and fortitude that have helped greatly in maintaining the keen efficiency of the flight. On one occasion when highly important information was being logged in the Rangoon area, one of the main sets became unserviceable. He was able to repair the fault in thirty minutes and obtain decisive results before leaving the target area. The arduous nature of the operations is shown by average durations of sorties carried out by this NCO being in excess of sixteen hours.

24 April 1945:

WHITE, Plt Off. John Anthony (J45138)—Distinguished Flying Cross, 159 Squadron.

In February 1945 this officer was the navigator of an aircraft detailed to attack an enemy bridge. In the run in to the target the aircraft was met with intense and accurate anti-aircraft fire. The navigator's compartment was pierced and Pilot Officer White was wounded in the chest. Despite this, he remained at his post and played and played his part worthily in the attack on the target. Although in pain and suffering greatly from the loss of blood, Pilot Officer White insisted on fulfilling his duties. Although he fainted twice he recovered quickly and continued to navigate the aircraft home. After a flight of several hours duration base was reached within a few minutes of the estimated time of arrival. This officer displayed outstanding courage, fortitude and determination.

22 May 1945:

CLARKE, Flt Lt Reginald Arnold (129222)—Distinguished Flying Cross, 159 Squadron.

Joint Citation—this officer and airman were pilot and bomb aimer respectively detailed for a mine-laying mission one night in March 1945. Just before turning to leave the target with their task accomplished, the aircraft was hit by anti-aircraft fire. The navigator was grievously wounded. Flight Sergeant Bailey immediately went to the assistance of his stricken comrade. Although he rendered most efficient first aid his efforts proved unavailing. Meanwhile, Flight Lieutenant Clarke set course for home. His aircraft had sustained damage. The aileron controls were affected and the artificial horizon had been rendered unserviceable. Nevertheless, this resolute pilot flew a considerable distance, at one period in the face of most adverse conditions, to reach base safely.

BAILEY, FS Bernard Frank (1336817)—Distinguished Flying Medal, 159 squadron.

Flight Sergeant Bailey has completed twenty two operations as a Bomb Aimer of Liberator aircraft. He has carried out his duties with considerable skill and enthusiasm. On the night of 22/23 March 1945, he in company with the remainder of his crew were detailed to lay mines in the Bangkok area. As the last mine was laid, the aircraft was hit by an explosive shell which exploded in the nose compartment, seriously wounding the Navigator whose right leg and arm were practically severed by the explosion. Flight Sergeant Bailey rendered immediate first aid, applying tourniquets, and did a most excellent job in an attempt to stop the serious loss of blood from these large wounds. However, all his efforts were unavailing in saving the life of the Navigator and the medical authorities have given the highest praise for his first aid rendered. At the same time Flight Sergeant Bailey rendered invaluable assistance to the captain of the aircraft in helping him navigate back to base. Throughout the emergency, he displayed great initiative and devotion to duty and, by his example, has been inspirational to the squadron.

14 June 1945:

BURCHMORE, Flt Lt Eric (49361)—Member, Order of the British Empire, 159 Squadron.

This officer has been engineering officer in the squadron and has been solely responsible for the exceptional standard of maintenance and the high degree of serviceability achieved. He has developed a maintenance section which, with its limited personnel and facilities, is equal to any in the command and time and again repairs and inspections have been carried out at high pressure in a most satisfactory manner. Flight Lieutenant Burchmore is an extremely good technical officer who has been a constant source of inspiration to his men.

20 July 1945:

ERCOLANI DSO, Wg Cdr Lucian Brett (62270)—Bar to Distinguished Service Order, 159 Squadron.

This officer is now on his third tour of operational duty and has served in both European and Far Eastern theatres of war. He has led his Squadron on numerous daylight bombing attacks against a wide variety of targets, and on many low level sorties against road and rail bridges. Wing Commander Ercolani has invariably displayed exceptional courage, tenacity and skill. Under his inspired leadership his unit has attained a high standard of operational efficiency and achieved many outstanding successes.

Ercolani was additionally awarded the Distinguished Flying Cross on 2 October 1945.

HULBERT, FS John (1254234)—Distinguished Flying Medal, 159 Squadron.

Flight Sergeant Hulbert has completed a tour of operations.... All sorties in which this NCO flew were more than twelve hours duration. The operations included high and low level bombing, dive bombing, mining and strafing of enemy shipping and railway installations. Some of these operations were carried out under very adverse weather conditions which called for a very high standard of navigation, but this NCO never failed to locate and bomb his objective. He was navigator of an aircraft which took part in the longest sortie ever undertaken by a heavy bomber, being in the air for more than seventeen hours.

9 October 1945:

POAG, Flt Lt John Herbert (J25926)—Distinguished Flying Cross, 159 Squadron.

Flight Lieutenant Poag has completed a tour of operational duty as captain of aircraft. His persistence and determination have frequently brought success to difficult missions. He has participated in two long range mine-laying operations, entailing round trips of eighteen and nineteen hours duration, which called for a high degree of skill. This officer has always shown courage and devotion to duty and his cheerfulness and enthusiasm have been an asset to his crew.

19 October 1945:

BARRETT, Fg Off. Francis (159496)—Distinguished Flying Cross, 159 Squadron.

Flying Officer Barrett was on a reconnaissance flight when he spotted a Japanese coastal vessel in a Liberator of the Strategic Eastern Command.... The vessel was bombed set on fire, blew up and disappeared...

11 December 1945:

WATSON, Sqn Ldr Thomas William (J6206)—Distinguished Flying Cross, 159 Squadron.

Squadron Leader Watson has a fine operational record. In the early stages of the fighting in the Far Eastern theatre, he completed very many sorties, flying in fighter aircraft, and was responsible for the destruction of at least two enemy aircraft. Three times this officer was himself shot down. On the last of these occasions he succeeded in escaping from Java just a few hours before the arrival of the enemy troops in the area. Some two years later, Squadron Leader Watson converted to heavy bomber aircraft in which type he has completed many attacks at various targets. On three separate occasions, vital bridges on the Bangkok–Singapore line were destroyed largely by the accurate bombing and repeatedly determined attacks of Squadron Leader Watson. This officer has set an outstanding example of courage and tenacity.

15 January 1946:

DREW, Fg Off. William (J44132)—Distinguished Flying Cross, 159 Squadron.

Flying Officer Drew has completed a tour of operational duty during which he has participated in numerous target marking and low level sorties. He is a bomb aimer of outstanding ability and skill, and on one occasion he was responsible for the destruction of an enemy depot ship at Satahib Bay. This officer also shared in the destruction of a span of the Kanchanaburi Bridge cutting the vital supply line between Bangkok and Moulmein. Throughout his tour Flying Officer Drew by his skill and devotion to duty has largely contributed to the successes achieved.

BORTHWICK, Flt Lt Roy McIntosh (J21490)—Distinguished Flying Cross, 159 Squadron.

This officer has completed a tour operational duty during which he has participated in numerous missions of a varied nature. On one occasion he took part in a minelaying operation at Penang. This involved flying a distance of approximately 3,000 miles. On another occasion during an attack at Satahib Bay whilst affording cover for aircraft attacking at low level he not only drew the fire of the defences but pressed home his own attack and obtained a hit on a 3,000-ton enemy depot ship, setting it on fire so that it finally sank. More recently Flight Lieutenant Borthwick during a low level attack destroyed a span of the Kanchanaburi Bridge on the important supply line between Bangkok and Moulmein. Throughout this officer has displayed cool judgement, courage and great devotion to duty.

WILLIAMS AFC, Flt Lt Clifford Frederick (J4867)—Distinguished Flying Cross, 159 Squadron

Throughout a large number of operational sorties this officer has proved to be an excellent captain of aircraft who has always pressed home his attacks with determination and skill. On one occasion during an attack against enemy shipping in Satahib Bay he made a second bombing run in the face of intense anti-aircraft fire and destroyed an enemy merchant ship. At all times Flight Lieutenant Williams has displayed outstanding enthusiasm and courage.

15 February 1946:

HOCKING DFC, Fg Off. Reginald Thomas (Aus407291)—Distinguished Flying Cross, 159 Squadron.

In October 1944 this officer was the mid-upper gunner of a Liberator aircraft detailed to make a low-level attack on rolling stock between Uttaradi and Pichai. Accurate anti-aircraft fire was encountered and the aircraft sustained damage. The mainplane was holed and set on fire and much height was lost. Flying Officer Hocking coolly informed his captain on the condition of the fire which was impossible to extinguish. The captain gave the order to abandon aircraft after gaining sufficient height. Three members of the crew were unable to leave immediately and Flying Officer Hocking remained behind assisting them and checking their equipment. Despite imminent danger he would not leave the aircraft until satisfied that the parachute equipment of each member was properly fitted and clipped into place. The cool behaviour and bravery of Flying Officer Hocking did much to save the lives of at least two members of the crew.

5 March 1946:

HAYCOCK, Flt Lt John Eustace (NZ422396)—Distinguished Flying Cross, 159 Squadron.

This officer has completed a highly successful tour of operations. This included many sorties against various objectives. Early in his tour during low-level attacks on a bridge [on 13 December 1944] his aircraft was attacked by an enemy fighter but by skilful manoeuvring and accurate fire he was able to destroy it. On another occasion [on 11 March 1945] when flying over Rangoon, his aircraft was seriously damaged by enemy action, with great skill and determination he regained control and successfully brought his damaged aircraft back to base, where he made a safe landing. Throughout his career Flying Officer Haycock has shown outstanding keenness, skill and great devotion to duty. In the incident over Rangoon mentioned above the Flight Engineer repaired the rudder control cables with parachute cords. On landing 197 holes were counted in the fuselage. The aircraft was so badly damaged it did not fly again.

JONES, Fg Off. David Arthur (174372)—Distinguished Flying Cross, 159 squadron.

This officer has completed two tours of operational flying in the Far Eastern theatre of war. On his first tour he participated in the early night bomber raids from India. Most of the flying took place in monsoon weather, thereby placing a good deal of responsibility on the navigator, but he completed the tour with the utmost success. Flying Officer Jones rejoined his old squadron as leading navigator, for his second tour of operations. Often the success of the mission depended on his skill and accurate timing, he never let either enemy opposition or adverse weather deflect him from completing his mission. By his courage and great devotion to duty, Flying Officer Jones has materially contributed to the success achieved by his squadron.

WILLIAMS, Sqn Ldr Robin Walton—Distinguished Flying Cross, 159 Squadron.

Squadron Leader Williams has set an example to the squadron of the highest order, and his leadership and example has considerably influenced the Squadron to success.

On 1 June at Satahib on a shipping strike, finding that the primary target was already beginning to sink, he saved the bombs for another target.... On another occasion an operation was planned to destroy the Kanchanaburi Bridge by low level bombing. For the successful conclusion of the mission it was essential that the considerable Ack-Ack defences should be silenced. This officer was selected to lead the flight with that objective in view. He personally remained over the target well within range of all their guns for over an hour, deliberately drawing their fire to distract them from the aircraft at low level, and then bombing them. It was persistent skill and complete lack of regards for his own personal safety that allowed the main force to attack and successfully conclude their mission with very little damage and no loss of life. His consistent devotion to duty and very real courage are worthy of high recognition.

SMITH, Plt Off. Fred (197075)—Distinguished Flying Cross, 159 Squadron.

Pilot Officer Smith has completed two tours of operations in the Burma theatre of war. These have included night sorties and low level bombing daylight raids. On his first tour, considerable fighter opposition was encountered over Rangoon, but, by his skill and accurate reporting, his captain was able to evade attacks and inflict damage on a number of enemy fighters. This officer is an excellent air gunner who, over a long period has displayed outstanding keenness for operational flying, great skill and devotion to duty.

1 October 1946:

RICHARDSON, FS Harry Frederick (R184955)—Mention in Despatches, 159 Squadron (deceased).

An air gunner, he was reported missing as of 5 October 1944 (Liberator B7978). Aircraft shot down by Japanese fighters, and, although he survived being adrift in a dinghy, he died as a prisoner of the Japanese. No citation other than ... In recognition of gallant and distinguished service whilst a prisoner of war in Japanese hands.

# Campaign Stars and Medals for Service over Burma

The pilots and air crews from within the Royal Air Force and Commonwealth Air Forces were issued with Campaign Medals to recognise service in the differing theatres of war. The vast majority of men who served in the Far East were most likely to have been awarded a Burma Star. The criteria for the award of medals to all those who had fought in the Second World War was only finalised in 1948. Eight Campaign Medals designed as six-pointed stars, pressed in bronze, were issued for the Second World War; the qualification period for each star is shown in brackets:

1939–1945 Star (3 September 1939–2 September 1945)
Atlantic Star (3 September 1939–8 May 1945)
Air Crew Europe Star (3 September 1939–4 June 1944)
Africa Star (10 June 1940–12 May 1943)
Pacific Star (8 December 1941–15 August 1945)
Burma Star (11 December 1941–2 September 1945)
Italy Star (11 June 1943–8 May 1945)
France and Germany Star (6 June 1944–8 May 1945)

No more than five Campaign Stars could be awarded to one individual. Those who would qualify for more were awarded a Clasp with the title of the Star to which they qualify. A recipient may qualify for both the Pacific and Burma Stars, but was only awarded one of these, which would have been the first Star earned. The recipient would then receive a Clasp, with the title of the second Star that was worn on the ribbon of the first. Therefore, it is commonly seen, particularly with Royal Air Force recipients, that the Burma Star supports a Pacific Clasp.

The campaign stars and medals most likely to be worn by Far East veterans who served in the air force are:

1939–1945 Star:
Awarded to personnel who had completed six months of service in specified
operational commands overseas between 3 September 1939 and 8 May 1945
(2 September 1945 in the Far East). Royal Air Force air crew qualified with two
months of service in an operational unit, including at least one operational sortie.

Burma Star:
Awarded for one or more days of service within Burma, those serving in Bengal, Assam,
India, China, Hong Kong, Malaya, or Sumatra between certain other specified dates
also qualified. Air crew personnel engaged on operations against the enemy also
qualified, provided that at least one operational sortie had been completed.

Pacific Star:
This medal was awarded to Royal Air Force air crew who participated in at least one
operational flight within the specified criteria area.

Defence Medal:
This medal was awarded to service and civilian defence personnel for three years'
service at home, one year's service in a non-operational area (India), or six months'
service overseas in territory subjected to air attack. Issued in cupro-nickel, although
the Canadian medal was silver.

War Medal 1939–45:
All full-time personnel of the Armed Forces wherever serving, provided they had
served for at least twenty-eight days. Issued in cupro-nickel, however, the Canadian
version was in silver.

Canadian and New Zealand Memorial Cross:
The Cross was announced by the New Zealand government in December 1946 and
formally instituted by King George VI on 12 September 1947. The award was intended
for widows and mothers of members of the New Zealand Armed Forces and merchant
seamen who were killed or died on active service during the Second World War. The
Cross is engraved with details of the casualty and owes it origins to a similar Memorial
Cross issued by the Canadian government following the First World War. The Canadian
Maple Leaf emblem appears on the Canadian issue medal, while the New Zealand Fern
is to be found on the New Zealand award. Unlike the widows and mothers of Canada
and New Zealand, the British Government issued no such award.

The General Service Medal (Army and Royal Air Force) 1918–64:
The General Service Medal was struck in silver and was awarded for service in various
parts of the world. Eighteen clasps or bars have been approved for this medal; it was
therefore never awarded without a clasp.

The Clasp 'Southeast Asia 1945–1946':

The Clasp was awarded to British personnel after the Japanese surrender of 15 August
1945. Primarily awarded for activities including guarding Japanese prisoners of
war, maintaining law and order, and recovery of Allied prisoners of war.

# Gallantry Awards Allocated to Heavy Bomber Squadrons over Burma

During the Second World War, the following heavy bomber squadrons primarily flew over Burma in the Eastern Air Command. The men who flew within these squadrons accumulatively received 266 individual Medals and Orders for Flying Gallantry. The numerical dissemination of the awards to those recipients within each squadron has been collated from *The London Gazette*.

No. 99 Squadron:
Forty-two Distinguished Flying Cross Medals
Twenty-three Distinguished Flying Medals
Two Distinguished Service Orders

159 Squadron:
Fifty-four Distinguished Flying Cross Medals
Sixteen Distinguished Flying Medals
Two Distinguished Service Orders

215 Squadron:
Fifty-four Distinguished Flying Cross Medals
Seven Distinguished Flying Medals
One Distinguished Service Order

355 Squadron:
Nine Distinguished Flying Cross Medals
Two Distinguished Flying Medals

356 Squadron:
Eight Distinguished Flying Cross Medals
One Distinguished Flying Medal
Three Distinguished Service Orders

One particular award to 356 Squadron illustrates a casualty not normally associated to the dangers of warfare. Acting Wg Cdr George Sparks was a Canadian who commanded 356 Squadron and compiled a list of targets attacked, which included four operations against the Burma–Thailand Railway and three to Bangkok. Setting an inspiring example to his squadron on 15 March 1945, bombing railway warehouses in northern Indochina, he was airborne for over fifteen hours. He later became infected with Polio and died on 11 August 1945. The posthumous award of the Distinguished Service Order was announced two months after his death and eventually presented to his next of kin in an award ceremony in 1949. He now lays in the Kranji war Cemetery, Singapore.

357 Squadron:
Forty-two Distinguished Flying Cross Medals
Eight Distinguished Flying Medals
One Conspicuous Gallantry Medal
Four Distinguished Service Orders

Excluded from these statistics of flying awards to personnel within Liberator squadrons are any awards of a Mention in Despatches. That particular award was awarded for acts of gallantry or valuable service. It has a long history, having arisen in the eighteenth century when a detached commander in the British Army sent a report to London. In a written despatch regarding the service of a deserving officer, the mention of the officer's name was published in *The London Gazette* to inform the public of the officer's bravery or merit. In effect, a process that still exists today.

The Mention in Despatches could also be awarded posthumously alongside the highest award for valour, the Victoria Cross. The author is aware of several instances where even though Victoria Cross recommendations had progressed through the system with well-evidenced material, a lesser award was granted and subsequently awarded. In some of these most exceptional cases where the individual was killed in action, the subsequent award was most likely to be the standard Mention in Despatches.

The Mention in Despatches was not a medal, but a small bronze oak leaf that was worn on the ribbon of the 1939–1945 War Medal. It was awarded with a small dedication certificate signed by, in the case of the Air Force, the Secretary of State for the Air. These small bronze oak leaf devices often beguile the status of this award as many instances exist where it was the only available option other than the Victoria Cross. It should be noted that the vast majority of Air Force Mention in Despatches awards were announced in *The London Gazette* without any squadron or theatre of war identifiers. An example being Wg Cdr Ercolani, his name was simply listed as being a recipient of a Mention in Despatches within the pages of *The London Gazette* published on 14 June 1945.

# Bibliography and References

## Books

Allison, L., and Hayward, H., *They Shall Grow Not Old*, (Commonwealth Air Training Plan Museum, 1992)

Battersby, P., *Thai-Australian Relations in the Twentieth Century*, (Bangkok: Kasetsart University, 2000)

Beaton, Lt-Col T. R., *A Travellers Guide to the Burma Railway*, (Department of Veteran's Affairs, 2003)

Beattie, R., *The Death Railway: A Brief History*, (Image Makers Co. Ltd, 2005)

Beckman, S., *War Crimes Studies Center*, (U.C. Berkeley Trial Records: WCSC, 2000)

Birdsall, S., *Log of the Liberators*, (Garden City, New York: Doubleday & Company, Inc., 1973)

Brett, Lt C. C. (Canadian First Corps), *SEATIC Bulletin 246*, (1946)

Clinton, C., *From Bradford to Burma and Back*, (Self-publication, 2005)

Council on Foreign Relations, *Burma, Vol. 1 Number 1*, (Foreign Affairs Association, 1944)

Davis, L., *B-24 Liberator in Action*, (Squadron/Signal Publications Inc., 1987)

Farquharson, R., *For Your Tomorrow: Canadians in the Burma Campaign, 1941 to 1945*, (Trafford Publishing, 2004)

Freeman, R. A., *Consolidated B-24J Liberator*, (Profile Publications, Inc., 1969)

Futamatsu, Y., *Across Three Pagodas Pass*, (Renaissance Books, 2013)

Gibson, Major E., and Kingsley Ward, G., *Courage Remembered*, (HMSO, 1989)

Gordon, Major L. L., *British Battles and Medals*, (London: Spink & Son Ltd, 1971), pp. 333-4,

Green, W., *Famous Bombers of the Second World War*, (Doubleday, 1959)

Gwynne-Timothy, J. R. W., *Burma Liberators*, (Next Level Press, 1991)

Hanson OBE, Group Captain C. M. (RNZAF), *By Such Deeds*, (Christchurch, New Zealand: Volplane Press, 2001)

Hearns, D., *Distinguished Service Order Air Awards*, (Naval and Military Press, 2011)

Johnson, F. A., *Consolidated B-24 Liberator, Vol. 1, Warbird Tech Series*, (Specialty Press, 1996)

Lamont-Brown, R., *Kempeitai Japan's Dreaded Military Police*, (Sutton Publishing, 1998)

Lloyd, A. T., *Liberator, Americas Global Bomber*, (Pictorial Histories, 1993)

Maton, M., *Honour Those Mentioned: The Air Forces*, (Token Publishing, 2004); *Honour Those Mentioned: Mentions in Despatches*, (Token Publishing 2010)

May, L. G., *Hellfire Pass Memorial Thailand–Burma Railway*, (Hall, 2002)

McDowell, E. R., *Consolidated B-24D-M Liberator IN USAAF-RAF-RAAF-MLD-IAF-CzechAF and CNAF Service*, (Arco Publishing Co., 1970)

Michno, G. F., *Death on the Hellships*, (US Naval Institute Press, 2001)

Probert, Air Commodore H., *The Forgotten Air Force*, (Brassey, 1995)

Robertson, B., *British Military Aircraft Serials, 1912-1969*, (Ian Allen, 1969)

Rowland, R., *Sugamo and the River Kwai*, (Princeton University, 2003)

Saunders, H. St G., *The Royal Air Force 1939-1945 'The Fight is Won'*, (HMSO Volume III, 1954)

Swanborough, G., and Bowers, P. M., *United States Military Aircraft Since 1909*, (Smithsonian, 1989)

Tanaka, Y., *Hidden Horrors: Japanese War Crimes in World War II*, (Boulder, 1966)

Taylor. M., *Jane's American Fighting Aircraft of the 20th Century*, (Mallard Press, 1991)

Trager, F., *Burma Japanese Military Administration Documents*, (University of Pennsylvania Press, 1971)

Wagner, R., *American Combat Planes*, Third Enlarged Edition, (Doubleday, 1982)

Wegg, J., *General Dynamics Aircraft and Their Predecessors*, (Naval Institute Press, 1990)

Royal Air Force Historical Society, *Bracknell Paper No. 6: A Symposium on the Far East War*, (Fotodirect Ltd, 1995)

# Archives

International Red Cross Archives: 19 Avenue de la paix, CH 1202, Geneva
Newspaper Archives, *Straits Times*, (17.7.1984)

## IWM Archives
Burma Thailand Map Tracing, IWM PJDT35
Private Papers Documents 1349, Innes-Ker, William McDonald
Private Papers Documents, Colonel Cyril Wild

## National Archives, Kew
Air 23/2016: Targets Bombing Routes into Burma
Air 27/1060 to Air 27/1064: 159 Squadron

Air 27/1579: 356 Squadron

Air 27/1754: 355 Squadron

Air 28: Station Operations Record Books

Air 29: Miscellaneous Units Operation Record Books

MSS EUR C614: Mitsuru, Col Sugii of the Burma National Army Advisory Department, History of the Minami Organ, (Compiled: 1944) Translated by Takahashi, H., (1954)

WO 203/6325: Brett Translation

WO 235/1009: The Trial of Okami Hiroshi

WO 235/1034: The F Force Trial

WO 325/88: Alexandra Hospital Massacre

# Publications

Fukubayashi, T., 'Verifying the Reality of Japan's Use of Allied POWs Based on Historical Records, Information Bureau of Japan', *The Asia-Pacific Journal*, Vol. 33-2-09, August 2009

Emperor Shōwa, 'Imperial Household Agency audio recording of the Emperor Showa declaration of surrender', *Japan Times*

Park, ACM Sir K., 'Air Operations in South East Asia: 3 May 1945-12 September 1945', *The London Gazette*, Supplement, 13 April 1951

Squadron Register 355/356, *Signed with Their Honour,* (Self-published after the war by members of the squadrons)

Information and Historical Service Headquarters Eighth Army, *Sugamo Prison, November 1945 to January 1947*. Published as document APO 343.